RAIL ATLAS
1939-1945

PETER WALLER

Ian Allan
PUBLISHING

Author's note:
The author would like to thank the World War 2 Railway Study Group for information supplied on wartime developments. As with the first edition of any atlas (particularly one as complex as this in trying to convey changes over an historical period), there will undoubtedly be errors; if you are aware of any, please make contact with the author via the publisher so that any future second edition can be corrected.

Front cover: A trainload of Covenanter tanks is seen here in transit on the LNER in October 1941. *Ian Allan Library*

Rear cover: The city of York, as a major railway junction and historic centre, was targeted on 28 April 1942. *Ian Allan Library*

Previous page: Middlesbrough suffered severe damage during the war. This view records the aftermath of a raid on 3 August 1942, which resulted in the partial demolition of the station's overall roof. The damage was ultimately not repaired and the remainder of the roof was subsequently dismantled. *Ian Allan Library*

Below: With the realisation that war was inevitable and that, following the experience of Europe, Britain's transport infrastructure would be an inevitable target for air attack, efforts were made to reduce the risk from bombing. This included the removal of glass from station roofs. Work is seen in progress here at Euston station in July 1940. *Ian Allan Library*

Below right: In order to improve the coastal defences of southeast England and Scotland, a number of armoured trains were constructed. One was built for the 15in-gauge Romney, Hythe & Dymchurch Railway, seen here on patrol with men from the Somerset Light Infantry. *Imperial War Museum (H4732)*

First published 2014

ISBN 978 0 7110 3630 7

Cartography © Ian Allan Publishing Ltd 2014
Text © Peter Waller 2014

Published by Ian Allan Publishing, Hersham, Surrey KT12 4RG.

Printed in Bulgaria.

Visit the Ian Allan Publishing website at www.ianallanpublishing.com

CONTENTS

INTRODUCTION

In September 1939, for the second time in less than a generation, Britain found itself at war in Europe. During World War 2, the country was faced by the 'total war' already inflicted on the Spanish town of Guernica during that nation's civil war, with cities and the civilian population targeted as directly as the military.

As in World War 1, the railways of Britain were to play a major role in the ultimate defeat of Germany. In doing so, however, they would be placed under enormous strain as ageing equipment and infrastructure endeavoured to cope with both the increased traffic that total war required and the constant threat of attack from the German air force.

On the outbreak of war, under the terms of the Emergency Powers (Defence) Act, the railways came under the control of the Railway Executive Committee. The REC had been established the previous year when the international situation suggested war was imminent, despite Neville Chamberlain's apparent success in securing the 1938 Munich Agreement with Hitler.

The arrangements in World War 2 were, however, subtly different to those of World War 1 in that the REC, chaired by Sir Ralph Wedgwood (the former Chief Officer of the LNER) from September 1939 until August 1941, was primarily a supervisory body with the day-to-day control of the railways left in the original management.

The 'Big Four' companies also took action to remove their London-based staff away from the Metropolis: the GWR to Beenham Grange, Aldermaston; the LMS to The Grove, Watford; the LNER to The Hoo, Hitchin; and the SR to the Deepdene Hotel, Dorking.

It was not only control of the railways which had been subject to prewar planning. Most important were the plans formulated to evacuate large numbers of vulnerable people – principally children and pregnant women – from major urban areas. While there had been a dry run earlier, the plans were realised on 31 August 1939 when the process of moving some 1.5 million people began over a three-day period. The railways were central to this. Not only were they involved in the evacuation of civilians, but the threat to the southeast also necessitated the removal of government departments and their staff, as well as the treasures of the nation's museums. (The collection from the National Gallery was, for example, shipped by rail to storage in North Welsh slate quarries for the duration of hostilities.)

Following this first evacuation, the so-called 'Phoney War' seemed to suggest that the military threat was not as severe as had been imagined and there was a gradual drift back to their homes by many evacuees. This situation changed following the spring 1940 defeat in France and retreat from Dunkirk – an evacuation that itself placed a major strain on the railways of southern England, as more than 330,000 British, Empire and Allied troops made their unscheduled appearance as a second phase of evacuating children from London, the southeast and any potential targets for German invasion began.

Between 13 and 18 June 1940 some 100,000 children were evacuated, compounded by the arrival of 30,000 civilians escaped from Europe and 25,000 from the Channel Islands between 20 and 24 June. In addition, the government's policy of interning the 'nationals' of enemy

Unlike World War 1, rail management in World War 2 remained largely in the hands of the main-line railways, with the Railway Executive Committee facilitating liaison between industry and government. The REC was chaired by Sir Ralph Wedgwood, ex-General Manager of the LNER, seen third from right. Most meetings of the REC were held in a disused Underground station at Down Street. Amongst other notable railwaymen present at this General Managers' Conference are Sir Eustace Missenden (Southern; extreme left), James Milne (GWR; second left) and Frank Pick (LPTB; fourth right). Pick retired from the LPTB in May 1940, as a result of ill health, and died in November 1941. *Ian Allan Library*

states, mainly on the Isle of Man, resulted in the movement of a substantial number of Germans and Italians towards the ports that served the island.

The process of evacuating civilians continued throughout the war in response to the German bombing of cities and, later, the use of the V-1 flying bombs and V-2 rockets against London and the Southeast. The policy of evacuation would cease in September 1944, but the official return of evacuees was not sanctioned until June 1945.

Back in the summer of 1940, however, with the surrender of France, German forces were now only 20-odd miles away. The frontline was now the English Channel. As part of Britain's defences, 12 armoured trains were constructed to serve coastal lines in the Southeast and Scotland. These were armed with six-pounder guns of World War 1 vintage, initially operated by the Royal Engineers and manned by the Royal Armoured Corps – although Polish troops took over in the southeast, from late 1940 until 1942, and the Home Guard manned the guns in Scotland until November 1944. In addition to the standard-gauge trains, there was also a miniature unit that operated over the 15in-gauge Romney, Hythe & Dymchurch Railway.

It was inevitable that the railways would become a target for German attack once the country was within the Luftwaffe's range. Preparations for war had been going on for some time and, from 1937 onwards, some £13 million was expended on ensuring the railways would be prepared for war. This work included the removal of much of the glass from station canopies and overall roofs, the bricking up of windows in signalboxes, the laying in of additional equipment to facilitate the quick repair of track and the creation of secure control rooms to be used in the event that existing facilities were destroyed. The blackout may now evoke Warden Hodges from *Dad's Army* with his 'Put that light out!', but it could have had serious consequences for the safe operation of the railways. It was, therefore, recognised that low-level lighting – the so-called 'gloomy glim' – was required even after an air-raid siren had been sounded.

Despite all such preparations, the destruction wrought by the war was significant. More than 9,200 incidents resulting in damage or delay to the railways were recorded. In terms of loss of equipment, eight locomotives were destroyed completely and a further 484 required repair after damage; similar respective figures for coaching stock were at 637 and 13,487 and for freight stock 3,321 and 20,294.

Many stations were hit during the raids – five main-line stations in London on 15 October 1940, for example. The viaduct on the approaches to Liverpool Exchange station was partially destroyed on 20 December 1940 and, on 10 May 1941, St Pancras station was hit by five bombs, resulting in complete closure for a week with its full reopening deferred until 7 June. On 19 April of that year,

With the city's famous minster in the background, York was another station where the vulnerable glass was removed from its roof. The city of York was subject to bombing during the war, with the station suffering severe damage. LNER 'A4' Pacific No 4469 *Sir Ralph Wedgwood* was destroyed on 6 June 1942, during one such raid. *Ian Allan Library*

a mine destroyed the girder bridge across Southwark Street, Blackfriars; the four-track line would be reopened in stages between 1 May and 29 June, with a new permanent structure built between January and December 1942.

The damage inflicted on the railways was nationwide: from Newton Abbot in Devon to York, Middlesbrough, Newcastle and Sunderland in the northeast, from Brighton in the southeast to Bristol and South Wales. It was essential, however, that they remained operational throughout and that railway staff were able, through preparation and experience, to repair much of the damage quickly and efficiently.

As Britain went onto a 'total war' footing, the railways played a crucial role not only in the movement of men and equipment, raw materials and goods, but also in the manufacture of arms and equipment by the railway workshops themselves. Tanks, aircraft parts and much else were produced at the major works, considerably aiding the nation's capacity to defend itself. Although operational staff were in a 'reserved occupation' and therefore exempt from conscription, other trades were not protected in this way and so large numbers of women were recruited to replace men called up for active service.

It was not only the railways that turned their workshops into munitions plants; across the length and breadth of the country, new factories sprang up – the so-called 'shadow factories' allocated to many well-known manufacturers – as well as new dedicated Royal Ordnance factories. These needed the railways to serve them, both

to bring in the raw materials and take out the finished goods, as well as to move the vast number of staff employed there. The new Royal Ordnance factory at Thorp Arch, West Riding of Yorkshire, for example, employed some 18,000 workers, their movement to and from the site placing considerable strain on the local railway branch. While the authorities exhorted the general population to avoid unnecessary journeys, the reality of the war was that traffic increased massively and known bottlenecks required improvement. Considerable investment therefore went into increasing railway capacity. This process became all the more important once the USA entered the war in December 1941, after which additional men and equipment from the US forces started to arrive, and in the build up to the D-Day landings of June 1944.

Alongside the infrastructure of the railways, there was also investment in locomotives and rolling stock. The Ministry of Supply ordered the construction of locomotives – the Austerity 0-6-0Ts, 2-8-0s and 2-10-0s – which were supplemented by various US-built counterparts, most notably the Class S160 2-8-0s. While many of these were ultimately destined for use on overseas railways, a large number were operated in Britain both to run them in and to increase the country's locomotive stock, at a time when the pressure on the rail network was at its most intense.

With the arrival of peace in 1945 came the final reckoning: the railways had helped to ensure Britain's survival, but at considerable cost. Apart from the direct loss of locomotives and rolling stock, a significant number

of buildings had suffered partial or complete destruction; lines and bridges that had been temporarily repaired during the war also required rebuilding. There was, moreover, a backlog of routine maintenance and the replacement of old equipment.

However, the importance of the railways to the ultimate Allied victory cannot be overstated. In 1945, Winston Churchill told the REC:

'Throughout the period of the heavy German air raids on this country, the arteries of the Nation – the railways – with their extensive dock undertakings, were subjected to intensive attacks. Yet the grim determination, unwavering courage, and constant resourcefulness of the railwaymen of all ranks have enabled the results of the damage to be overcome very speedily, and communications restored without delay. Thus, in spite of every enemy effort, the traffic has been kept moving, and the great flow of munitions proceeds. Results such as the railways have achieved are only won by blood and sweat, and on behalf of the Nation I express gratitude to every railwayman who has participated in this great transport effort which is contributing so largely towards final victory.'

This book is not intended as a comprehensive account of the railways at war during the period from September 1939 through to August 1945, but rather an exploration mapping the changes wrought upon the railway network during those years. The maps themselves are designed to show the state of the railway industry on the outbreak of war and how it evolved over that historic period. The comprehensive gazetteer is designed to record stations – public and non-timetabled passenger stations, freight and military – that existed during this period. The following text describes the significant opening and closing dates, where known, of the railways during the period, as well as the background to some of the military lines that played a significant role in the war. Once again, this cannot be comprehensive. However, readers are referred to the bibliography for some of the myriad books that explore in more detail aspects of the railway's role during the war.

The signalbox at Northallerton demonstrates three facets of wartime contingency: the windows have been bricked up, but note also the removal of the nameboard, and the sandbags on the roof. *Ian Allan Library*

MILITARY RAILWAYS

There were a number of military railways in Britain of both standard and narrow gauge, some of which remain extant. Within the confines of this book it is not possible to describe all in detail, but the following are the most significant – in particular those that underwent development or expansion during World War 2.

• Bicester

Prior to the outbreak of war, there had been some efforts by the military to improve upon the nation's existing – but inadequate – five Central Ordnance Depots (Branston, Chilwell, Didcot, Weedon and Woolwich) with new facilities such as Donnington in Shropshire, then already under construction. Once the war had started, there remained a need for a large new depot with good road and rail access in Southern England. Despite opposition from the LMS, a site at Bicester was identified. With all the associated work, this has been described as the single largest military project undertaken in the UK. Work commenced on the construction of the site in 1941, including the building of a new 660-wagon marshalling yard at Swanbourne on the Bletchley-Oxford line. On 16 January 1943, by which date the first 30.25 miles of track had been laid and with locomotives available, operations commenced. Passenger services commenced in June of that year. Development of the site continued through the war and, by mid-1945, the railway network extended to some 47.5 miles. Postwar, the site remained important and the railway is still extant, with some 40 miles of track in use. The base is home to the section of the Royal Logistics Corps tasked with training military personnel in railway operation and maintenance.

It was not only above ground that precautions against aerial bombing were taken. On the London Underground, the LPTB, in conjunction with the Ministry of Transport, undertook a significant programme of emergency work costing some £1 million. This included the installation of electrically operated floodgates at Waterloo and Charing Cross stations. This view, taken in October 1939, shows the work in progress. In the event of use, the gates were capable of closing within three minutes and withstanding a force of 800 tons. *Ian Allan Library*

• Bramley

The Bramley Central Ammunition Depot – originally known as the Bramley Ordnance Depot – was originally established during World War 1 and was located to the east and west of the Reading-Basingstoke line. It was served by an intricate network of lines some 30 miles in length, passing under the main line in two short tunnels. In addition to the running of ammunition trains, there was also a workmen's service from Bramley station into the CAD, although this was suspended during World War 2. Workmen's services to the site finally ceased altogether in 1970, with the transport of armaments to and from the depot concluding on 1 March 1987. The site is now used as a training camp.

• Cairnryan

With ports in the south and west under the threat of direct attack following the collapse of France in 1940, the military sought out sites for ports that would be in less jeopardy. Amongst the locations examined were Cairnryan and Faslane. As part of the project to construct Military Port No 2 at Cairnryan, a seven-mile branch from the Dumfries-Stranraer line was constructed. Surveying work started on the line in November 1940 and construction in January the following year. The official opening date was July 1942, although there had been some limited operations beforehand and King George VI travelled over the line with Queen Elizabeth in June 1942. The port became fully operational in July 1943; by 1944, however, the preparations for D-Day meant that the port's role – other than in the construction of sections for Mulberry harbour – was reduced. The branch was used postwar for

With the threat of invasion all too real after the defeat of France in 1940, the British government constructed countless concrete bunkers as part of its strategic defence of the nation. As Commander-in-Chief of Home Forces, General Edmund Ironside was tasked with drawing up lines of defence that often included rivers and railway lines. Strategically important buildings, such as the 'B' control at Bletchley (seen here in 1944), were also constructed in concrete. Buildings like this were usually left exposed, the rationale being that, if hit by a bomb, the ordnance would bounce and explode safely away from the structure. If the building was encased in earth, however, the bomb itself would be embedded and the force of any explosion would be transmitted into the structure. *Ian Allan Library*

the movement of live ammunition to be destroyed at sea. Military use ceased in 1959, but the line itself survived until its final closure and lifting in 1967.

• Calshot RAF Railway
The 2ft 0in-gauge line serving the RAF's seaplane and flying boat station at Calshot, near Fawley in Hampshire, opened in 1919. Until its closure in 1945, it linked Calshot Spit (the seaplane and flying boat station) with Eaglehurst Camp.

• Catterick Camp Military Railway
Construction of Catterick Camp commenced shortly after the outbreak of World War 1 in 1914, with the first soldiers arriving in late 1916. A 2ft 0in-gauge line was built to assist in construction of the site and this was converted to standard gauge by late 1915. The decision was taken to make the camp permanent after the war, although the railway was cut back in 1919, when California and Scotton stations were closed and some track was lifted. Effectively, the line now ran from a junction on the LNER Richmond branch at Catterick Bridge to Camp Centre. Inevitably, World War 2 saw an increase in traffic with numerous troop trains running. The line finally closed completely on 26 October 1964.

• Chattenden Naval Tramway
Constructed by the Admiralty following a Light Railway Order of 24 July 1901, the CNT was a two-mile standard-gauge line that connected Lodge Hill eastwards to Sharnal Street. A second line, authorised before World War 1 but not opened until 1915, ran eastwards from Sharnal Street to Kingsnorth. Following an agreement of 14 August 1924, the Kingsnorth Light Railway worked the line from 24 July 1926, later taking ownership following an order dated 25 July 1929. The line closed at some date between 1945 and 1957, while the original CNT closed in 1961.

• Chattenden & Upnor Railway
Pre-dating the CNT, the Chattenden & Upnor Railway ran

south from Lodge Hill to Upnor. Originally built as a standard-gauge line in the 1870s, it was converted to 2ft 6in by the Royal Engineers in the 1890s before transfer to the Admiralty on 1 April 1906. The line survived the two world wars before final closure on 31 December 1961.

• Chilmark
Located to the west of Salisbury on the line towards Exeter, Dinton was the centre of a network of lines serving military installations in the area. An RAF depot was opened adjacent to the station on 10 July 1938. There had been a previous railway serving the station, the Fovant Military Railway, which ran some two miles southwards to serve an army camp. The line was built in 1915 and dismantled in 1926, after closure in February 1924. Located west of Dinton station, on the north side of the line, an RAF bomb store was opened in a disused limestone quarry at Chilmark in 1937. This was served by a standard-gauge line from Dinton and nine miles of 2ft-gauge track. East of Dinton station, there were also Admiralty sidings at Baverstock. The narrow-gauge system at Chilmark remained operational until 1995. Evidence of the now-closed facilities at Dinton, including rusting track and buildings, is still visible from services on the Salisbury-Exeter line.

• Devonport Dockyard Railway
The first broad gauge lines were laid in Devonport dockyard in 1860, extended in 1865 and again in 1876 (when track was laid through the tunnel between Keyham and the South Yard); the network was converted to standard gauge in 1892. During the late 19th century, the dockyard expanded considerably and a passenger service was introduced, operating until May 1966. Although reduced in scope, the Devonport Dockyard Railway remains in operation to serve the naval base.

• Faslane
Opened in 1941 to serve Military Port No 1 at Faslane, this double-track branch ran for 2.5 miles from its junction on

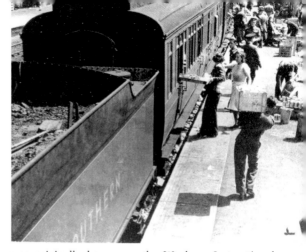

Apart from evacuation in the early part of the war, the next emergency that required running a significant number of unplanned services was the aftermath of the retreat from Dunkirk, in the period 26 May to 3 June 1940. Following the repatriation of more than 330,000 British, Empire and Allied troops from France, these soldiers were dispersed to camps across the nation. Here we see a train of returned soldiers stopping whilst refreshments are provided. Although the scene is on the Southern Railway, the leading vehicle is an ex-Midland Railway clerestory coach. *Ian Allan Library*

the West Highland line between Helensburgh and Garelochhead. Unusually for a British line, it operated with right-hand running, apparently to familiarise staff with continental railway practices. Faslane ceased to be a military port in April 1946 – although it subsequently became the base for submarines carrying Britain's nuclear deterrent – with operation of the line transferred to the LNER. The line was singled on 30 May 1946 and used to serve ship-dismantling facilities. The branch finally closed in 1983.

• Kineton
Situated on the erstwhile Stratford-upon-Avon & Midland Junction Railway line between Fenny Compton and Stratford, the military base at Kineton developed from 1941 onwards. Originally one of the additional Central Ammunition Depots, it also served as a transit camp for Czech and Polish soldiers. The site, now part of the Defence Storage & Distribution Agency, remains operational with a rail link to Fenny Compton. Apart from military use, it has also housed redundant main-line locomotives and rolling stock in recent years.

• Long Marston
A 455-acre site at Long Marston was laid out for military use in 1940, primarily by the Royal Engineers. The railway network linked to the GWR Stratford-Honeybourne line was integral to the site's operation. The site itself remained in postwar military use, although a section was latterly used as a scrapyard by Bird's of Stratford until 1999, with the remainder used as the Central Engineer's Depot until closure, once again in 1999. The site was put up for sale in 2001 and has subsequently been used for storage of redundant main-line locomotives and rolling stock.

• Longmoor
The first railway at Longmoor was a 4.5-mile/1ft 6in tramway, constructed in the early years of the 20th century between Longmoor Camp and Bordon. This line was converted to standard gauge between 1905 and 1907. It

was originally known as the Woolmer Instructional Military Railway, becoming the Longmoor Military Railway in 1935. The line was extended south to Liss in 1933, with a loop line from Longmoor Camp to Whitehill Junction via Hopkins Bridge opening in 1942. At its maximum extent the LMR stretched over 70 track miles. It was used primarily for training soldiers in the construction and operation of railways, with sections of the line regularly lifted and re-laid. The LMR survived World War 2 but would close on 31 October 1969, with the rationalisation of Britain's defence requirements. There were plans to preserve the line and a number of ex-BR steam locomotives were based at the site, but efforts to save the section from Liss to Liss Forest Road were thwarted by the opposition of local residents.

• Longtown
During World War 1 Gretna was the site of one of Britain's most important cordite factories. Opened in April 1916, it employed almost 17,000 (mostly female) workers at its peak. The factory closed after the war and most of the land it occupied was sold off. However, land remained in military ownership around Longtown, Eastriggs and Smalmstown, with new Central Ammunition Depots established on these sites during the late 1930s. These were linked to the LNER main line from Carlisle to Edinburgh and the LMS line from Gretna to Annan. In order to improve connections at the Longtown end, a new signalbox was opened at Bush Junction on 8 June 1942. The Eastriggs site is still served by a 2ft 0in internal railway. The Longtown site remains in military use, although it is reduced in scale, with rail access from Mossband Junction on the West Coast main line. Rail access to Eastriggs is also still possible via the Gretna-Annan line.

• Marchwood
Planning and preparation for the D-Day landings of 1944 were inevitably essential for the Allies' ultimate victory in World War 2. The landings were and remain the single largest seaborne invasion in history, requiring the

movement of vast numbers of men and their equipment across the English Channel to Normandy. Essential work included the construction of a temporary harbour (the Mulberry harbour) in sections in the UK, for ultimate use in France as the invading force secured the beachhead. In order to facilitate this massive undertaking a new military port was built at Marchwood, to be served by a new railway line constructed off the Southern Railway branch to Fawley. Construction of the dock and railway was completed in 1943, the latter opening on 28 November of that year. Following the successful invasion of France in June 1944, the relatively small port (which possessed at this stage only a single jetty) was used for the movement of reinforcements across the Channel. The port remains in military use today, as a base for the Royal Fleet Auxiliary, and is still served by the branch. However, recent reductions in Britain's defence budget have resulted in a threat of closure, and an increase in non-military (particularly container) traffic has been observed.

• **Shoeburyness**

The Board of Ordnance acquired the site at Shoeburyness in 1849 and, in 1863, a School of Gunnery was established. The first section of the military railway opened in 1884 and the network was to be considerably extended between then and 1925. In 1953, when the line was at its peak, it employed some 20 standard-gauge steam and diesel locomotives. Since the early 1990s its importance has declined, with much of the line now closed, although the northern section remains extant in part to serve a QinetiQ facility at Pig's Bay and partly as a storage site for redundant rolling stock.

There were also a number of lines constructed to serve some of the Royal Ordnance Factories built during the war. One of these served the ROF at Thorp Arch, northeast of Leeds, where transport was required for 18,000 workers who made their way daily to the factory. In order to serve the site, the LNER constructed a circular railway around the exterior of its 642 acres. The first two stations were opened in November 1941, followed by the full circular line on 19 April 1942. The ROF remained operational until closure in April 1958.

Top: It was inevitable that the railways would be targeted by the Luftwaffe during World War 2 and that a significant amount of damage would be inflicted. During the Blitz on London in 1940, the LNER warehouse at Goodman's Yard was severely damaged. This view shows the resulting damage to the building and some of the rolling stock at the yard. *Ian Allan Library*

Above: Suburban and main-line services out of King's Cross were disrupted in late 1940, when the footbridge over the lines at Hornsey station collapsed into a bomb crater. *Ian Allan Library*

Right: The Plessey company was able to utilise part of the unopened eastward extension of the Central Line for the production of aircraft parts and munitions for the War Office. *Plessey Company*

LINES TAKEN OVER BY THE MILITARY

Apart from the lines either already constructed for use by the military or added to the military network during the war, there were a number that passed from the control of the Railway Executive to the War Department during the period. These included:

• Shropshire & Montgomeryshire

There were a number of railways that remained independent after the Grouping of 1923. One such was the Shropshire & Montgomeryshire Light Railway, which had a somewhat chequered career both before and after its reopening under the control of Colonel Holman F. Stephens in 1911. Passenger services were suspended on 6 November 1933 for financial reasons and never resumed. On 1 September 1939, the railway's management was informed that it was one of 11 independent lines to be placed under government control as a result of the Defence of the Realm regulations introduced that year. Following a survey in 1940, it was decided that the line would be a suitable location for a new ordnance depot. The War Office, under the auspices of the No 1 Railway Group, formally took over operation of the S&M main line – but not the Criggion branch – on 1 June 1941. Prior to opening of the exchange sidings at Hookagate, near Shrewsbury, on 29 January 1942, traffic started to flow to the S&M. The line would ultimately play host to 206 rail-served depots, with additional halts constructed to serve the military-operated passenger services and camps established along the line. Postwar, the line remained primarily to serve the Central Armaments Depot at Nesscliff, until the decision was taken to close the site by 1960. The Criggion branch closed on 4 January that year, the main line effectively closing from 29 February. Following closure, the line was transferred to the British Transport Commission, under whose auspices it was dismantled.

• Cleobury Mortimer & Ditton Priors

Passenger services on the Cleobury Mortimer & Ditton Priors Light Railway – which had been taken over by the GWR at Grouping in 1923 – were withdrawn on 24 September 1938, after which the line carried a single daily freight train. However, its importance increased with construction of the Royal Naval Armament Depot at Ditton Priors. This was supplemented during the war by

Above: The LNER warehouse at New Bridge Street in Newcastle, then regarded as one of the most modern in the country, was wrecked by bombing in 1941. *Ian Allan Library*

Below: In September 1941, King's Cross shed (Top Shed) was severely damaged during the Blitz on London, but the original caption of this picture, passed by the wartime censor, noted how 'the work went on'. Visible in the damaged building are 'V2s' Nos 4883 and 4797. *Ian Allan Library*

Right: LNER Class O3 2-8-0 No 3462 was damaged during the Blitz of 1940. Although it was one of two locomotives hit during this particular raid, No 3462 was quickly repaired and restored to service. *Ian Allan Library*

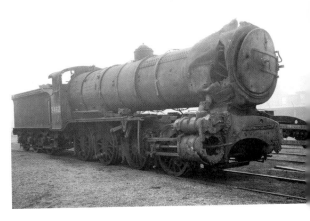

Below right: Southern Railway Class D3 0-4-4T No 2365 achieved fame on 28 November 1942 when it became the only steam locomotive to destroy an enemy aircraft. Travelling between Brighton and Chichester, it came under attack from a German bomber. Although No 2365 was severely damaged during the assault, the aircraft was flying so low that it hit the locomotive's dome. Engulfed by steam, the plane crashed, killing its pilot – although the footplate crew survived. No 2365 was soon repaired and survived until withdrawal in December 1952. *Ian Allan Library*

further dumps along the line. The commercial freight service was suspended from 11 September 1939, after which the GWR operated supply trains as far as Cleobury North, where RNAD locomotives took over. The line remained in the ownership of the GWR, and then BR, until 1 May 1957, when it was transferred to the Admiralty. It closed completely with the demise of the RNAD in 1965.

• **Chellaston East Junction/Ashby-de-la-Zouch**
Known as the Melbourne Military Railway, this ex-Midland Railway branch in Derbyshire and Leicestershire was handed over to the military on 19 November 1939 to become No 2 Railway Training Centre. The railway's headquarters were established at Chellaston East Junction, where a shed accommodating eight locomotives was built, while soldiers were based at a camp at Weston-on-Trent. Sidings were laid at Kings Newton, where a bridge-building school was established. The railway was used at first for the training of individuals but eventually entire companies were trained, with each company operating the line for a week at a time. From July 1941, soldiers who had received their initial training at Longmoor were transferred to Melbourne for its completion. Apart from the military traffic, which most provided stores to and from Kings Newton and Tonge, the line was also used to move coal and lime from New Lount Colliery and Cloud Hill. Towards the end of the war, military requirements diminished and the line was returned to civilian control on 1 January 1945.

Below: The city of York, as a major railway junction and historic centre, was subjected to a number of raids, in particular the Baedeker Blitz of April-June 1942 that also targeted other historic cities – Bath, Canterbury, Exeter and Norwich – following the RAF's destruction of the German city of Lübeck at the end of March. York was targeted on 28 April; amongst the structures that suffered significant damage was York station. This was the view recorded the following day, showing the burnt-out remains of the 10.15pm express from King's Cross to Edinburgh. *Ian Allan Library*

PASSENGER LINES CLOSED DURING THE WAR

During World War 2, a number of passenger lines had their services either withdrawn completely, effectively continuing the process of rationalisation that began during the late 1920s, or suspended for the duration of hostilities. The latter was the case with the Didcot, Newbury & Southampton, although the DN&S's temporary closure resulted from the need to upgrade the line in connection with the volume of military traffic, central to the strategic build-up of men and equipment in the period prior to D-Day.

Airdrie-Whifflet (Upper)	3 May 1943
Alcester-Bearley (North Junction)	25 September 1939
Note: Workmen's services operated between Birmingham and Great Alne until 3 July 1944.	
Aldgate East (St Mary's Junction)-Shadwell (Whitechapel Junction)	6 October 1941
Aldwych-Holborn	22 September 1940
Note: service reintroduced 1 July 1946.	
Angel Road-Lower Edmonton (Low Level)	11 September 1939
Arnside-Hincaster Junction	4 May 1942
Note: Line used for occasional excursions to Windermere until September 1963.	
Banavie Pier-Fort William (Banavie Junction)	4 September 1939
Beckton-Custom House	7 September 1940
Beighton (Killamarsh Junction)-Langwith Junction	10 September 1939
Bishop Auckland (East Junction)-Spennymoor	4 December 1939
Bottesford (West Junction)-Newark	11 September 1939
Brentford-Southall	4 May 1942
Brocketsbrae (Alton Heights Junction)-Douglas West (Poniel Junction)	11 September 1939
Brynmawr-Pontypool (Trevethin Junction)	5 May 1941
Canada Dock-Spellow (Atlantic Dock Junction)	5 May 1941
Canterbury (West) (Harbledown Junction)-Lyminge	2 December 1940
Carstairs (Dolphinton Junction)-Dolphinton	4 June 1945
Catrine-Mauchline (Brackenhill Junction)	3 May 1943
Dalkeith-Millerhill (Glenesk Junction)	5 January 1942
Darvel-Strathaven (Central)	11 September 1939
Denham-Uxbridge (Vine Street)	1 September 1939
Dumfries (Cairn Valley Junction)-Moniaive	3 May 1943
Eardisley-Titley	1 July 1940
Earl's Court-Willesden Junction	20 October 1940
Note: Closure caused by bomb damage.	
East Finchley-Highgate	3 March 1941
Note: service withdrawn following opening of the LPTB Northern Line link from East Finchley to Highgate.	
East Putney-Point Pleasant Junction	5 May 1941
Edgware-Finchley (Church End)	11 September 1939
Note: Reopened Mill Hill East to Finchley (Church End; renamed Central on 1 April 1940) with electrification as part of the extended Northern Line of the LPTB on 18 May 1941.	
Egginton Junction-Derby (Friargate)	4 December 1939
Ellesmere-Wrexham	8 June 1940
Note: Services restored May 1946.	
Ferryhill (Tursdale Junction)-Leamside	28 July 1941
Firsby-Spilsby	10 September 1939
Fishponds (Kingswood Junction)-Montpelier (Ashley Hill Junction)	31 March 1941
Forncett-Wymondham	10 September 1939
Fort George-Gollanfield	5 April 1943
Gallions-Custom House	8 September 1940
Girvan-Turnberry	2 March 1942
Haverton Hill-Port Clarence	11 September 1939
Hay-Pontrilas	15 December 1941
Heanor-Ilkeston (Stanton Junction)	4 December 1939
Hertford (North)-Stevenage (Langley Junction)	10 September 1939
Kensington (Uxbridge Road Junction)-Kensington (Latimer Road)	20 October 1940
Note: Closure caused by bomb damage.	
Kew Bridge-South Acton (Bollo Lane Junction)	12 September 1940
Killin-Loch Tay	9 September 1939
Lybster-Wick	1 April 1944
Nottingham (London Road Low Level)-Nottingham (Trent Lane West Junction)	22 May 1944
Nunhead-Crystal Palace (High Level) & Upper Norwood	22 May 1944
Note: Reopened 4 March 1946.	
Plymouth (Cornwall Junction)-Plymouth (Devonport Junction)	23 April 1941
Plymouth (Millbay)-Plymouth (North Road)	23 April 1942
Poplar (East India Road)-Dalston Junction	15 May 1944
Note: Replaced by buses until 23 April 1945.	
Portishead-Weston-super-Mare	20 May 1940
Ravelrig-Balerno-Slateford (Balerno Junction)	1 November 1943
Stafford-Uttoxeter (Bromshall Junction)	4 December 1939
Stratford Low Level (Channelsea Junction)-Victoria Park	2 November 1942
Thornbury-Yate	19 June 1944
Weymouth Quay-Weymouth Junction	25 July 1940
Note: Last train operated 6 September 1939; line reopened postwar.	
Windermere Lakeside-Ulverston (Plumpton Junction)	31 August 1941
Note: Full passenger service ceased 26 September 1938; thereafter summer season only. Ran alternate Sundays only in 1941. Reopened 3 June 1946.	

FREIGHT LINES CLOSED DURING THE WAR

During the was a limited number of freight-only liness closed. These included:

Calderbank-Airdrie	31 July 1941
Calderbank-Chapelhall	1939
Caersws-Van	4 November 1940
Cleobury Mortimer-Ditton Priors	11 September 1939
Gelli Tarw Junction-Dare Junction-Nantymelin Colliery	1 September 1939
Giffen-Glengarnock High	1 March 1945

Left Although the war put a considerable amount of pressure on the nation's railway network, there were a number of closures of passenger and, to a lesser extent, freight lines during hostilities. One of the most notable casualties was the Weston, Clevedon & Portishead line, which closed completely on 20 May 1940. In June 1937, before the outbreak of war, WC&P No 5 is seen passing Wick St Lawrence station with a service from Portishead to Weston-super-Mare. *Ian Allan Library*

Right: A trainload of Covenanter tanks is seen here in transit on the LNER in October 1941. The Covenanter was designed by the LMSR and entered production in 1939, with production handled by the LMS's works at Crewe and Horwich; more than 500 were completed there by 1942, as well as at English Electric and Leyland. The Covenanter tank was, with few exceptions, rarely deployed outside the UK, but was used to re-equip the 1st Armoured Division (following its retreat from Dunkirk) and other UK-based units. The tank, of which almost 1,200 were built, was declared obsolete in 1943. *Ian Allan Library*

Left: The D-Day landings were the greatest seaborne invasion in history, requiring the deployment of vast quantities of men and materials. In the period before, during and after the landings, the railways of Britain shipped both to the ports of southern England for embarkation to Europe. In this view, a War Department ex-GWR 'Deans Goods' 0-6-0, fitted with the side tanks from an 0-6-0PT, shunts wagons onboard US vessels prior to shipment to France. *Ian Allan Library*

STATIONS CLOSED 1939-1945

Name	Passengers	Goods	Completely
Abbeydore	15 December 1941	3 June 1957	3 June 1957
Abersychan & Talywain	5 May 1941	23 August 1965	23 August 1965
Airdrie (LMS)	3 May 1943	6 July 1964	6 July 1964
All Stretton Halt*	4 January 1943	n/a	9 June 1958
Almeley	1 July 1940	1 July 1940	1 July 1940
Ashcombe Road	20 May 1940	20 May 1940	20 May 1940
Ashwellthorpe	10 September 1939	4 August 1951	4 August 1951
Aston Botterell Siding	Already closed	11 September 1939	11 September 1939
Aston Cantlow Halt	25 September 1939	n/a	25 September 1939
Astwood Halt	25 September 1939	n/a	25 September 1939
Bacton	15 December 1941	2 February 1953	2 February 1953
Baglan Sands Halt	25 September 1939	n/a	25 September 1939
Bala Lake Halt	25 September 1939	n/a	25 September 1939
Balerno	1 November 1943	4 December 1967	4 December 1967
Banavie Pier	4 September 1939	1951	1951
Bangor-on-Dee*	10 June 1940	10 September 1962	10 September 1962
Bankhead (LMS)	2 June 1945	1 November 1950	1 November 1950
Barham	1 December 1940	1 October 1947	1 October 1947
Baron's Lane Halt & Siding	10 September 1939	1 April 1953	1 April 1953
Barton Stacey Halt (Military)	2 December 1940	n/a	2 December 1940
Battersea (WLE)	21 October 1940	n/a	21 October 1940
Beckton	29 December 1940	Already closed	29 December 1940
Bentley Crossing (Workmen)	c1943	n/a	c1943
Billinge Green	2 March 1942	n/a	2 March 1942
Birkenhead Town	7 May 1945	n/a	7 May 1945
Bishopsbourne	1 December 1940	1 October 1947	1 October 1947
Bishopstone Beach Halt	1 January 1942	Already closed	1 January 1942
Blaenavon (LMS)	5 May 1941	28 September 1964	28 September 1964
Blaengwynfi	26 February 1968	October 1941	26 February 1968
Blowick	25 September 1939	1964	1964
Botolph's Bridge Road	1939	n/a	1939
Bow	23 April 1945	?	?
Bow Road*	21 April 1941/	7 December 1964	7 December 1964
Brentford (GW)	4 May 1942	n/a	4 May 1942
Bridge	1 December 1940	1 October 1947	1 October 1947
Brighton Road	27 January 1941	n/a	27 January 1941
Bristol Road	20 May 1940	n/a	20 May 1940
Broadstone	20 May 1940	n/a	20 May 1940
Bromshall	Already closed	September 1942	September 1942
Brookwood Cemetery North	15 May 1941	n/a	15 May 1941
Brookwood Cemetery South	15 May 1941	n/a	15 May 1941
Broughton Cross	2 March 1942	n/a	2 March 1942
Burdett Road	21 April 1941	n/a	21 April 1941
Burley Fields & Doxey Siding (Stafford)	n/a	1940	1940
Burmash Road	30 June 1940	n/a	30 June 1940
Burwarton Halt & Siding	Already closed	11 September 1939	11 September 1939
Byers Green	4 December 1939	2 June 1958	2 June 1958
Cadbury Road	20 May 1940	20 May 1940	20 May 1940
Caersws (Van)	Already Closed	4 November 1940	4 November 1940

Name	Passengers	Goods	Completely
Calder	3 May 1943	3 April 1967	3 April 1967
Calderbank	Already closed	31 July 1941	31 July 1941
Calderwood Glen Platform (Excursions)	September 1939	n/a	September 1939
Camber Sands	4 September 1939	4 September 1939	4 September 1939
Camel's Head Halt	4 May 1942	n/a	4 May 1943
Camp Hill	27 January 1941	n/a	27 January 1941
Canada Dock (Liverpool)	5 May 1941 *(due to enemy action)*	?	?
Canterbury South	1 December 1940	1 October 1947	1 October 1947
Catcliffe	11 September 1939	1 March 1955	1 March 1955
Catrine	3 May 1943	6 July 1964	6 July 1964
Central (PLA)	8 September 1940	n/a	8 September 1940
Cerist	Already closed	4 November 1940	4 November 1940
Chelsea & Fulham (WLE)	21 October 1940	n/a	21 October 1940
Chartley	4 December 1939	5 March 1951	5 March 1951
Childwall	Already closed	6 August 1943	6 August 1943
Chilton Halt & Siding	Already closed	11 September 1939	11 September 1939
Churn	10 September 1962	14 April 1943	10 September 1961
Churwell	2 December 1940	n/a	2 December 1940
Clapton Road	20 May 1940	n/a	20 May 1940
Cledford Bridge Halt	2 March 1942	n/a	2 March 1942
Cleobury North Crossing	Already closed	11 September 1939	11 September 1939
Cleobury Town Halt & Siding	Already closed	11 September 1939	11 September 1939
Clevedon	20 May 1940	20 May 1940	20 May 1940
Clevedon (All Saints)	20 May 1940	n/a	20 May 1940
Clevedon East	20 May 1940	n/a	20 May 1940
Clifford	15 December 1941	2 January 1950	2 January 1950
Clowne South	10 September 1939	4 July 1960	4 July 1960
Cloy Halt*	10 June 1940	n/a	10 September 1962
Cold Norton	10 September 1939	1 April 1953	1 April 1953
Colehouse Lane	20 May 1940	n/a	20 May 1940
Colinton	1 November 1943	4 December 1967	4 December 1967
Connaught Road (PLA)	8 September 1940	n/a	8 September 1940
Cotham	11 September 1939	3 February 1964	3 February 1964
Coundon	4 December 1939	September 1956	September 1956
Creswell & Welbeck	10 September 1939	28 November 1949	28 November 1949
Crossford	3 May 1943	4 July 1949	4 July 1949
Crystal Palace (High Level) & Upper Norwood*	22 May 1944	20 September 1954	20 September 1954
Currie	1 November 1943	4 December 1967	4 December 1967
Cwmffrwdoer Halt	5 May 1941	n/a	5 May 1941
Dalkeith	5 January 1942	10 August 1964	10 August 1964
Dare Junction	n/a	1 September 1939	1 September 1939
Detton Ford Siding	Already closed	11 September 1939	11 September 1939
Ditton Priors Halt	Already closed	11 September 1939	11 September 1939
Dolphinton (LMS)	2 June 1945	1 November 1950	1 November 1950
Dorstone	15 December 1941	2 February 1953	2 February 1953
Drumclog	11 September 1939	11 September 1939	11 September 1939
Dundee Esplanade	2 October 1939	n/a	2 October 1939
Dunscore	3 May 1943	4 July 1949	4 July 1949
Dunsyre	2 June 1945	1 November 1950	1 November 1950
East Putney (SR)	5 May 1941	n/a	5 May 1941
Ebdon Lane	20 May 1940	n/a	20 May 1940
Edgware (LNER)	11 September 1939	1 June 1964	1 June 1964
Edwalton	28 July 1941	1 November 1965	1 November 1965
Elham	1 December 1940	1 October 1947	1 October 1947
Elson Halt*	10 June 1940	n/a	10 September 1962
Esholt	28 October 1940	28 October 1940	28 October 1940
Esplanade (Dundee)	2 October 1939	n/a	2 October 1939
Etwall	4 December 1939	4 March 1968	4 March 1968
Fairfield Halt	11 September 1939	n/a	11 September 1939
Finchley Road (Met)	Open	1 August 1941	Open

Name	Passengers	Goods	Completely
Finedon	2 December 1940	6 July 1964	6 July 1964
Five Ways	2 October 1944	n/a	2 October 1944
Flushdyke	5 May 1941	Mid-1948	Mid-1948
Folkestone Warren Halt	25 September 1939	n/a	25 September 1939
Ford Halt (Plymouth) (GWR)	6 October 1941	n/a	6 October 1941
Fort George	5 April 1943	11 August 1958	11 August 1958
Fushiebridge	4 October 1943	1 January 1959	1 January 1959
Gallions (PLA)	8 September 1940	n/a	8 September 1940
Garndiffaith	5 May 1941	n/a	5 May 1941
Garn-yr-Erw	5 May 1941	n/a	5 May 1941
Garth & Van Road	Already closed	4 November 1940	4 November 1940
Gartsherrie (LMS)	28 October 1940	28 October 1940	28 October 1940
Gillett's Crossing Halt	11 September 1939	n/a	11 September 1939
Girtford Halt & Siding	17 November 1940	1 November 1951	1 November 1951
Glengarnock High	Already closed	1 March 1945	1 March 1945
Golden Hill Platform	5 February 1940	n/a	5 February 1940
Golf Links (RC)	4 September 1939	n/a	4 September 1939
Gorleston North	5 October 1942	5 October 1942	5 October 1942
Grainsby Halt	October 1939	n/a	1939
Grassmoor	28 October 1940	28 October 1940	28 October 1940
Great Alne	25 September 1939	25 September 1939	25 September 1939
Great Houghton Halt & Goods	10 September 1951	1 March 1944	10 September 1951
Greatstone*	30 June 1940	n/a	30 June 1940
Green's Siding	15 December 1941	2 January 1950	2 January 1950
Greenodd*	16 September 1940	2 December 1963	2 December 1963
Grindley	4 December 1939	5 March 1951	5 March 1951
Grinkle	11 September 1939	11 September 1939	11 September 1939
Haggerston	6 May 1940	n/a	6 May 1940
Hailes Halt	1 November 1943	n/a	1 November 1943
Halton Holgate	10 September 1939	1 December 1958	1 December 1958
Ham Lane	20 May 1940	20 May 1940	20 May 1940
Handsworth Wood	5 May 1941	n/a	5 May 1941
Hassop	17 August 1942	5 October 1964	5 October 1964
Haverthwaite*	16 September 1940	24 April 1967	24 April 1967
Hazelwell	27 January 1941	1 March 1965	1 March 1965
Heanor (LNER)	4 December 1939	7 October 1963	7 October 1963
Hemsworth & South Kirkby	Already closed	1 April 1940	1 April 1940
Heversham	4 May 1942	n/a	4 May 1942
Hightown Halt	10 June 1940	n/a	10 September 1962
High Westwood	4 May 1942	n/a	4 May 1942
Holiday Camp (Jesson)*	30 June 1940	n/a	30 June 1940
Holtby	11 September 1939	1 January 1951	1 January 1951
Homerton	15 May 1944	n/a	15 May 1944
Honor Oak	22 May 1944	20 September 1954	20 September 1954

The effect of massive recruitment of men to serve in the armed forces was that large numbers of women were employed in traditionally male trades. This view, taken at the LNER's Temple Mills wagon shops, shows an improvised adjustable lever in use to enable the women employed to swing heavy axleboxes with minimum effort. *Ian Allan Library*

Name	Passengers	Goods	Completely
Hornsey Road	3 May 1943	n/a	3 May 1943
Husborne Crawley Halt	5 May 1941	n/a	5 May 1941
Ingestre	4 December 1939	5 March 1951	5 March 1951
Iron Acton	19 June 1944	10 June 1963	10 June 1963
Irongray	3 May 1943	4 July 1949	4 July 1949
Junction Road	3 May 1943	n/a	3 May 1943
Juniper Green	1 November 1943	11 August 1958	11 August 1958
Kelvinside	1 July 1942	6 July 1964	6 July 1964
Kempston & Elstow Halt	5 May 1941	n/a	5 May 1941
Kew Bridge (NSWJ)	12 September 1940	n/a	12 September 1940
King's Cross (Met)	16 October 1940	n/a	16 October 1940
King's Heath	27 January 1941	2 May 1966	2 May 1966
Kingston Road	20 May 1940	n/a	20 May 1940
Kinmel Bay Halt	2 September 1939	n/a	2 September 1939
Kirkby ROF Halt (Workmen)	c1943	n/a	c1943
Kirkland	3 May 1943	4 July 1949	4 July 1949
Lade Halt*	30 June 1940	n/a	30 June 1940
Lamesley	4 June 1945	14 September 1959	14 September 1959
Leman Street	7 July 1941	n/a	7 July 1941
Lifford	30 September 1940	1964	1964
Lipson Vale Halt	22 March 1942	n/a	22 March 1942
Little Drayton Halt	6 October 1941	n/a	6 October 1941
Little Stretton Halt*	4 January 1943	n/a	9 June 1958
Littlestone Holiday Camp*	30 June 1940	n/a	30 June 1940
Llanyblodwell	1951	May 1941	1951
Loch Tay	9 September 1939	9 September 1939	9 September 1939
Lochanhead	25 September 1939	1947	1947
Long Ashton Halt	6 October 1941	n/a	6 October 1941
Longdon Road	Already closed	1 June 1941	1 June 1941
Lord's (Met)	20 November 1939	n/a	20 November 1939
Lordship Lane*	22 May 1944	n/a	20 September 1954
Loudounhill	11 September 1939	11 September 1939	11 September 1939
Lower Edmonton, Low Level	11 September 1939	1964	1964
Lybster	1 April 1944	1 April 1944	1 April 1944
Lyminge*	3 May 1943	1 October 1947	1 October 1947
Lyonshall	1 July 1940	1 July 1940	1 July 1940
Maldon West	10 September 1939	1959	1959
Manor Way (PLA)	8 September 1940	n/a	8 September 1940
Marchwiel*	10 June 1940	4 September 1972	4 September 1972
Marlborough Road (Met)	20 November 1939	n/a	20 November 1939
Meickle Earnock Halt & Goods	12 December 1943	1953	1953
Methley Junction	4 October 1943	4 October 1943	4 October 1943
Mickleover	4 December 1939	1964	1964
Mickleton Halt	6 October 1941	n/a	6 October 1941
Mid Clyth	1 April 1944	1 April 1944	1 April 1944
Mill Hill (The Hale)	11 September 1939	1964	1964
Milton Road	20 May 1940	n/a	20 May 1940
Minshull Vernon	2 March 1942	n/a	2 March 1942
Moniaive	3 May 1943	1949	1949
Monks Lane Halt	11 September 1939	n/a	11 September 1939
Monkton	28 October 1940	1960	1960
Moore	1 February 1943	n/a	1 February 1943
Moseley (LMS)	27 January 1941	n/a	27 January 1941
Mount Vernon South	16 August 1943	1965	1965
Neepsend	28 October 1940	n/a	28 October 1940
Nelson, Glam (TV)	Already closed	End 1939	End 1939
Newbigging (LMS)	2 June 1945	1960	1960
Newby Bridge	12 September 1939	n/a	12 September 1939
Newby Wiske	11 September 1939	1963	1963
Newhouse (Workmen)	31 July 1941	n/a	31 July 1941
Newton Road	7 May 1945	n/a	7 May 1945

Name	Passengers	Goods	Completely
Newtonairds	3 May 1943	1949	1949
Ninian Park Platform	10 September 1939	n/a	10 September 1939
Norwich (Trowse)	5 September 1939	Post 1978	Post 1978
Nottingham London Road (Low Level)	25 May 1944	4 December 1972	4 December 1972
Occumster	1 April 1944	1 April 1944	1 April 1944
Old Ford (NL)	23 April 1945	n/a	23 April 1945
Old Oak Common Coal Depot	n/a	March 1942	March 1942
Orton Waterville	5 October 1942	1964	1964
Overton-on-Dee*	10 June 1940	10 September 1962	10 September 1962
Overtown (LMS)	5 October 1942	n/a	5 October 1942
Palterton & Sutton	Already closed	December 1939	December 1939
Parkside Halt	1 April 1944	n/a	1 April 1944
Penmaen Halt	25 September 1939	n/a	25 September 1939
Pentrepoid Halt	5 May 1941	n/a	5 May 1941
Pentwyn Halt	5 May 1941	n/a	5 May 1941
Peterchurch	15 December 1941	1953	1953
Pickhill Halt*	10 June 1940	n/a	10 September 1962
Plaidy	22 May 1944	22 May 1944	22 May 1944
Plymouth Millbay	23 April 1941	1966	1966
Poplar (East India Road) (NL)	23 April 1945	n/a	23 April 1945
Poplar (GWR)	n/a	October 1940	October 1940
Port Clarence	11 September 1939	1964	1964
Portishead (WCP)	20 May 1940	n/a	20 May 1940
Portishead South	20 May 1940	n/a	20 May 1940
Prescott Siding	Already closed	11 September 1939	11 September 1939
Princes Dock (LOR)	13 March 1941	n/a	13 May 1941
	(due to enemy action)		
Queenborough Pier	Already closed	1939	1939
Ravenscraig	1 February 1944	1949	1949
Red House	Already closed	4 November 1940	4 November 1940
Riby Street Platform (Workmen)	14 April 1941	n/a	14 April 1941
Richborough Castle Halt	September 1939	n/a	September 1939
Rigg	1 November 1942	1956	1956
Roster Road Halt	1 April 1944	n/a	1 April 1944
Rye (RC)	4 September 1939	4 September 1939	4 September 1939
Ryeland	11 September 1939	11 September 1939	11 September 1939
St Ann's Road	9 August 1942	n/a	9 August 1942
St Quintin Park & Wormwood Scrubs	3 October 1940	n/a	3 October 1940
Salt & Sandon	4 December 1939	n/a	4 December 1939
Sandside	4 May 1942	1968	1968
Saughtree*	1 December 1944	1 September 1958	1 September 1958
Scotby (Mid)	1 February 1942	1 February 1942	1 February 1942
Seaham Harbour	11 September 1939	n/a	11September 1939
Sesswick Halt*	10 June 1940	n/a	10 September 1962
Shadwell & St George's East	7 July 1941	n/a	7 July 1941
Sherburn Colliery	28 July 1941	1959	1959
Shincliffe	28 July 1941	1963	1963
Shoreditch (NL)	4 October 1940	n/a	4 October 1940
Shoreham Airport (Bungalow Town Halt)	15 July 1940	n/a	15 July 1940
Soho Road	5 May 1941	n/a	5 May 1941
South Bromley (NL)	23 April 1945	n/a	23 April 1945
South Marston Halt (Workmen)	1944	n/a	30 June 1957
Spiersbridge	Already closed	September 1941	September 1941
Spilsby	10 September 1939	1958	1958
Spinkhill	10 September 1939	4 January 1965	4 January 1965
Stafford Common	4 December 1939	1968	1968
Stansfield Halt	31 July 1944	n/a	31 July 1944
Stapleford (LNER)	10 September 1939	1966	1966
Steelend	n/a	1 July 1941	1 July 1941
Stepford	3 May 1943	1949	1949
Stottesdon Halt & Siding	Already closed	11 September 1939	11 September 1939

Name	Passengers	Goods	Completely
Stow St Mary Halt	10 September 1939	n/a	10 September 1939
Strap Lane Halt*	6 October 1941	n/a	5 June 1950
Stretton-on-Fosse	Already closed	1 June 1942	1 June 1942
Sutton Weaver	Already closed	30 April 1942	30 April 1942
Swiss Cottage (Met)	18 August 1940	n/a	18 August 1940
Tan-y-Grisiau (Fest)	16 September 1939	1946	1946
Tarbolton	4 January 1943	1964	1964
The Pilot*	30 June 1940	n/a	30 June 1940
Thornbury (Mid)	19 June 1944	1966	1966
Thrumster	1 April 1944	1 April 1944	1 April 1944
Tidal Basin (GE)	15 August 1943	n/a	15 August 1943
Tovil	15 March 1943	15 March 1943	15 March 1943
		(Maidstone (Tovil Siding)	
Trecynon	n/a	1 September 1939	1 September 1939
Trefeglwys	Already closed	4 November 1940	4 November 1940
Trench Halt & Siding	10 June 1940	2 April 1941	10 September 1962
Trentham Gardens	11 September 1939	11 September 1939	11 September 1939
Turnberry	2 March 1942	1955	1955
Tytherington	19 June 1944	1963	1963
Ulbster	1 April 1944	1 April 1944	1 April 1944
Ullock	Already closed	1 July 1943	1 July 1943
Upper Sydenham*	22 May 1944	n/a	20 September 1954
Uxbridge High Street	1 September 1939	1964	1964
Uxbridge Road	20 October 1940	n/a	20 October 1940
Varteg Halt	5 May 1941	n/a	5 May 1941
Victoria Park (LNER)	1 November 1942	n/a	1 November 1942
Victoria Park (NL)	8 November 1943	n/a	8 November 1943
Vowchurch	15 December 1941	1953	1953
Waenavon	5 May 1941	1954	1954
Wainfelin Halt	5 May 1941	n/a	5 May 1941
Walton Park	20 May 1940	20 May 1940	20 May 1940
Walton-in-Gordano	20 May 1940	20 May 1940	20 May 1940
Washingborough	29 July 1940	29 July 1940	29 July 1940
Waterloo Road (Stoke)	4 October 1943	n/a	4 October 1943
Watton-at-Stone	10 September 1939	1965	1965
Weaste	19 October 1942	1947	1947
Weelsby Road Halt	1 January 1940	n/a	1 January 1940
Welsh's Crossing Halt	By May 1941	n/a	By May 1941
Wern Hir Halt (Workmen)	21 October 1940	n/a	21 October 1940
West Brompton (WLE)	21 October 1940	n/a	21 October 1940
West Rounton Gates	13 September 1939	n/a	13 September 1939
West Tinsley	11 September 1939	1960	1960*
Westbrook	15 December 1941	1950	1950
Westhall Milk Platform (Workmen)	2 June 1945	n/a	2 June 1945
Westwood	28 October 1940	28 October 1940	28 October 1940
Wick St Lawrence	20 May 1940	20 May 1940	20 May 1940
Windermere Lakeside	31 August 1941	6 April 1964	6 April 1964
Wood Green (Old Bescot)	5 May 1941	n/a	5 May 1941
Woodhead Dam (Workmen)	1944	n/a	1944
Woodkirk	25 September 1939	25 September 1939	25 September 1939
Wootton Broadmead Halt	5 May 1941	n/a	5 May 1941
Worle Town	20 May 1940	20 May 1940	20 May 1940
Wreay	16 August 1943	16 August 1943	16 August 1943

* Stations reopened to passenger services postwar.

PASSENGER STATIONS OPENED
1939-1945

Arncott (Military)	1940
Cairn Point (Military)	May 1942
Cairnryan (Military)	May 1942
Canley Halt	30 November 1940
Charlesfield Halt (Workmen)	10 August 1942
Chittening Platform (Workmen)	27 October 1941
Cold Meece (Workmen)	10 August 1941
Eryholme (Military)	17 February 1944
Ford Halt (Military)	1940
Ford Houses (Workmen)	5 August 1941
Glascoed East Access Halt (Workmen)	3 January 1943
Glascoed West Access Halt (Workmen)	12 June 1941
Gregson Lane Halt (Workmen)	Unknown date during war
Halliford Halt	1 May 1944; renamed Upper Halliford Halt 22 May 1944
Heighington ROF Demons Bridge	14 December 1941
Heighington ROF Simpasture	18 January 1942
Hillington West	1 January 1940
Hirwaun Pond Halt (Workmen)	23 July 1941
Idmiston Halt	3 January 1943
Innermessan (Military)	May 1942
Kidwelly Flats Halt (Workmen)	6 August 1941
King George V Dock (Troopships)	Used during World War 2 but dates uncertain
Kinnerley Halt	1941
Kirkby ROF Halt	9 December 1940
Larkhill Camp (Military)	c1940
Lemsford Road Halt (Workmen)	1 August 1942

Preparation was essential in ensuring that Britain's railways were restored as quickly as possible when damaged. This view, taken on the LNER, shows an ARP exercise in early 1943. *Ian Allan Library*

Llanbadarn	27 July 1945 (reopened)
Llandow Wick Road Halt	19 April 1943
London Road (Military)	May 1942
Longcross Halt (Military)	c1940; became public station 21 September 1942
Lutnor (Military)	c1942
Manor Road	15 May 1940
Millway (Workmen)	October 1944
Mulberry Halt (Military)	1943
Nesscliff Camp (Military)	1941
Nesscliff Halt (Military)	1941
Old House Point (Military)	May 1942
Parkhouse Halt (Military)	7 July 1941
Pentre Halt (Military)	1941
Piddington (Military)	June 1943
Port Gate Platform (Military)	1943
Risley (Workmen)	2 April 1940
Risley (Workmen)	July 1941; branch from Newchurch
Ruddington Factory Halt (Workmen)	1 September 1941
Shrawardine Halt (Military)	1941
Singer Workers Platform (Workmen)	c1942
South Marston Halt (Workmen)	5 June 1941
St John's Wood (Bakerloo)	20 November 1939
Stanlow & Thornton	Opened 23 December 1940 for oil workers; opened to public 24 February 1941
Swiss Cottage (Bakerloo)	20 November 1939
Tinker's Green Halt	16 October 1939
Treforest Estate	5 January 1942
Ulceby Aerodrome Platform (Military)	by June 1943
Upnor (Military)	1942
Urlay Nook Halt (Workmen)	4 October 1943; renamed Allens West Halt 22 May 1944
Wilhamstead (Workmen)	Uncertain
Woodcroft Halt (Military)	26 August 1943

Below left: **Although the public were urged not to make unnecessary journeys during the war, conventional timetabled services still operated and most of the prewar passenger network was maintained. Seen here on the left, 'Lord Nelson' No 865** *Sir John Hawkins* **awaits departure from Waterloo on 7 August 1942, with the 10.50am service to the West of England; on the right, 'Paddlebox' No 445 stands at the head of the 10.54am semi-fast service to Salisbury.** *Ian Allan Library*

Below right: **During World War 2 the railways were required to move vast quantities of men and equipment. It was estimated that each 1,000 bomber raid required 650 tanks of fuel, as well as 362 wagons of bombs; in the three months following the D-Day landings in June 1944, 100 million gallons of fuel were used by RAF and USAAF aircraft flying from the airfields of East Anglia alone. Here three large naval guns are being moved by the LNER.** *Ian Allan Library*

TRACK MODIFICATIONS

At the outbreak of war, the British railway network stretched for some 20,300 route miles, of which 10,800 were double-track and 7,500 single-track. World War 2 would impose new traffic patterns upon the railways and also the need to ensure that traffic could be safely and efficiently diverted away from lines – such as the West London Railway and the City Widened lines – perceived to be at high risk in the event of enemy action against the country's transport infrastructure.

Other work was designed to increase the capacity of the rail network. In 1941, authority was granted to quadruple the six-mile section line from Lansdown Junction, Cheltenham, to Engine Shed Junction, Gloucester. Work commenced in September 1941 and included the installation of some 15 miles of track and pointwork, completed in June 1942. The line between Severn Tunnel Junction and Newport was also quadrupled, with work undertaken between August and November 1941. The LNER main line between York and Northallerton had been upgraded during the 1930s, but there were surviving bottlenecks at Skelton Bridge, Raskelf, Sessay and Thirsk. Work here was undertaken in two stages: firstly, the 6.45-mile stretch of line between Pilmoor and Thirsk was quadrupled; secondly, a 27-mile down slow line was built from Skelton Bridge to Thirsk. Improvement work, with an additional bridge, was also undertaken at Skelton Bridge.

Generally speaking, improvements to lines were undertaken without the withdrawal of services, which proved impractical. However, when it came to doubling of the Didcot, Newbury & Southampton line of the GWR, the build-up of men and equipment required for the planned D-Day landings rendered the capacity of the single-track DN&S inadequate. Passenger services over the line were suspended between 4 August 1942 and 8 March 1943, to facilitate improvements. Completion of the doubling from Didcot to Newbury was completed on 18 April 1943, and from Woodhay to Winchester Junction on 5 May. Doubling of the line from Didcot to Newbury and thence on to Woodhay, the first station south of Newbury, was completed in stages through the winter and spring of 1942/43. Beyond Woodhay the single line was retained but with extended, re-instated or new passing loops provided. There was a totally new connection for Up trains between Winchester Junction (SR) and the DNS stopping place at Worthy Down.

There were also a number of branches constructed to serve military installations and Royal Ordnance factories. These included:

* Caerwent branch – to serve the Royal Naval Propellant Factory – opened 1939
* Glascoed ROF branch – opened 6 October 1940
* Moreton-on-Lugg – opened 12 September 1943 to serve a US Army depot; vacated by the US in 1945 and became No 42 Ordnance Depot.

The following examines in more detail the various curves and spurs constructed during World War 2:

Location and lines, (Date opened), [Fate]

KING'S CROSS – connection installed by the LPTB between the Widened Lines and the Circle Line to the east of King's Cross Metropolitan Line station, (20 November 1939)

HARRINGAY – Harringay Park Junction on the Tottenham & Hampstead Joint to Harringay West Junction on the ECML, (11 March 1940, [Still in use as a freight-only line]

GOSPEL OAK – double-track connection between the Tottenham & Hampstead Joint line and the WCML at Gospel Oak Junction, (11 March 1940), [Still in use as a freight-only line]

ROMFORD – Connection between the LMS branch from Upminster and the LNER Romford-Shenfield line, (21 July 1940), [Still in use as a passenger line]

SANDY – double-track connection from Tempsford on the ECML to Blunham on the Cambridge-Bedford line, (13 September 1940), [Closed January 1961; used briefly as sidings thereafter]

CALVERT – double-track connection from Calvert on the GC main line to Claydon on the Oxford-Bedford line, (14 September 1940), [Still in use as a freight-only line]

STAINES MOOR – single-track connection between Staines Moor Junction on the Staines-Windsor line and Yeoveney on the Staines West-West Drayton line, (15 September 1940), [Closed 16 December 1947]

OXFORD – direct connection between the GWR and LMS lines north of the station; previously the connection could only be made via exchange sidings, (8 November 1940), [Link retained post World War 2 and used in 1951 when all passenger services diverted into the ex-GWR station in Oxford to permit the closure of Oxford (Rewley Road). The link was slightly relocated in the early 1970s. Still in use today for the Bicester Town-Oxford service]

ST BUDEAUX – connection between St Budeaux Junction on the GW main line to the west of Plymouth and St Budeaux Victoria Road, (21 March 1941), [Still in use as a passenger line following the closure of the ex-LSWR route into Plymouth]

CANTERBURY – Link between the Faversham-Dover and Ashford-Margate lines to facilitate movement of rail-borne batteries; restored a link that had previously existed between 5 May 1918 and November 1920, (2 March 1941), [Last used 28 November 1946 but not officially closed until October 1951; reopened 23 February 1953 due to flooding. Final closure occurred on 20 May 1953]

READING – double-track connection from Reading New Junction on the GWR main line to Reading Spur Junction on the SR line from Reading to Ascot, (1 June 1941), [Still in use for both passenger and freight services]

BORDESLEY – doubling of the goods branch between the LMS and GWR, (13 July 1941), [Still in use for passenger and freight traffic]

DORKING – An emergency curve from the Dorking-Redhill line to the Dorking-Horsham line, (3 September 1941), [Probably never used]

NORTHALLERTON – Connection between the northbound Northallerton loop line and the northbound ECML to provide a diversionary route for ECML traffic away from the station. The line passed under the Hawes branch; as a result of the difference in height being only 5ft a temporary removable bridge was installed on the branch over the connection, (November 1941), [Closed]

WESTBURY – Connection between Heywood Road Junction (on the Westbury-Pewsey line) and Hawkeridge Junction (on the Westbury-Trowbridge line), (30 July 1942), [Still in use as a passenger line]

BLETCHLEY – single-track connection between the down fast WCML and the Oxford-Bedford line, (31 August 1942), [Survived until the layout through Bletchley was modernised as part of the West Coast electrification scheme in the early 1960s]

BROOM – Connection from the Broom-Stratford line to the Broom-Evesham line, (28 September 1942), [Closed 13 June 1960]

MICKLE TRAFFORD – Connection between the Chester-Warrington line and the Chester (Northgate)-Altrincham line, (4 October 1942), [Finally closed 1992]

CRAYFORD – Crayford Spur A Junction to Crayford Spur B Junction, (11 October 1942), [Still in use as a freight-only line]

ROCHESTER – The original bridge, disused from 1927, was restored to use in case of damage to the existing bridge at a cost of £70,400. The modified structure was designed to handle both road and rail traffic, (November 1942), [Probably never used; dismantled after the war]

WREXHAM – Connection between the GWR line north of General station and the LNER line north from Exchange, (9 February 1943), [Still in use as a freight-only line]

CARLISLE – The section of line from Caldew Junction to Etterby Junction was quadrupled to increase capacity for goods traffic; this resulted in the construction of a new double-track viaduct across the River Eden. Also access to and from Kingmoor shed was improved, (14 March 1943), [The viaduct remains in use for freight traffic]

SOUTHAMPTON – double-track link from Redbridge to Southampton's New Docks, (19 April 1943), [Still in use as a freight-only line serving the docks]

KING'S WORTHY – single-track connection between the Didcot, Newbury & Southampton line and the SR Basingstoke-Winchester line at Winchester Junction, (5 May 1943), [Closed officially by November 1951, but not used for some period prior to actual closure]

LAUNCESTON – connection between the GWR and SR lines to the east of the town, (22 September 1943), [Closed 28 February 1966]

YEOVIL – double-track connection between the GWR line to the south of Pen Mill station and the SR line from Yeovil Junction to Yeovil Town, (13 October 1943), [Still in use as a freight-only line]

LYDFORD – connection between the GWR Plymouth-Launceston line and the SR main line to the south of Lydford station, (15 November 1943), [Closed 28 February 1966]

BOUNDS GREEN – single-track connection between the branch terminus at Palace Gates and Bowes Park on the Wood Green-Hertford North line, (9 July 1944), [Still in use as access from the north to Bounds Green depot]

Above: Created shortly before the outbreak of war, the Ministry of Supply included a Directorate of Transport Engineers. This department was headed by Robert A. Riddles, formerly Mechanical & Electrical Engineer for the LMS in Scotland. He was tasked with designing locomotives that were easy to build and maintain, resulting in two classes of tender locomotive – the first of which was the 2-8-0. Having rejected such designs as the LNER 'O2' and the GWR '28xx', construction of the LMS '8F' was initially continued by all of the 'Big Four' companies. The later Austerity 2-8-0 was designed in 1942 and the first models ordered later that year. No 7035 was one of the initial batch of 50 ordered from North British and completed in April 1943. It was loaned to the LMS between construction and January 1945; after return to the War Department, it was subsequently loaned to the LNER in August 1947 and passed to BR ownership in December 1948. Renumbered 90131, it remained in service until March 1965. *C. C. B. Herbert*

Above right The second class of tender locomotive designed by Robert A. Riddles was the Austerity 2-10-0. A total of 150 of the type were constructed by North British between 1943 and 1945. No 73777 is seen here on 14 July 1945, running light engine, tender first, at

Trumpington in Cambridgeshire. This particular locomotive was constructed in June 1945 and loaned to the LNER when new. It returned to the War Department in October 1946, before becoming BR No 90753 in December 1948. It was finally withdrawn for scrap in July 1961. *E. R. Wethersett*

Left: The third class of Austerity locomotive was a 0-6-0ST shunter designed by the Hunslet company of Leeds. Although the War Department had initially planned to use the LMS 'Jinty' 0-6-0T as the basis of its standard shunting locomotive, Hunslet was successful in getting its design adopted and a total of 377 were built between 1943 and 1947, on orders placed during the war. With the cessation of hostilities, the number of locomotives required was significantly reduced and the War Department sold a number of them – including 75 that passed to the LNER to become that railway's Class J94. One of these, LNER No 8027, is seen here at Darlington in August 1947. It was originally built by Hunslet in 1945. *H. C. Casserley*

BIBLIOGRAPHY

British Railways Press Office, *British Railways in Peace and War*, 1944

British Railways Press Office, *It Can Now Be Revealed: More about British Railways in Peace and War*, 1945

Bryan, Tim, *Railways in Wartime*, Shire 2011

Burkhalter, Paul, *Devonport Dockyard Railway*, Twelveheads Press 1996

Christiansen, Mike, *The Shropshire & Montgomeryshire Light Railway under Military Control 1940-1960*, Lightmoor, 2011

Cooper, Alan, Leggot, Peter and Sprenger, Cyril, *The Melbourne Military Railway*, Oakwood 1990

Crump, Norman, *By Rail to Victory*, LNER 1947

Johnson, Peter, *An Illustrated History of the Shropshire and Montgomeryshire Light Railway*, OPC 2008

Lawton, E. R. and Sackett, M. W., *The Bicester Military Railway*, OPC 1992

Ludlam, A. J., *The Catterick Camp Military Railway and the Richmond Branch*, Oakwood 1993

Nash, George C., *The LMS at War*, LMSR 1946

Nock, O. S., *Britain's Railways at War 1939-1945*, Ian Allan 1971

Price, M. R. C., *The Cleobury Mortimer & Ditton Priors Light Railway*, Oakwood 1995

Ronald, D. W. and Carter, R. J., *Longmoor Military Railway*, David & Charles 1974

Ronard, D. W. and Christiansen, Mike, *The Longmoor Railway, A New History Volume 2: World War 2 and the Cold War Era*, Lightmoor, 2013

Rowledge, Peter, *Austerity 2-8-0s & 2-10-0s*, Ian Allan 1987

Smith, W. and Beddoes, K., *The Cleobury Mortimer and Ditton Priors Light Railway*, OPC 1980

Above: Of the 800 'S160s' delivered to the UK in 13 batches during 1942 and 1943, almost 400 were initially allocated to the main-line companies, in part to get them run in and partly to replace equipment and increase capacity. The latter 400 were largely stockpiled at Ebbw Vale pending the D-Day landings. One of the 50 allocated to the LMSR was No 2244, seen here at Berkhamsted on 14 June 1944. Following the D-Days landings, the locomotives allocated to the UK railways were gradually transferred to Ebbw Vale and then shipped across to Europe. *H. C. Casserley*

Below: The 'S100' class 0-6-0T was another class of US-built steam locomotive to see service on Britain's railways during the war, of which 382 were built between 1942 and 1944 by the Davenport locomotive works, H. K. Porter and Vulcan iron works, to the design of Colonel Howard G. Hill. Shipped to Britain prior to D-Day, 15 were eventually acquired by the Southern Railway – of which 14 ultimately entered service, with four surviving into preservation. Taken at Newbury on 29 March 1947, this view records 10 of the ex-WD locomotives awaiting disposal. *H. C. Casserley*

Key to map pages

─────────	Passenger line
● THURSO	Passenger station
─────────	Line closed completely 1.9.39 - 31.8.45
● LYBSTER	Station closed completely 1.9.39 - 31.8.45
─────────	Freight line
● BODDAM	Freight station
─────────	Passenger service withdrawn 1.9.39 - 31.8.45
● FORT GEORGE	Station closed to passenger services 1.9.39 - 31.8.45
─────────	Freight - only line closed 1.9.39 - 31.8.45
● CHILDWELL	Freight - only station closed 1.9.39 - 31.8.45
─────────	Military line
● BISLEY CAMP	Military station
	Line constructed for use during war
● HALLIFORD HALT	Station opened during war
─────────	Line taken over by military exclusively during war
● WORTHINGTON	Station taken over by military exclusively during war

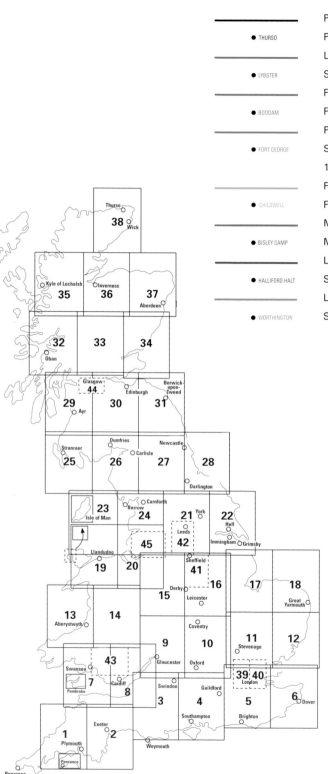

27

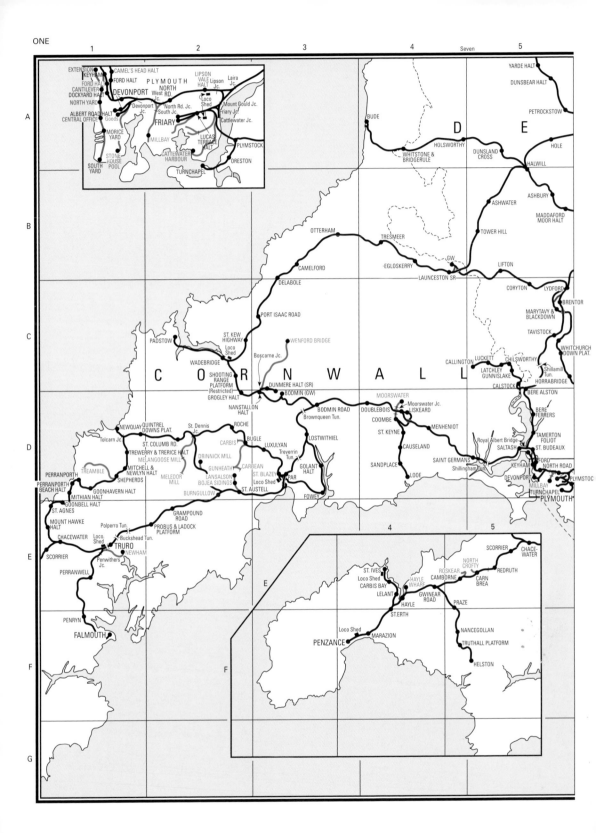

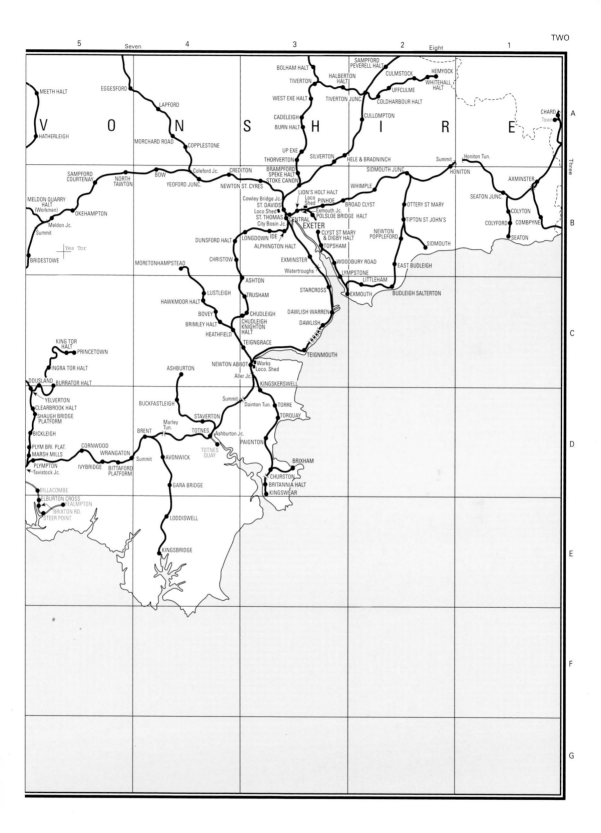

5   Seven   4   3   2   Eight   1

MEETH HALT
EGGESFORD
LAPFORD

V   O   N   S   H   I   R   E

BOLHAM HALT
SAMPFORD PEVERELL HALT
TIVERTON
HALBERTON HALT
CULMSTOCK
HEMYOCK
WHITEHALL HALT
WEST EXE HALT
TIVERTON JUNC.
UFFCULME
COLDHARBOUR HALT

CHARD Town

HATHERLEIGH

MORCHARD ROAD
COPPLESTONE

CADELEIGH
BURN HALT
CULLOMPTON

SAMPFORD COURTENAY
NORTH TAWTON
BOW
Coleford Jc.
CREDITON

UP EXE
THORVERTON
SILVERTON
HELE & BRADNINCH
Summit
Honiton Tun.

A

Three

YEOFORD JUNC.
NEWTON ST. CYRES
BRAMPFORD SPEKE HALT
STOKE CANON
SIDMOUTH JUNC.
HONITON
AXMINSTER

MELDON QUARRY HALT (Workmen)
OKEHAMPTON
LION'S HOLT HALT
Loco Shed
WHIMPLE

Meldon Jc.
Cowley Bridge Jc.
ST. DAVIDS
Loco Shed
ST. THOMAS
City Basin Jc.
PINHOE
BROAD CLYST
Exmouth Jc.
POLSLOE BRIDGE HALT
SEATON JUNC.
OTTERY ST MARY
TIPTON ST JOHN'S
COLYTON
COLYFORD
COMBPYNE

Summit
EXETER
CENTRAL
CLYST ST MARY & DIGBY HALT
NEWTON POPPLEFORD
SIDMOUTH
SEATON

BRIDESTOWE
Yes Tor
DUNSFORD HALT
LONGDOWN   IDE
ALPHINGTON HALT
TOPSHAM
WOODBURY ROAD
EAST BUDLEIGH

B

MORETONHAMPSTEAD
CHRISTOW
EXMINSTER
Watertroughs
LYMPSTONE
BUDLEIGH SALTERTON

ASHTON
STARCROSS
LITTLEHAM
LUSTLEIGH
TRUSHAM
EXMOUTH

HAWKMOOR HALT
BOVEY
BRIMLEY HALT
CHUDLEIGH
CHUDLEIGH KNIGHTON HALT
DAWLISH WARREN

KING TOR HALT
PRINCETOWN
HEATHFIELD
TEIGNGRACE
DAWLISH

C

INGRA TOR HALT
ASHBURTON
NEWTON ABBOT
Works
Loco. Shed
TEIGNMOUTH

DOUSLAND
BURRATOR HALT
Aller Jc.
KINGSKERSWELL

YELVERTON
CLEARBROOK HALT
SHAUGH BRIDGE PLATFORM
BUCKFASTLEIGH
Summit
Dainton Tun.
TORRE
TORQUAY

BICKLEIGH
STAVERTON

PLYM BRI. PLAT.
MARSH MILLS
CORNWOOD
WRANGATON
BRENT
Marley Tun.
TOTNES
Ashburton Jc.
PAIGNTON

D

PLYMPTON
IVYBRIDGE
BITTAFORD PLATFORM
AVONWICK
TOTNES QUAY
BRIXHAM

Tavistock Jc.
BILLACOMBE
ELBURTON CROSS
YEALMPTON
BRIXTON RD.
STEER POINT
GARA BRIDGE
CHURSTON
BRITANNIA HALT
KINGSWEAR

LODDISWELL

E

KINGSBRIDGE

F

G

29

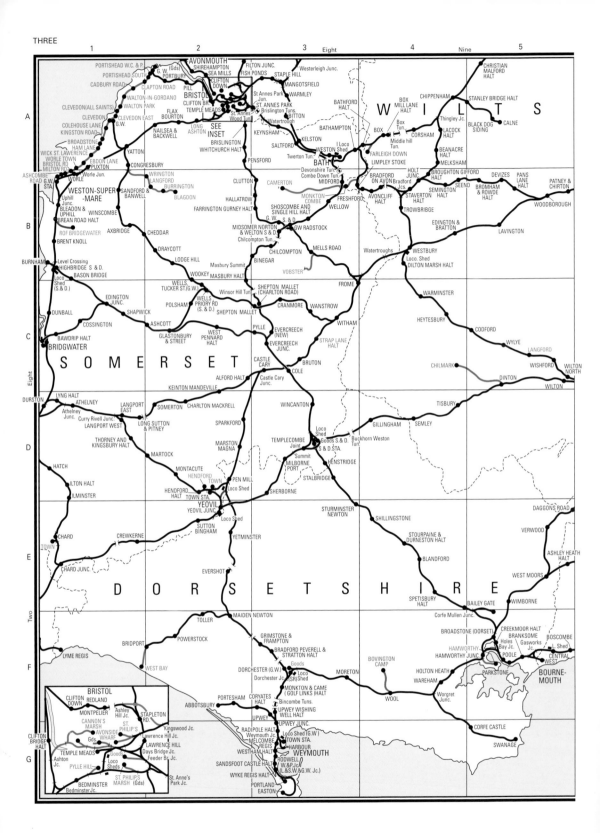

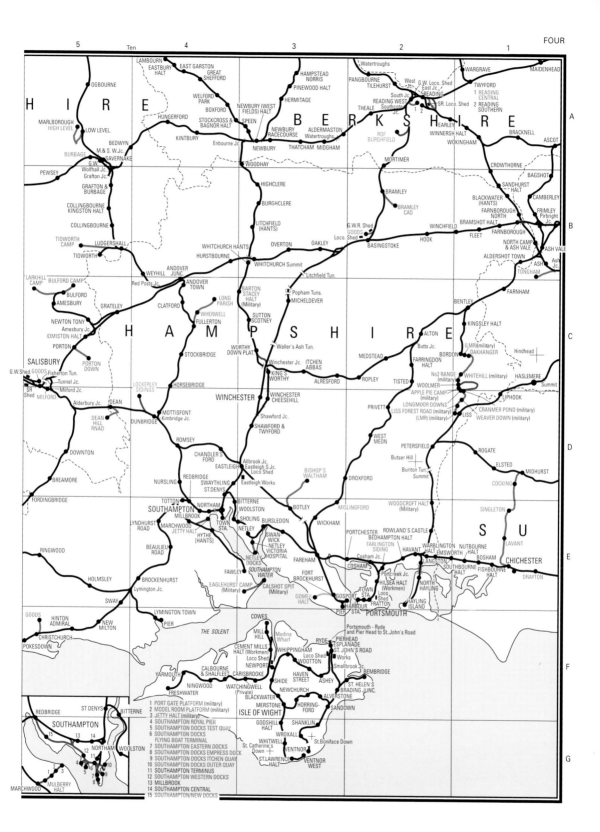

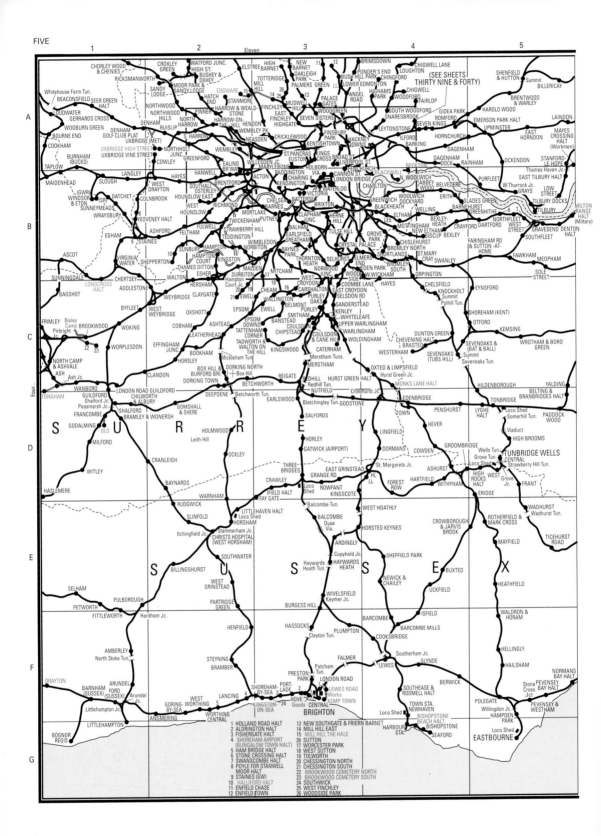

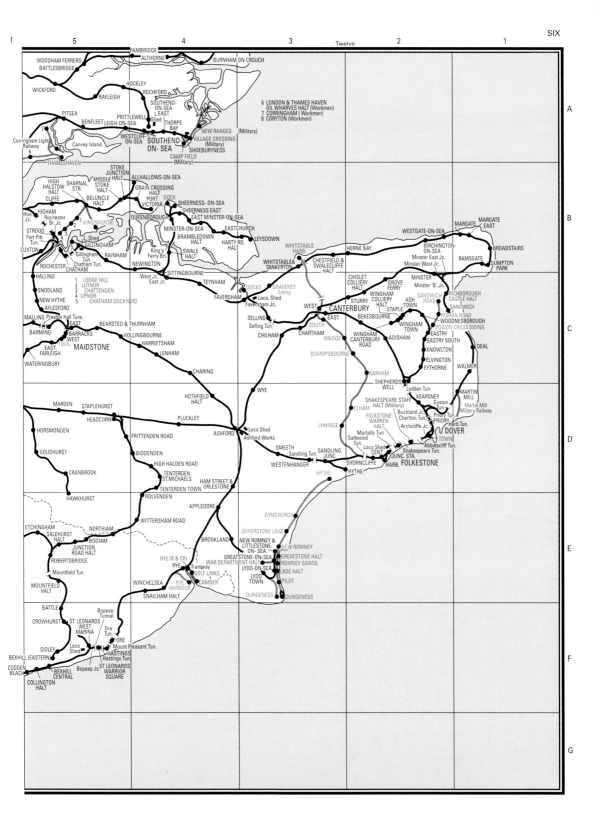

5 4 3 Twelve 2 1

A

B

C

D

E

F

G

FAMBRIDGE
WOODHAM FERRERS
BATTLESBRIDGE
ALTHORNE
BURNHAM ON CROUCH
WICKFORD
HOCKLEY
RAYLEIGH
ROCHFORD
SOUTHEND-
ON-SEA
L.EAST
PITSEA
BENFLEET
LEIGH-ON-SEA
PRITTLEWELL
THORPE
BAY
Shed
WESTCLIFF-
ON-SEA
SOUTHEND-
ON- SEA
VILLAGE CROSSING
(Military)
SHOEBURYNESS
Corringham Light
Railway
Canvey Island
NEW RANGES
(Military)
CAMP FIELD
(Military)
THAMESHAVEN

6 LONDON & THAMES HAVEN
  OIL WHARVES HALT (Workmen)
7 CORRINGHAM (Workmen)
8 CORYTON (Workmen)

STOKE
JUNCTION
HIGH
HALSTOW
HALT
SHARNAL
STR.
MIDDLE
STOKE
HALT
BELUNCLE
HALT
ALLHALLOWS-ON-SEA
GRAIN CROSSING
HALT
DOCK
CLIFFE
Hoo
Jc.
Rochester
Br. Jc.
PORT
VICTORIA
SHEERNESS-ON-SEA
SHEERNESS EAST
EAST MINSTER-ON-SEA
STROOD
Fort Pitt
Tun.
KINGSNORTH
QUEENBOROUGH
MINSTER-ON-SEA
EASTCHURCH
WESTGATE-ON-SEA
MARGATE
MARGATE
EAST
CUXTON
ROCHESTER
L. Shed
GILLINGHAM
Chatham Tun.
CHATHAM
RAINHAM
King's
Ferry Bri.
BRAMBLEDOWN
HALT
SWALE
HALT
HARTY RD.
HALT
LEYSDOWN
HERNE BAY
BIRCHINGTON-
ON-SEA
Minster East Jc.
Minster West Jc.
RAMSGATE
BROADSTAIRS
DUMPTON
PARK
HALLING
1 LODGE HILL
2 LUTNOR
3 CHATTENDEN
4 UPNOR
5 CHATHAM DOCKYARD
NEWINGTON
West Jc.
East Jc.
SITTINGBOURNE
WHITSTABLE
HARB.
WHITSTABLE &
TANKERTON
CHESTFIELD &
SWALECLIFFE
HALT
SNODLAND
NEW HYTHE
AYLESFORD
TEYNHAM
DOCKS
GRAVENEY
Siding
CHISLET
COLLIERY
HALT
GROVE
FERRY
MINSTER
Minster 'B' Jc.
RICHBOROUGH
CASTLE HALT
MALLING
Preston Hall Tuns.
BARMING
EAST
BARRACKS
WEST
TOVIL
FAVERSHAM
Faversham Jc.
SELLING
Selling Tun.
WEST
EAST
CANTERBURY
SOUTH
WINGHAM
COLLIERY
HALT
STURRY
BEKESBOURNE
STAPLE
ASH
TOWN
SANDWICH
ROAD
ROMAN ROAD
SANDWICH
WOODNESBOROUGH
POISON CROSS SIDING
MAIDSTONE
BEARSTED & THURNHAM
HOLLINGBOURNE
HARRIETSHAM
EAST
FARLEIGH
WATERINGBURY
LENHAM
CHARING
CHILHAM
CHARTHAM
BRIDGE
WINGHAM
CANTERBURY
ROAD
ADISHAM
WINGHAM
TOWN
EASTRY
EASTRY SOUTH
KNOWLTON
DEAL
WALMER
BISHOPSBOURNE
ELVINGTON
EYTHORNE
MARDEN
STAPLEHURST
HEADCORN
HOTHFIELD
HALT
PLUCKLEY
WYE
BARHAM
SHEPHERDS
WELL
Lydden Tun.
KEARSNEY
MARTIN
MILL
HORSMONDEN
GOUDHURST
FRITTENDEN ROAD
BIDDENDEN
ASHFORD
Loco Shed
Ashford Works
SMEETH
SHAKESPEARE STAFF
HALT (Military)
ELHAM
FOLKESTONE
WARREN
HALT
Guston
Tun.
Buckland Jc.
Charlton Tun.
Archcliffe Jc.
Priory Tun.
PRIORY
DOVER
Harb. Tun.
Martin Mill
Military Railway
CRANBROOK
LYMINGE
Martello
Tun.
Saltwood
Tun.
Loco Shed
CENT.
Abbotscliff Tun.
Shakespeare Tun.
TOWN
HIGH HALDEN ROAD
SANDLING
JUNC.
Sandling Tun.
WESTENHANGER
SHORNCLIFFE
HARB.
FOLKESTONE
HAWKHURST
TENTERDEN
ST.MICHAELS
TENTERDEN TOWN
HAM STREET &
ORLESTONE
HYTHE
HYTHE
ROLVENDEN
APPLEDORE
WITTERSHAM ROAD
DYMCHURCH
ETCHINGHAM
SALEHURST
HALT
NORTHIAM
BODIAM
JUNCTION
ROAD HALT
ROBERTSBRIDGE
Mountfield Tun.
RYE (R & CR)
RYE
BROOKLAND
JEFFERSTONE LANE
NEW ROMNEY &
LITTLESTONE-
ON-SEA
NEW ROMNEY
GREATSTONE-ON-SEA
GREATSTONE HALT
ROMNEY SANDS
WAR DEPARTMENT HALT
MOUNTFIELD
HALT
WINCHELSEA
Tramway
GOLF LINKS
CAMBER
RYE
HARBOUR
SNAILHAM HALT
LYDD-ON-SEA
LADE HALT
LYDD
TOWN
PILOT
DUNGENESS
DUNGENESS
BATTLE
CROWHURST
Bopeep
Tunnel
ST. LEONARDS
WEST
MARINA
Ore
Tun.
Mount Pleasant Tun.
SIDLEY
Loco
Shed
ORE
HASTINGS
Hastings Tun.
BEXHILL (EASTERN)
COODEN
BEACH
BEXHILL
CENTRAL
Bopeep Jc.
ST LEONARDS
WARRIOR
SQUARE
COLLINGTON
HALT

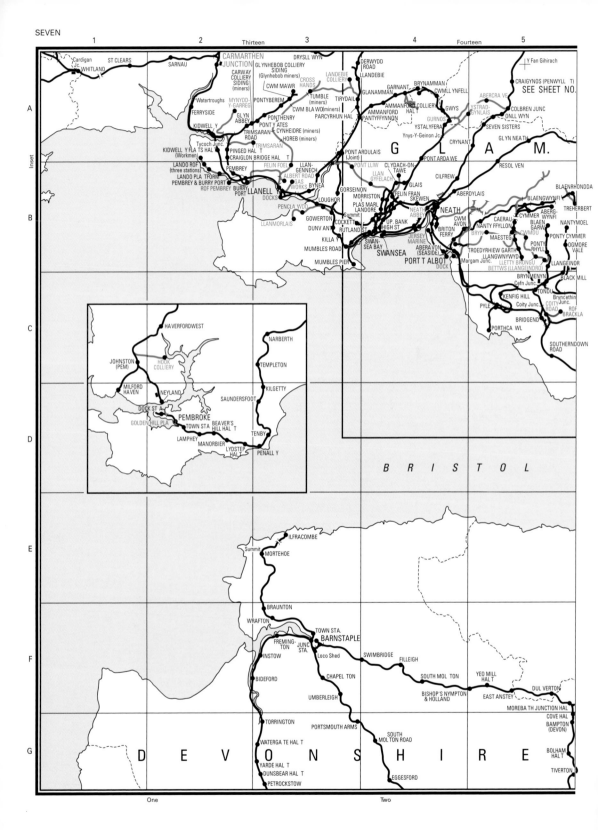

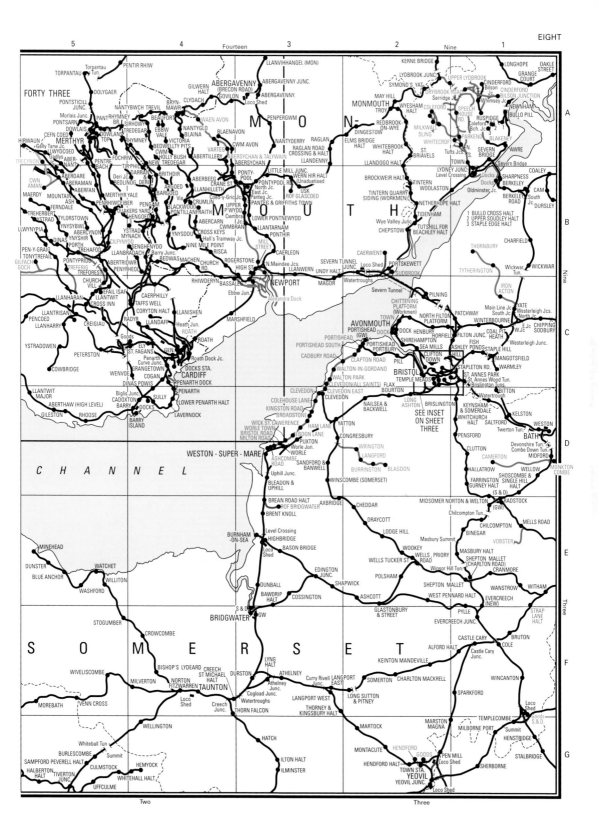

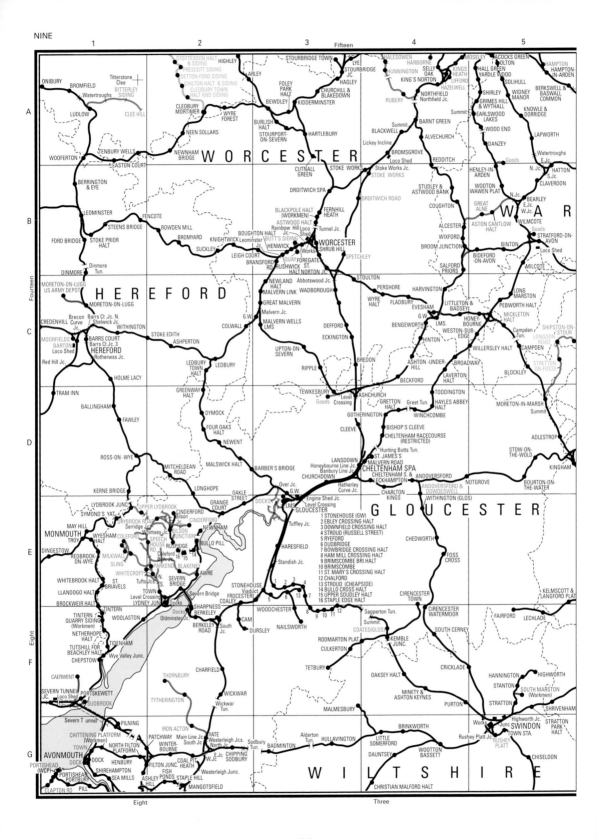

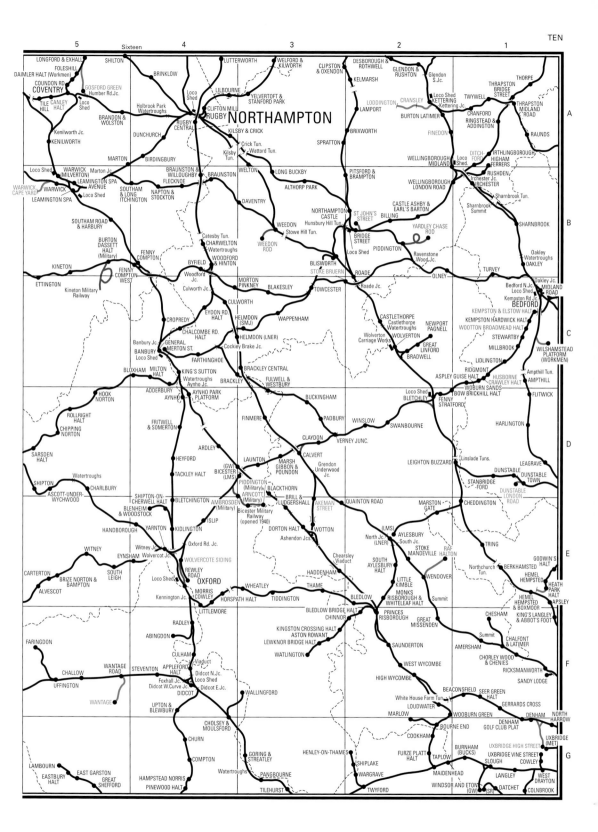

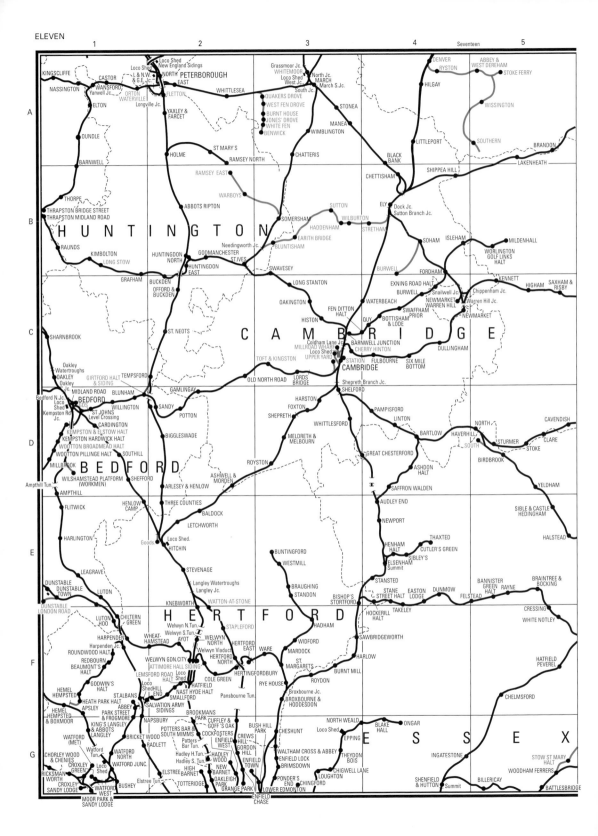

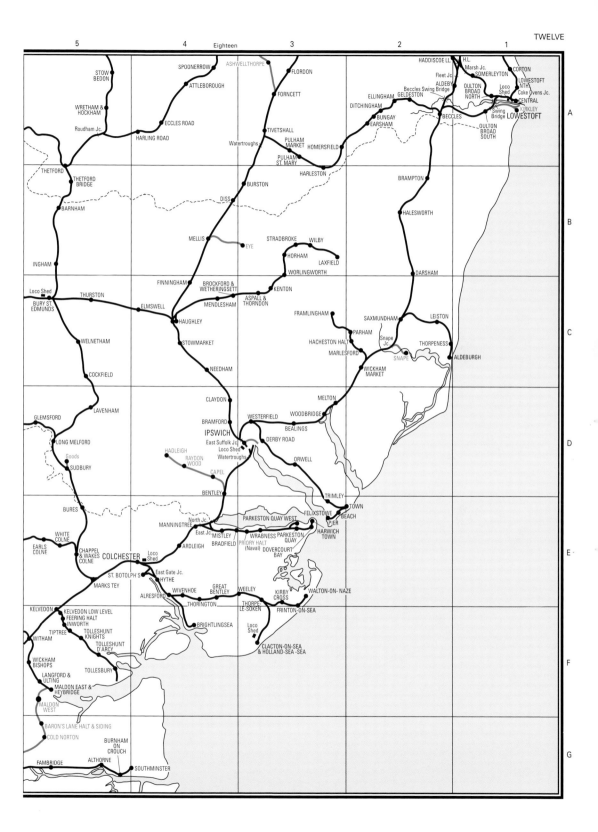

1 2 3 4 5

Nineteen

A

BIRMINGHAM DISTRICT
(INSET ON SHEET No. FIFTEEN)

PRIESTFIELD
Goods
DARLASTON
Goods
Goods
WALSALL
DYFFRYN - ON - SEA
TALYBONT HALT
LLANABER HALT
Barmouth
Bridge
BARMOUTH
BILSTON
BILSTON
East Jc.
West Jc.
BARMOUTH JUNC.
FAIRBOURNE.
ARTHOG
DAISY BANK
& BRADLEY
WOOD GREEN
(OLD BESCOT)
South Jc.
Cader
Idris
DEEPFIELDS
PRINCE'S
END &
COSELEY
Goods
Goods
Loco
Shed
West Jc.
BESCOT
LLWYNGWRIL
NEWTON ROAD
GREAT BARR
ABERGYNOLWYN
Goods Branch Jc.
WEDNESBURY
LLANGELYNIN HALT
DOLGOCH
TIPTON (LMS)
GREAT
BRIDGE
(LMS)
GREAT
BRIDGE
(GW)
North Jc.
TONFANAU
BRYNGLAS
RHYDYRONEN
PENDRE
TIPTON
(GW)
Horsleyfield Jc.
DUDLEY PORT (L.L.)
HIGH LEV. STA.
SWAN VILLAGE
PERRY BARR
WHARF STA.
TOWYN
PENHELIG
HALT
GOGARTH
HALT
ABERTAFOL
HALT
Sedgley Jc.
Handsworth Jc.
WITTON
ALBION
Goods
WEST BROMWICH
HANDSWORTH
WOOD
ASTON
Loco
Shed
ABERDOVEY
DUDLEY CASTLE
DUDLEY
Goods
OLDBURY &
BROMFORD LANE
THE HAWTHORNS
(Football)
Handsworth Jc.
SOHO ROAD
Soho Pool Jc.
SALTLEY
Loco Shed
YNYSLAS
BLOWERS GREEN
NETHERTON
OLDBURY
SPON LANE
SMETHWICK JUNC.
HANDSWORTH &
SMETHWICK
SMETHWICK
SOHO POOL
BORTH
BAPTIST END HALT
Galton Jc.
SOHO
Soap Works Jc.
SOHO & WINSON
GREEN
VAUXHALL &
DUDDESTON
WINDSOR STR.
WHARF
Saltley Jc.
LLANDRE
WINDMILL END
LANGLEY GREEN
& ROOD END
SOHO
Soho East Jc.
HOCKLEY
Aston Curve Jc.
BOW STREET
WITHYMOOR BASIN
DARBY
END
HALT
WINSON GREEN
CURZON STR.
LAWLEY STR.
LLANBADARN
LLANRHYSTYD
RD.
OLD HILL
HIGH STREET
HALT
Harborne
Jc.
MONUMENT
LANE
Loco Shed
SNOW HILL
Prodhouse Jc.
ADDERLEY PARK
LOCO
Shed
GLANRAFON
CAPEL
BANGOR
OLD
HILL
CENTRAL
FIVE WAYS
NEW
ST.
MOOR
ST.
Curzon
Str.Jc. St. Andrew's Jc.
BORDESLEY
Bordesley
Jc.
ABERYSTWYTH
LLANILAR
ROWLEY REGIS &
BLACKHEATH
HAGLEY RD.
CAMP HILL
Camp Hill Jc.
CAMP HILL
TRAWSCOED
HARBORNE
BRIGHTON RD.

B

C

D

ABERAYRON
LLANERCH-AYRON HALT

CROSSWAYS HALT
CILIAU AERON HALT

PONT LLANIO

FELIN FACH
TALSARN HALT
OLMARCH
HALT

E

C A R D I G A N

BLAENPLWYF HALT
SILIAN HALT
LLANGYBI
DERRY ORMOND
Aberayron Jc.
LAMPETER

CARDIGAN

PENCARREG HALT

LLANYBYTHER

Fishguard-Waterford
Fishguard-Rosslare } G.W.R.

KILGERRAN

HENLLAN

FISHGUARD &
GOODWICK

FISHGUARD
HARBOUR

NEWCASTLE
EMLYN

PENTRECOURT
PLATFORM

LLANDYSSUL MAESYCRUGIAU

BRYN TEIFY

BONCATH

PENCADER

F

P E M B R O K E

C A R M A R T H E N

JORDANSTON
HALT
Letterston Jc.

TRECWYN
SIDINGS

PUNCHESTON

CRYMMYCH ARMS

GLOGUE

LLANPUMPSAINT

LETTERSTON
ROSEBUSH
LLANFYRNACH

MATHRY ROAD

MAENCLOCHOG
RHYDOWEN
CONWIL
BRONWYDD ARMS
TALLEY ROAD

WELSH HOOK HALT
WOLFS CASTLE
HALT
Spittal Tun.
Clarbeston Jc.

LLAN-Y-CEFN
BEAG FAIR
SIDING

LOGIN

LLANGLYDWEN

ABERGWILI

GOLDEN
GROVE
LLANDILO
BRI.
LLANDILO

FFAIRFACH

G

CLARBESTON ROAD
Cardigan
Jc.

LLANFALTEG

SARNAU

TOWN STA.

NANTGAREDIG
LLANARTHNEY
DRYSLLWYN

DERWYDD
ROAD

CLYNDERWEN
WHITLAND
ST. CLEARS
JUNC. STA.
CARMARTHEN
Myrtle Hill Jc.
Loco Shed

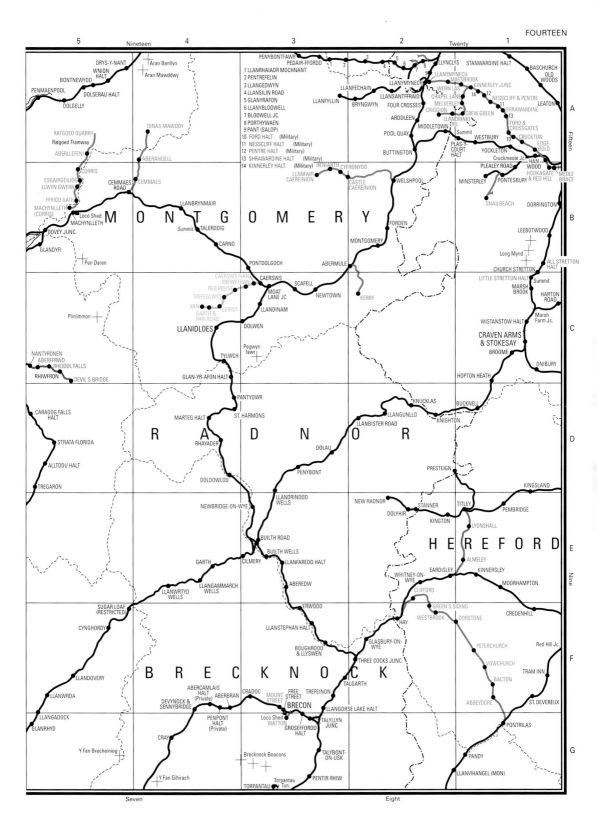

1 LLANRHAIADR MOCHNANT
2 PENTREFELIN
3 LLANGEDWYN
4 LLANSILIN ROAD
5 GLANYRAFON
6 LLANYBLODWELL
7 BLODWELL JC.
8 PORTHYWAEN
9 PANT (SALOP)
10 FORD HALT (Military)
11 NESSCLIFF HALT (Military)
12 PENTRE HALT (Military)
13 SHRAWARDINE HALT (Military)
14 KINNERLEY HALT (Military)

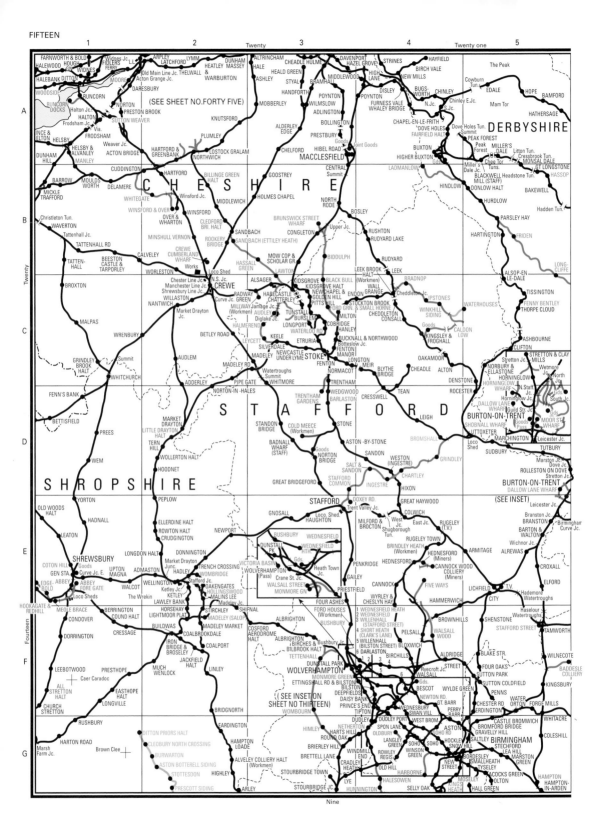

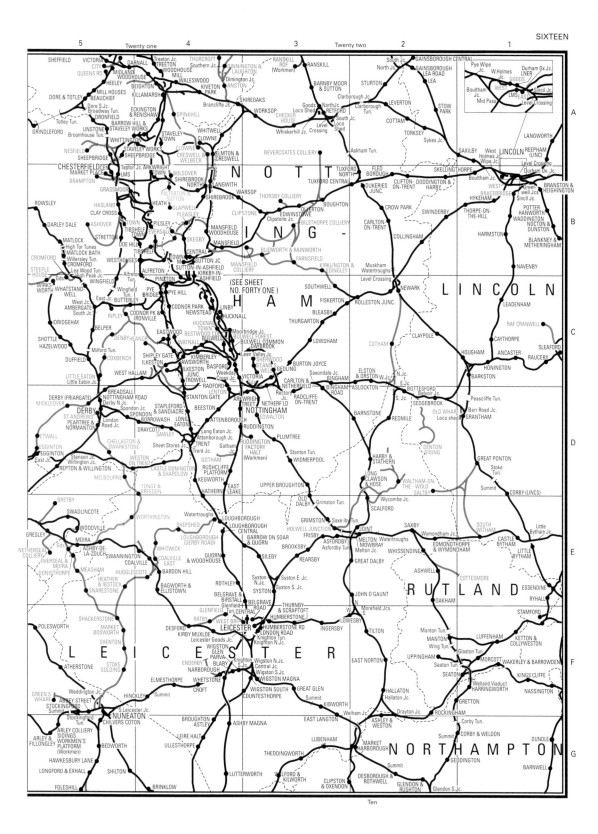

1   2   3   4   5

A
B
C
D
E
F
G

MARKET RASEN
SALTFLEETBY
FOTHERBY HALT
GRIMOLDBY
LOUTH
Loco Shed
THEDDLETHORPE
HALLINGTON
WITHCALL
SOUTH WILLINGHAM & HAINTON
WICKENBY
LEGBOURNE ROAD
MABLETHORPE
SNELLAND
EAST BARKWITH
DONINGTON-ON-BAIN
AUTHORPE
ABY
SUTTON-ON-SEA
WRAGBY
ALFORD TOWN
LANGWORTH
KINGTHORPE
MUMBY ROAD
LINCOLN CENTRAL (LMS)
REEPHAM
WASHINGBOROUGH
FIVE MILE HOUSE
PELHAM STREET
WILLOUGHBY
Durham Ox. Jc.
BRANSTON
LINCOLN ST MARKS (LNER)
BARDNEY
HORNCASTLE
BURGH-LE-MARSH
POTTER HANWORTH
SOUTHREY
WADDINGTON
STIXWOULD
SPILSBY
FIRSBY
NOCTON & DUNSTON
WOODHALL SPA.
HALTON HOLGATE
Firsby S. Jc.
SKEGNESS
BLANKNEY & METHERINGHAM
WOODHALL JUNC.
LITTLE STEEPING
THORPE CULVERT
SEACROFT
NAVENBY
SCOPWICK & TIMBERLAND
TATTERSHALL
CONINGSBY
STICKNEY
MIDVILLE
Bellwater Jc.
WAINFLEET
HAVENHOUSE
DIGBY
DOGDYKE
TUMBY WOODSIDE
NEW BOLINGBROKE
EAST VILLE
CRANWELL (RAF)
RUSKINGTON
North Jc.
LANGRICK
HALL HILLS (Workmen)
OLD LEAKE
ANCASTER
RAUCEBY
SLEAFORD
HECKINGTON
HUBBERT'S BRIDGE
SWINESHEAD
Loco Shed
BOSTON
SIBSEY
East Jc.
South Jc.
Sleaford Jc.
DOCKS
ASWARBY & SEDRINGHAM
HELPRINGHAM
KIRTON
HUNSTANTON
DOCKING
BILLINGBOROUGH & HORBLING
DONINGTON ROAD
ALGARKIRK & SUTTERTON
HEACHAM
SEDGEFORD
GOSBERTON
SURFLEET
SNETTISHAM
RIPPINGALE
DERSINGHAM
WOLFERTON
CORBY (LINCS)
MORTON ROAD
PINCHBECK
HOLBEACH
WHAPLODE
FLEET
HILLINGTON
NORTH WOOTTON
SPALDING ST JOHNS
South Jc.
North Jc.
SPALDING
MOULTON
GEDNEY
LONG SUTTON
GRIMSTON ROAD
COUNTER DRAIN
NORTH DROVE
WESTON
Sutton Bridge Jc.
SUTTON BRIDGE
Loco Shed
KING'S LYNN
GAYTON ROAD
CASTLE BYTHAM
Little Bytham Jc.
East Jc.
Cuckoo Jc.
Welland Bank Jc.
TERRINGTON
MIDDLETON TOWERS
BOURNE
West Jc.
TWENTY
WALPOLE
CLENCHWARTON
SOUTH LYNN
HARDWICK ROAD SIDING
EAST WINCH
LITTLE BYTHAM
THURLBY
WILSTHORPE CROSSING HALT
COWBIT
TYDD
NARBOROUGH & PENTNEY
BRACEBOROUGH SPA HALT
LITTLEWORTH
FERRY
ESSENDINE
POSTLAND
FRENCH DROVE & GEDNEY HILL
MAGDALEN ROAD
RYHALL
DEEPING ST JAMES
WISBECH ST.MARY
WISBECH NORTH
EMNETH
SMEETH ROAD
MIDDLE DROVE
STOW BARDOLPH
STAMFORD
TALLINGTON
HELPSTON
PEAKIRK
Level Crossing
MURROW
WISBECH EAST
ELMBRIDGE
BOYCES BRI.
OUTWELL BASIN
KETTON & COLLYWESTON
UFFINGTON & BARNACK
THORNEY
WRYDE
COLDHAM
GUYHIRNE
OUTWELL VILLAGE
DOWNHAM
Werrington Watertroughs
Werrington Jc.
EYE GREEN
UPWELL
WALTON
ABBEY & WEST DEREHAM
Loco Shed
New England Sidings
DENVER
RYSTON
KINGSCLIFFE
WANSFORD
Loco Shed
NORTH
L. & N.W. & G.E. Jc.
PETERBOROUGH
Grassmoor Jc.
WHITEMOOR
Loco Shed
West Jc.
North Jc.
MARCH
March S.Jc.
HILGAY
STOKE FERRY
CASTOR
EAST
WHITTLESEA
South Jc.
March Jc.
NASSINGTON
Yarwell Jc.
ORTON WATERVILLE
FLETTON
QUAKERS DROVE
WEST FEN DROVE
STONEA
WISSINGTON
ELTON
Longville Jc.
YAXLEY & FARCET
BURNT HOUSE
JONES' DROVE
WHITE FEN
MANEA
OUNDLE
BENWICK
WIMBLINGTON
LITTLEPORT
SOUTHERN
BRANDON
BARNWELL
HOLME
ST MARY'S
RAMSEY NORTH
CHATTERIS
BLACK BANK
LAKENHEATH

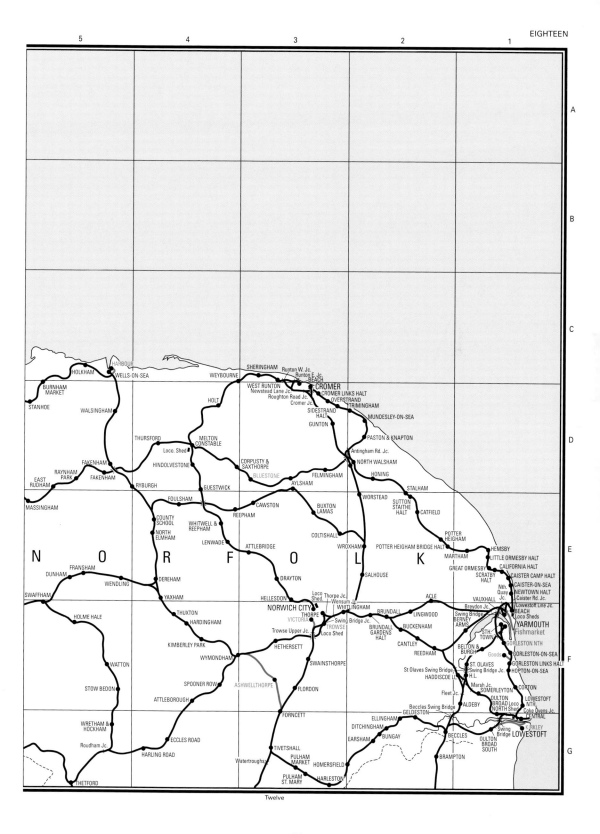

NORFOLK

HOLKHAM
WELLS-ON-SEA
HARBOUR
BURNHAM MARKET
STANHOE
WALSINGHAM
SHERINGHAM
WEYBOURNE
WEST RUNTON
Runton W. Jc.
Runton E. Jc.
BEACH
CROMER
Newstead Lane Jc.
CROMER LINKS HALT
Roughton Road Jc.
OVERSTRAND
Cromer Jc.
TRIMINGHAM
HOLT
SIDESTRAND HALT
MUNDESLEY-ON-SEA
GUNTON
THURSFORD
MELTON CONSTABLE
PASTON & KNAPTON
Loco. Shed
Antingham Rd. Jc.
FAKENHAM
HINDOLVESTONE
CORPUSTY & SAXTHORPE
NORTH WALSHAM
RAYNHAM PARK
BLUESTONE
HONING
EAST RUDHAM
FAKENHAM
RYBURGH
GUESTWICK
FELMINGHAM
STALHAM
MASSINGHAM
FOULSHAM
CAWSTON
AYLSHAM
WORSTEAD
SUTTON STAITHE HALT
COUNTY SCHOOL
REEPHAM
BUXTON LAMAS
CATFIELD
DUNHAM
FRANSHAM
NORTH ELMHAM
WHITWELL & REEPHAM
COLTISHALL
POTTER HEIGHAM
HEMSBY
WENDLING
LENWADE
ATTLEBRIDGE
WROXHAM
POTTER HEIGHAM BRIDGE HALT
LITTLE ORMESBY HALT
SWAFFHAM
DEREHAM
DRAYTON
SALHOUSE
MARTHAM
GREAT ORMESBY
CALIFORNIA HALT
YAXHAM
SCRATBY HALT
CAISTER CAMP HALT
HOLME HALE
THUXTON
HELLESDON
Loco. Shed
Thorpe Jc.
ACLE
VAUXHALL
Nth. Quay Jc.
CAISTER-ON-SEA
NEWTOWN HALT
Caister Rd. Jc.
Wensum Jc.
WHITLINGHAM
Lowestoft Line Jc.
HARDINGHAM
NORWICH CITY
THORPE
BRUNDALL
LINGWOOD
Breydon Jc.
BEACH
KIMBERLEY PARK
VICTORIA
Swing Bridge Jc.
BRUNDALL GARDENS HALT
BUCKENHAM
Swing Bridge
BERNEY ARMS
Loco Sheds
YARMOUTH
Fishmarket
WYMONDHAM
HETHERSETT
Trowse Upper Jc.
TROWSE
Loco Shed
CANTLEY
BELTON & BURGH
STH. TOWN
GORLESTON NTH
SPOONER ROW
ASHWELLTHORPE
SWAINSTHORPE
REEDHAM
Goods
GORLESTON-ON-SEA
STOW BEDON
FLORDON
St Olaves Swing Bridge
ST. OLAVES
GORLESTON LINKS HALT
WATTON
HADDISCOE LL
Swing Bridge Jc.
H.L.
HOPTON-ON-SEA
ATTLEBOROUGH
FORNCETT
Marsh Jc.
SOMERLEYTON
CORTON
Fleet Jc.
OULTON BROAD Loco
LOWESTOFT NTH.
WRETHAM & HOCKHAM
ELLINGHAM
Beccles Swing Bridge
ALDEBY
NORTH Shed
CENTRAL
Roudham Jc.
ECCLES ROAD
DITCHINGHAM
GELDESTON
Coke Ovens Jc.
KIRKLEY
HARLING ROAD
TIVETSHALL
EARSHAM
BUNGAY
BECCLES
Swing Bridge
LOWESTOFT
Watertroughs
PULHAM MARKET
HOMERSFIELD
OULTON BROAD SOUTH
THETFORD
PULHAM ST. MARY
HARLESTON
BRAMPTON

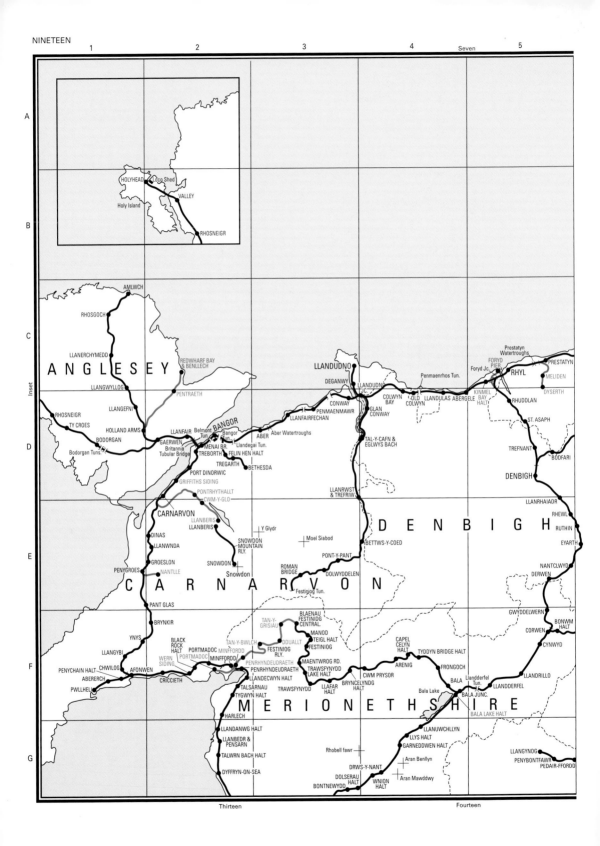

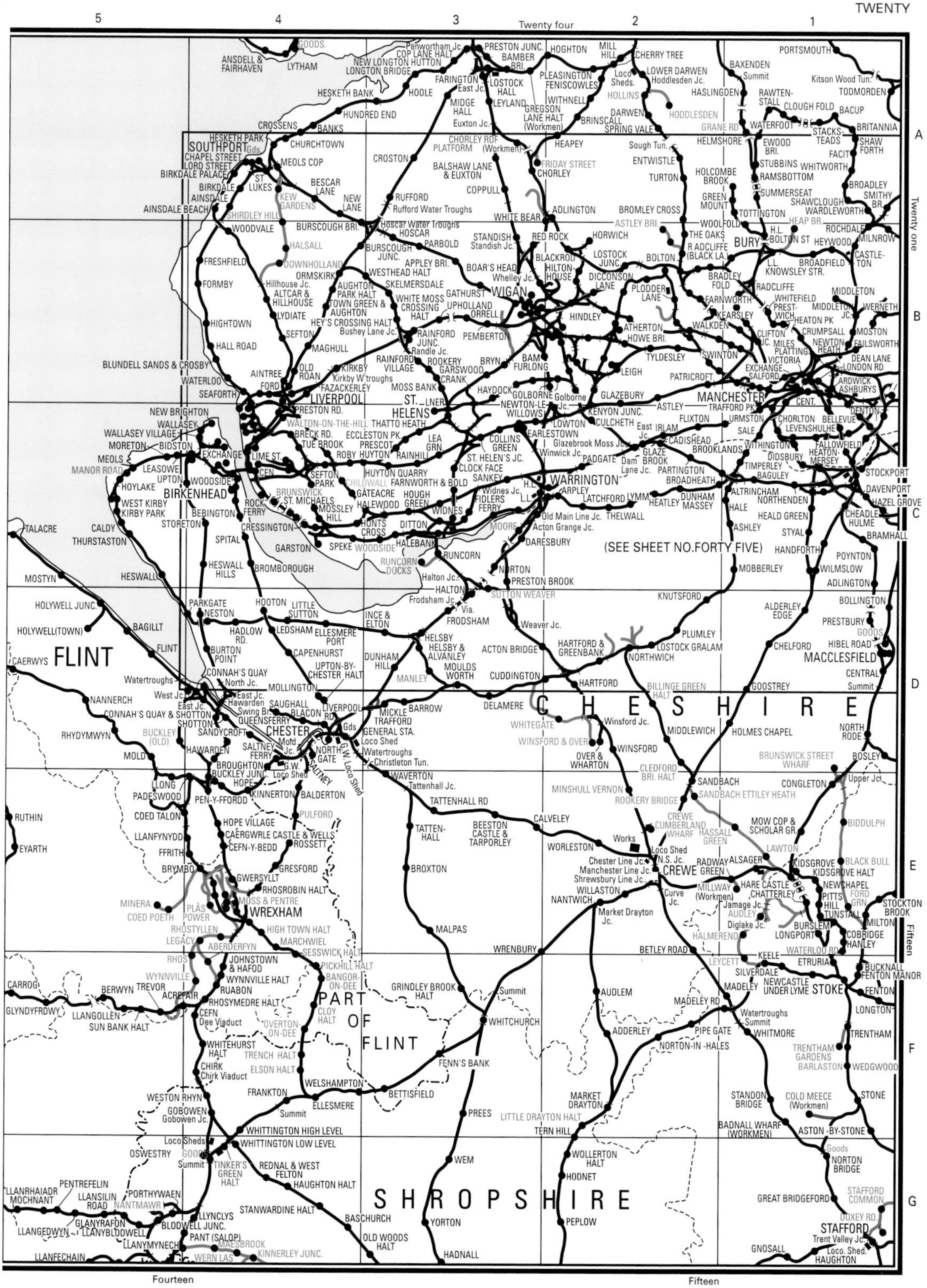
5
4
3
2
1
Twenty four
Twenty one
Fifteen
Fourteen
Fifteen
A
B
C
D
E
F
G
FLINT
CHESHIRE
PART OF FLINT
SHROPSHIRE
(SEE SHEET NO.FORTY FIVE)
SOUTHPORT
LIVERPOOL
BIRKENHEAD
ST. HELENS
WIGAN
BOLTON
BURY
MANCHESTER
WARRINGTON
CHESTER
WREXHAM
CREWE
MACCLESFIELD
STOCKPORT
STOKE
STAFFORD
PRESTON JUNC.
LYTHAM
ANSDELL & FAIRHAVEN
HESKETH BANK
HOOLE
CROSSENS
BANKS
CHURCHTOWN
MEOLS COP
BIRKDALE PALACE
BIRKDALE
AINSDALE
AINSDALE BEACH
FRESHFIELD
FORMBY
HIGHTOWN
HALL ROAD
BLUNDELL SANDS & CROSBY
WATERLOO
SEAFORTH
NEW BRIGHTON
WALLASEY
WALLASEY VILLAGE
MORETON
MEOLS
MANOR ROAD
HOYLAKE
WEST KIRBY
KIRBY PARK
TALACRE
MOSTYN
HOLYWELL JUNC.
HOLYWELL(TOWN)
BAGILLT
FLINT
CAERWYS
NANNERCH
RHYDYMWYN
MOLD
RUTHIN
EYARTH
ORMSKIRK
AUGHTON PARK HALT
TOWN GREEN & AUGHTON
MAGHULL
AINTREE
KIRKBY
RAINFORD JUNC.
HUYTON
PRESCOT
RAINHILL
WIDNES
DITTON
HALEBANK
SPEKE
GARSTON
RUNCORN
HALTON
FRODSHAM
HELSBY
DUNHAM HILL
ELLESMERE PORT
HOOTON
LEDSHAM
CAPENHURST
MOLLINGTON
QUEENSFERRY
SALTNEY
WAVERTON
TATTENHALL RD
BEESTON CASTLE & TARPORLEY
CALVELEY
WORLESTON
NANTWICH
WRENBURY
WHITCHURCH
MALPAS
BROXTON
ELLESMERE
WELSHAMPTON
BETTISFIELD
FENN'S BANK
PREES
WEM
YORTON
HADNALL
OSWESTRY
GOBOWEN
WESTON RHYN
CHIRK
RUABON
LLANGOLLEN
BERWYN
CARROG
GLYNDYFRDWY
LLANFECHAIN
LLANYMYNECH
BASCHURCH
MARKET DRAYTON
TERN HILL
HODNET
PEPLOW
AUDLEM
ADDERLEY
NORTON-IN-HALES
PIPE GATE
MADELEY RD
WHITMORE
STANDON BRIDGE
NORTON BRIDGE
GREAT BRIDGEFORD
GNOSALL
HAUGHTON
STONE
TRENTHAM
WEDGWOOD
BARLASTON
LONGTON
FENTON
KEELE
SILVERDALE
NEWCASTLE UNDER LYME
ETRURIA
HANLEY
BURSLEM
TUNSTALL
KIDSGROVE
ALSAGER
SANDBACH
CONGLETON
BOSLEY
NORTH RODE
HOLMES CHAPEL
GOOSTREY
MIDDLEWICH
WINSFORD
NORTHWICH
HARTFORD
ACTON BRIDGE
CUDDINGTON
DELAMERE
KNUTSFORD
PLUMLEY
LOSTOCK GRALAM
MOBBERLEY
CHELFORD
ALDERLEY EDGE
WILMSLOW
HANDFORTH
STYAL
POYNTON
ADLINGTON
BOLLINGTON
PRESTBURY
ALTRINCHAM
HALE
ASHLEY
SALE
URMSTON
FLIXTON
IRLAM
GLAZEBROOK
PATRICROFT
ECCLES
SWINTON
WALKDEN
FARNWORTH
KEARSLEY
LEIGH
TYLDESLEY
ATHERTON
HINDLEY
NEWTON-LE-WILLOWS
EARLESTOWN
GOLBORNE
DARESBURY
NORTON
PRESTON BROOK
HORWICH
ADLINGTON
CHORLEY
LEYLAND
DARWEN
HASLINGDEN
RAWTENSTALL
BACUP
TODMORDEN
ROCHDALE
HEYWOOD
MIDDLETON
OLDHAM
RADCLIFFE
RAMSBOTTOM
HELMSHORE
ENTWISTLE
TURTON
PORTSMOUTH

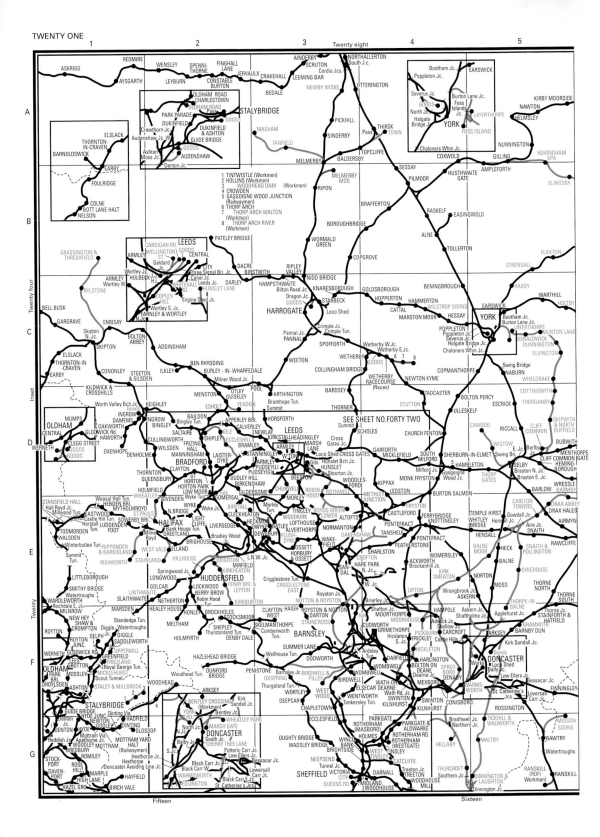

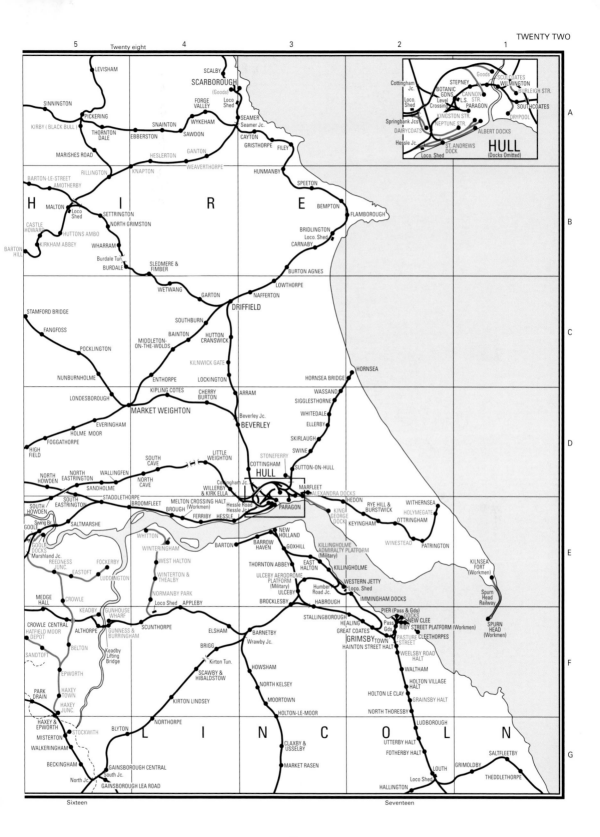

HULL
(Docks Omitted)

Goods
Cottingham Jc.   STEPNEY   SCULCOATES
BOTANIC   WILMINGTON
GDNS.   CANNON   BURLEIGH STR.
Loco.   Level   L.S. STR.
Shed   Crossing   PARAGON   SOUTHCOATES
KINGSTON STR.
Springbank Jcs.   NEPTUNE STR.   DRYPOOL
DAIRYCOATS
ALBERT DOCKS
Hessle Jc.   ST. ANDREWS
DOCK
Loco. Shed

LEVISHAM
SCALBY
SCARBOROUGH
(Goods)
SINNINGTON   FORGE   Loco
PICKERING   VALLEY   Shed
KIRBY (BLACK BULL)   SNAINTON   WYKEHAM   SEAMER
THORNTON   SAWDON   Seamer Jc.
DALE   EBBERSTON   CAYTON
MARISHES ROAD   HESLERTON   GRISTHORPE   FILEY
RILLINGTON   WEAVERTHORPE
BARTON-LE-STREET   KNAPTON   HUNMANBY
AMOTHERBY
H   I   R   E   SPEETON
MALTON   Loco   SETTRINGTON   BEMPTON
Shed
CASTLE   NORTH GRIMSTON   FLAMBOROUGH
HOWARD   HUTTONS AMBO   BRIDLINGTON
BARTON   KIRKHAM ABBEY   WHARRAM   Loco. Shed
HILL   CARNABY
Burdale Tun.   SLEDMERE &
BURDALE   FIMBER   BURTON AGNES
WETWANG   LOWTHORPE
STAMFORD BRIDGE   GARTON   NAFFERTON
FANGFOSS   DRIFFIELD
SOUTHBURN
POCKLINGTON   BAINTON   HUTTON
MIDDLETON-   CRANSWICK
ON-THE-WOLDS
KILNWICK GATE
NUNBURNHOLME   ENTHORPE   LOCKINGTON   HORNSEA
KIPLING COTES   ARRAM   HORNSEA BRIDGE
LONDESBOROUGH   CHERRY   WASSAND
BURTON   SIGGLESTHORNE
MARKET WEIGHTON   Beverley Jc.   WHITEDALE
EVERINGHAM   BEVERLEY   ELLERBY
HOLME MOOR   SKIRLAUGH
FOGGATHORPE   SWINE
HIGH   LITTLE   SUTTON-ON-HULL
FIELD   SOUTH   WEIGHTON   STONEFERRY
CAVE   COTTINGHAM
NORTH   NORTH   WALLINGFEN   HULL
HOWDEN   EASTRINGTON   NORTH   Cottingham Jc.   MARFLEET
SANDHOLME   CAVE   WILLERBY   ALEXANDRA DOCKS
STADDLETHORPE   & KIRK ELLA   HEDON
SOUTH   SOUTH   MELTON CROSSING HALT   Hessle Road   KING   RYE HILL &   WITHERNSEA
HOWDEN   EASTRINGTON   BROOMFLEET   (Workmen)   Hessle Jc.   GEORGE   BURSTWICK
Swing Br.   BROUGH   PARAGON   DOCK   HOLYMEGATE
GOOLE   SALTMARSHE   FERRIBY   HESSLE   KEYINGHAM   OTTRINGHAM
GOOLE   WHITTON   NEW
DOCKS   HOLLAND   WINESTEAD   PATRINGTON
Marshland Jc.   WINTERINGHAM   BARTON   BARROW   GOXHILL
REEDNESS   WEST HALTON   HAVEN   KILNSEA
UNC.   FOCKERBY   EAST   KILLINGHOLME   FORT
MEDGE   EASTOFT   WINTERTON &   THORNTON ABBEY   HALTON   ADMIRALTY PLATFORM   (Workmen)
HALL   LUDDINGTON   THEALBY   (Military)   Spurn
CROWLE   NORMANBY PARK   ULCEBY AERODROME   Humber   WESTERN JETTY   Head
KEADBY   Loco Shed   APPLEBY   PLATFORM   Road Jc.   Loco. Shed   Railway
CROWLE CENTRAL   GUNHOUSE   (Military)   IMMINGHAM DOCKS
HATFIELD MOOR   WHARF   ULCEBY
DEPOT   ALTHORPE   GUNNESS &   SCUNTHORPE   BROCKLESBY   HABROUGH   PIER (Pass & Gds)
BURRINGHAM   DOCKS   SPURN
SANDTOFT   Keadby   STALLINGBOROUGH   NEW CLEE   HEAD
BELTON   Lifting   ELSHAM   HEALING   Pass.   RIBY STREET PLATFORM (Workmen)   (Workmen)
EPWORTH   Bridge   BARNETBY   GREAT COATES   Gds   PASTURE   CLEETHORPES
PARK   HAXEY   BRIGG   Wrawby Jc.   GRIMSBY TOWN   STREET
DRAIN   TOWN   Kirton Tun.   HAINTON STREET HALT   WEELSBY ROAD
HAXEY   HOWSHAM   HALT
JUNC.   SCAWBY &   WALTHAM
HAXEY &   HIBALDSTOW   NORTH KELSEY   HOLTON VILLAGE
EPWORTH   STOCKWITH   HALT
MISTERTON   BLYTON   KIRTON LINDSEY   MOORTOWN   HOLTON LE CLAY   GRAINSBY HALT
WALKERINGHAM   NORTHORPE   HOLTON-LE-MOOR   NORTH THORESBY
L   I   N   C   O   L   N   LUDBOROUGH
BECKINGHAM   CLAXBY &   UTTERBY HALT   SALTFLEETBY
GAINSBOROUGH CENTRAL   USSELBY   FOTHERBY HALT
South Jc.   MARKET RASEN   GRIMOLDBY   THEDDLETHORPE
North Jc.   GAINSBOROUGH LEA ROAD   LOUTH
Loco Shed
HALLINGTON

A

B

C

D

E

F

G

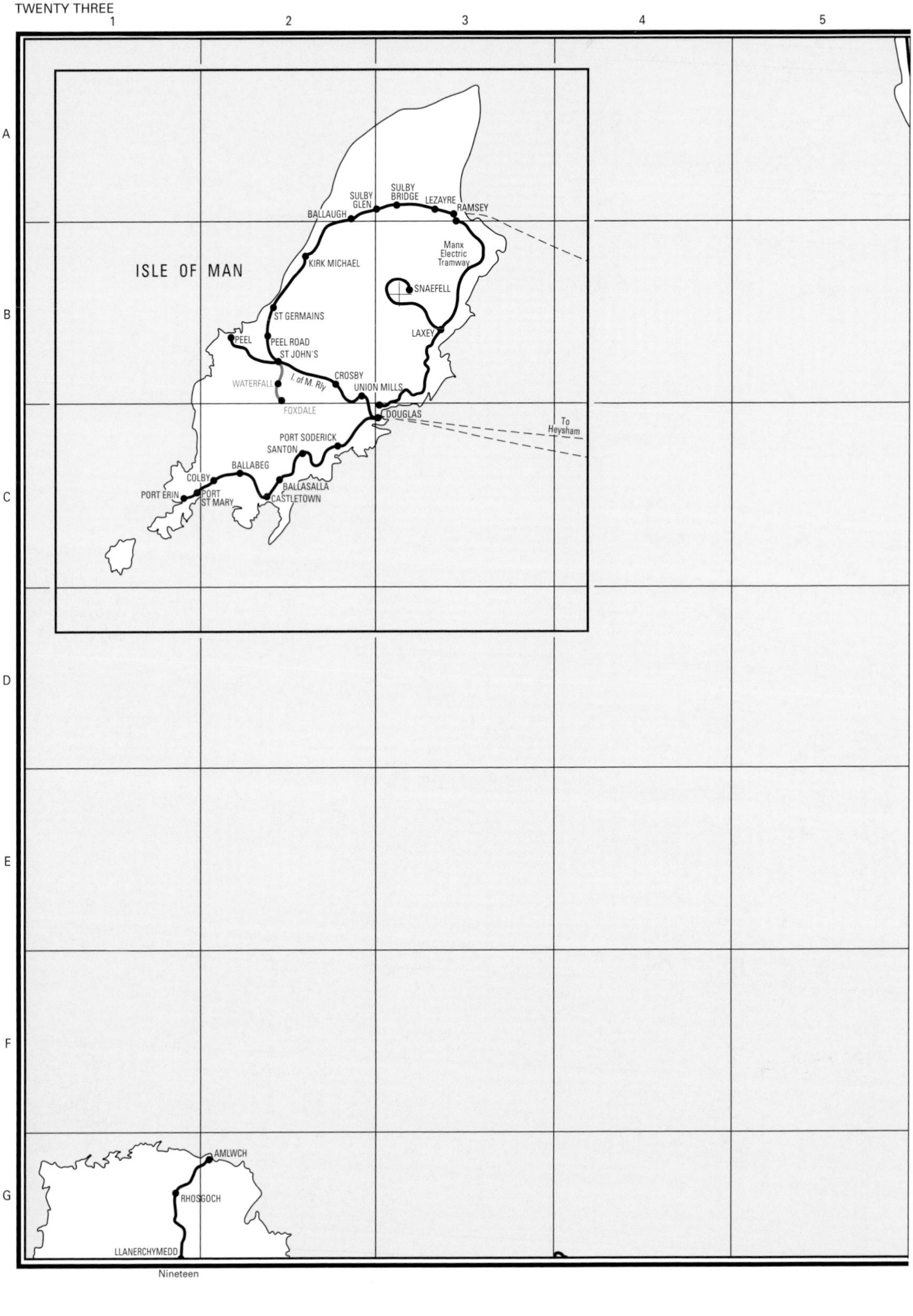
1
2
3
4
5
A
B
C
D
E
F
G
ISLE OF MAN
SULBY GLEN
SULBY BRIDGE
LEZAYRE
RAMSEY
BALLAUGH
KIRK MICHAEL
Manx Electric Tramway
SNAEFELL
ST GERMAINS
LAXEY
PEEL
PEEL ROAD
ST JOHN'S
WATERFALL
I. of M. Rly
CROSBY
UNION MILLS
FOXDALE
DOUGLAS
To Heysham
PORT SODERICK
SANTON
BALLABEG
COLBY
PORT ERIN
PORT ST MARY
BALLASALLA
CASTLETOWN
AMLWCH
RHOSGOCH
LLANERCHYMEDD
Nineteen

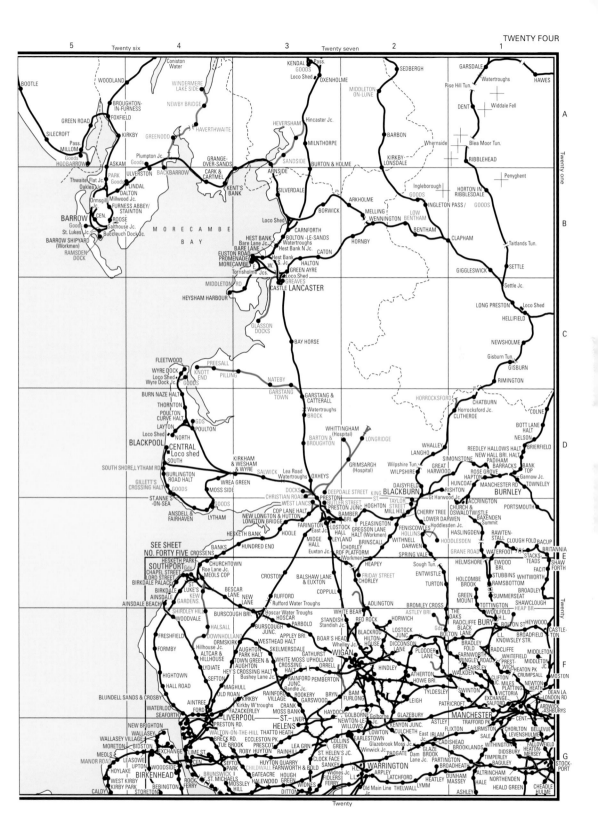

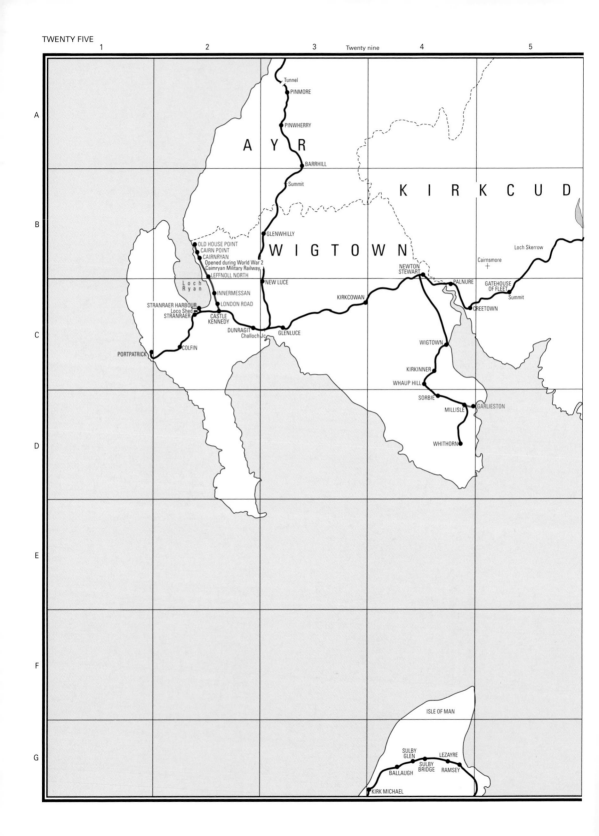

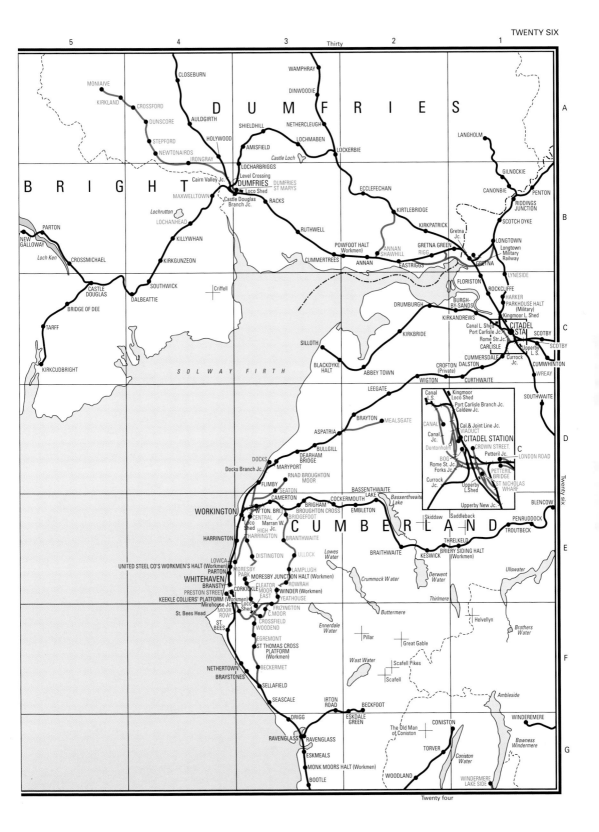

5   4   3   Thirty   2   1

MONIAIVE
KIRKLAND
CROSSFORD
CLOSEBURN
WAMPHRAY
DINWOODIE

D U M F R I E S   A

DUNSCORE
AULDGIRTH
STEPFORD
NEWTONAIRDS
HOLYWOOD
IRONGRAY
SHIELDHILL
NETHERCLEUGH
LANGHOLM

AMISFIELD
LOCHMABEN
LOCKERBIE
GILNOCKIE

B R I G H T
Cairn Valley Jc.
Level Crossing
LOCHARBRIGGS
Castle Loch
Dumfries
ST MARYS
ECCLEFECHAN
CANONBIE
PENTON

DUMFRIES
Loco Shed
MAXWELLTOWN
Castle Douglas
Branch Jc.
RACKS
KIRTLEBRIDGE
RIDDINGS
JUNCTION
SCOTCH DYKE

Lochrutton
LOCHANHEAD
KIRKPATRICK
Gretna
Jc.
LONGTOWN   B
Longtown
Military
Railway

PARTON
RUTHWELL
KIRKPATRICK
GRETNA GREEN
RIGG

NEW
GALLOWAY
KILLYWHAN
POWFOOT HALT
(Workmen)
ANNAN
SHAWHILL
EASTRIGGS
GRETNA

Loch Ken
CROSSMICHAEL
KIRKGUNZEON
CUMMERTREES
ANNAN
FLORISTON
LYNESIDE

CASTLE
DOUGLAS
SOUTHWICK
Criffell
DRUMBURGH
BURGH-
BY-SANDS
ROCKCLIFFE
HARKER
PARKHOUSE HALT
(Military)

BRIDGE OF DEE
DALBEATTIE
KIRKANDREWS
Kingmoor L. Shed
CITADEL
STA   C

TARFF
SILLOTH
KIRKBRIDE
Canal L. Shed
Port Carlisle Jc.
Rome Str.Jc.
CARLISLE
Upperby
L.S.
SCOTBY
SCOTBY

KIRKCUDBRIGHT
BLACKDYKE
HALT
ABBEY TOWN
CUMMERSDALE
DALSTON
Currock
Jc.
CUMWHINTON
WREAY

S O L W A Y   F I R T H
WIGTON
CROFTON
(Private)
CURTHWAITE

LEEGATE
SOUTHWAITE

BRAYTON
MEALSGATE
Canal
L.S.
Kingmoor
Loco Shed
Port Carlisle Branch Jc.
Caldew Jc.

ASPATRIA
CANAL
Cal.& Joint Line Jc.   D
VIADUCT
Canal
Jc.
CITADEL STATION

BULLGILL
DEARHAM
BRIDGE
Dentonholm
CROWN STREET.
LONDON ROAD
C

DOCKS
Docks Branch Jc.
MARYPORT
RNAD
BROUGHTON
MOOR
BOG
Rome St. Jc.
Forks Jc.
Petteril Jc.
PETTERIL
BRIDGE
ST NICHOLAS
WHARF

FLIMBY
Currock
Jc.
Upperby
L Shed

SEATON
CAMERTON
BASSENTHWAITE
LAKE
Bassenthwaite
Lake
Upperby New Jc.
BLENCOW

WORKINGTON
W.TON. BRI.
BRIGHAM
BROUGHTON CROSS
COCKERMOUTH
EMBLETON
Skiddaw
Saddleback
PENRUDDOCK

CENTRAL
Loco
Shed
Marran W.
HIGH
Jc.
BRIDGEFOOT
C U M B E R L A N D
TROUTBECK
E

HARRINGTON
HARRINGTON
BRANTHWAITE
THRELKELD

LOWCA
DISTINGTON
ULLOCK
Lowes
Water
BRAITHWAITE
KESWICK
BRIERY SIDING HALT
(Workmen)

UNITED STEEL CO'S WORKMEN'S HALT
MORESBY
PARK
(Workmen)
LAMPLUGH
MORESBY JUNCTION HALT (Workmen)
Derwent
Water
Ullswater

PARTON
WHITEHAVEN
CLEATOR
MOOR
ROWRAH
Crummock Water

BRANSTY
PRESTON STREET
CORKICKLE
MOOR
EAST
WINDER (Workmen)
YEATHOUSE
Thirlmere

KEEKLE COLLIERS' PLATFORM (Workmen)
Loco
Shed
FRIZINGTON
C.MOOR
Buttermere
Helvellyn

Mirehouse Jc.
MOOR
ROW
CROSSFIELD
WOODEND
Ennerdale
Water
Pillar
Great Gable
Brothers
Water

St. Bees Head
ST.
BEES
EGREMONT
Wast Water
Scafell Pikes

NETHERTOWN
ST THOMAS CROSS
PLATFORM
(Workmen)
BECKERMET
Scafell
F

BRAYSTONES
SELLAFIELD
Ambleside

SEASCALE
IRTON
ROAD
BECKFOOT
WINDERMERE

DRIGG
ESKDALE
GREEN
The Old Man
of Coniston
CONISTON
Bowness
Windermere

RAVENGLASS
RAVENGLASS
TORVER
Coniston
Water
WINDERMERE
LAKE SIDE

ESKMEALS
WOODLAND   G

MONK MOORS HALT (Workmen)

BOOTLE

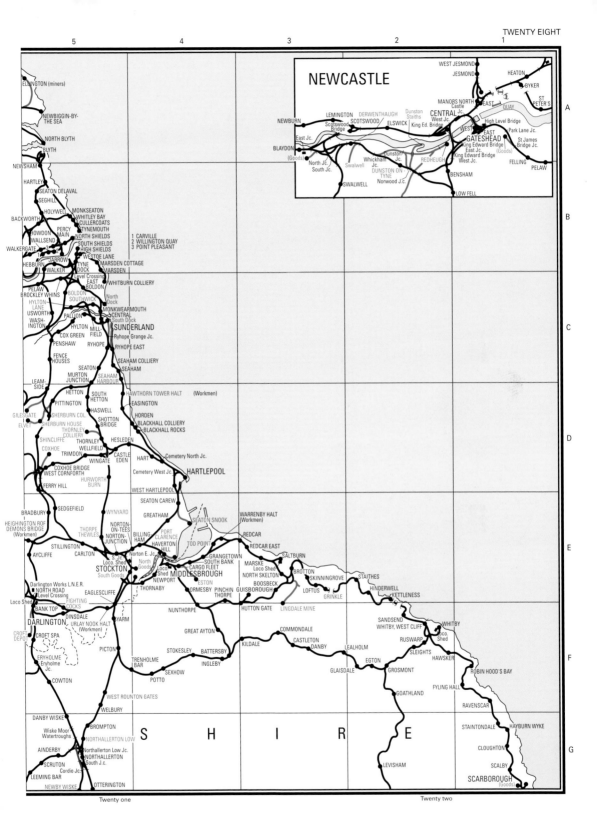

1 2 3 4 5

To INVERARY

LOCHGOILHEAD

Loch Goil

CARRICK CASTLE

Loch Long

Summit

To ARROCHAR

Ben Lomond

ROWARDENNAN

ABERFOYLE

DOUNE

GARTMORE

BUCHLYVIE

KIPPEN

PORT OF MENTEITH

FAIRFIELD SIDING

GARGUNNOCK

LADYLANDS SIDING

CRARAE

FASLANE PORT

WHISTLEFIELD

GARELOCHHEAD

SHANDON

(Mil.)

FASLANE PLATFORM

(Workmen)

Gare Loch

DUM-BARTON

Loch Lomond

BALMAHA

S T I R L

BALFRON

GARTNESS

KILLEARN

DUMGOYNE

DRYMEN

CALDARVAN

BLANEFIELD

STRATHBLANE

Campsie Fells

MILTON OF CAMPSIE

LENNOXTOWN

CAMPSIE GLEN

KILSYTH (Pass.)

(Gds)

TWECHAR

ARDENTINNY

RHU

HELENSBURGH (UPPER)

Loco. Shed

HELENSBURGH

BALLOCH PIER

BALLOCH

JAMESTOWN

CAMPSIE FELLS

MILNGAVIE

BALMORE

TORRANCE

GARTSHORE

KIRKINTILLOCH

Waterside Jc.

ARDNADAM

BLAIRMORE

COVE

KILMUN

KIRN

DUNOON

PORT MATILDA

PRINCES PIER

CENTRAL

CRAIGENDORAN

CARDROSS

RENTON

DALREOCH

BONHILL

DUMBARTON

DUMBUCK SIDING

DUHBUCK (Gds)

BOWLING

KILPATRICK

DALMUIR

SINGER

HILLFOOT

BEARSDEN

BARDOWIE

SUMMERSTON

LENZIE

Milngavie Jc.

MARYHILL

Campsie Bch. Jc.

Bridgend

SPRINGBURN PK

STEPPS

BISHOPBRIGGS

ST ROLLOX W.

ROBROYSTON

BLAIRHILL

GARNKIRK

SHETTLESTON

BARGEDDIE

ORMIDALE

COLINTRAIVE

INELLAN

LYNEDOCH/OVERTON

BOGSTON

UPPER PORT GLASGOW

PORT GLASGOW

LANGBANK

BISHOPTON

ROF BISHOPTON

KILBOWIE

CLYDEBANK

YOKER

SCOTSTOUN

GEORGETOWN

SCOTSTOWN

PARTICK

GOVAN

CLYDE

QUEEN ST

CENTRAL

ST ENOCH

IBROX

CARNTYNE

MT VERNON

BROOMHOUSE

1 UPPER GREENOCK
2 GREENOCK WEST

INVERKIP

WEMYSS BAY

KILMACOLM

BRIDGE OF WEIR

JOHNSTONE NORTH

KILBARCHAN

HOUSTON

LINWOOD

PAISLEY

RENFREW

ABERCORN

ELDERSLIE

CROOKSTON

CROSSMYLOOF

NITSHILL

POTTERHILL

CARDONALD

BUCHANAN ST

R E N F R E W

MILLIKEN PARK

HOWWOOD

JOHN-STONE

CATHCART

CAMBUSLANG

MUIREND

CLARKSTON

BURNSIDE

RUTHERGLEN

CARMYLE

KIRKHILL

NEWTON

BLANTYRE

BOTHWELL

BARRHEAD

THORNLIEBANK

GIFFNOCK

PATTERTON

WHITE-CRAIGS

NETHERTON

THORNTONHALL

BUSBY

BLANTYRE HIGH

L.S.

TIGHNABRUAICH

PORT BANNATYNE

ROTHESAY

B U T E

FIRTH OF CLYDE

Hill of Stake

LOCHWINNOCH

LOCHSIDE

NEILSTON

CALDWELL

UPLAWMOOR

East Jc.

HAIRMYRES

EAST KILBRIDE

MEIKLE EARNOCK

QUARTER

To TARBERT etc.

LARGS

KILBIRNIE

BEITH NORTH.

BEITH

BARRMILL

GIFFEN

GLENGARNOCK

SWINLEES

GLENGARNOCK HIGH

GREE DEPOT

DUNLOP

SEE SHEET NO: FORTY FOUR

KILCHATTAN BAY

MILL-PORT

FAIRLIE PIER

FAIRLIE

WEST KILBRIDE

DALRY

Dalry Jc.

AUCHENMADE

LISSENS

STEWARTON

GLASSFORD

STRATHAVEN NTH.

CEN.

RYELAND

LOCHRANZA

KILWINNING

SALTCOATS

Dubbs Jc.

MONTGREENAN

CUNNINGHAMHEAD

KILMAURS

NEWMILNS

LOUDONHILL

L A

CORRIE

ARDROSSAN

MONTGOMERIE PIER

WINTON PIER

SOUTH BEACH

STEVENSTON

MOORPARK

ARDEER WORKS

PLATFORM

(Workmen)

BOGSIDE

IRVINE

DREGHORN

CROSSHOUSE

SPRINGSIDE

ST MARNOCK

KILMARNOCK

Kaypark Jc.

HURLFORD

GALSTON

DARVEL

DRUMCLOG

County Boundary Jc.

BRODICK

A R R A N

IRVINE HARBOUR

GAILES

DRY. GATEHEAD

BRIDGE

Bellfield Jc.

RICCARTON & CRAIGIE

FAIRLIE

BARLEITH

LAMLASH

HARBOUR

TROON

GOODS

Pass.

BARASSIE

Lochgreen Jc.

MONKTON

GARROCHBURN SIDING

MAUCHLINE

CATRINE

MUIRKIRK

Loco. Shed

KING'S CROSS

PRESTWICK

Mossblown Jc.

TARBOLTON

LUGAR

GASWATER MINE

CRONBERRY

WHITING BAY

NEWTON-ON-AYR

HARBOUR

AYR GOODS

Falkland Jc.

Blackhouse Jc.

Hawkhill Jc.

Pass.

ALLOWAY

L.C.

ANNBANK

TRABBOCH

Brackenhill Jc.

AUCHINLECK

SKARES

OLD CUMNOCK

COMMONDYKE

Logan Jc.

NEW CUMNOCK

HEADS OF AYR

DUNURE

Alloway Jc.

DRONGAN

OCHILTREE

DUMFRIES HOUSE

Belston Jc.

CUMNOCK

GREENHAM CASTLE

DALRYMPLE

DALRYMPLE JUNCTION

HOLLYBUSH

RANKINSTON

HOLEHOUSE

Watertroughs

KNOWESIDE

BALCHRISTON SIDING

CASSILLIS

PATNA

A Y R S H I R E

Blackcraig Hill

GLENSIDE

MAYBOLE

WATERSIDE

MAIDENS

TURNBERRY

DIPPLE SIDING

DAILLY

KIL KERRAN

DALMELLINGTON

KILLOCHAN

GIRVAN OLD

GIRVAN

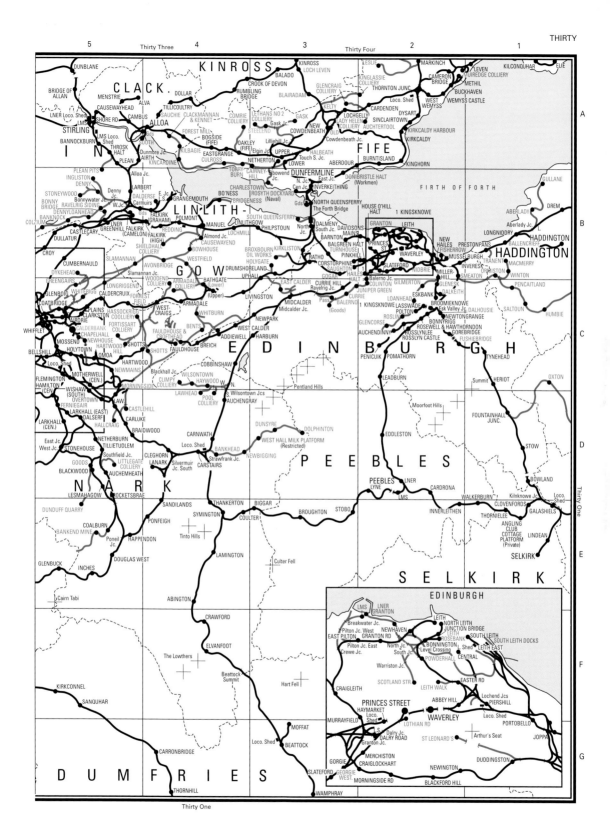

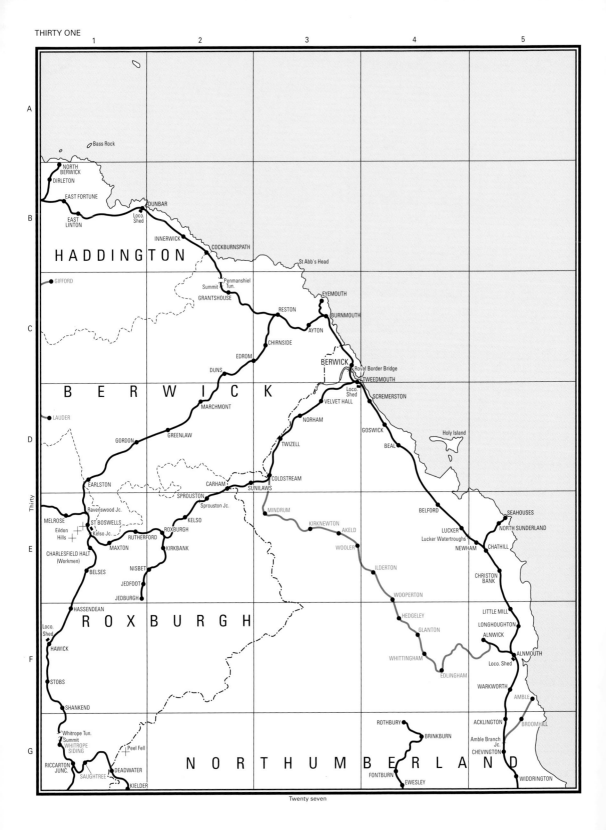

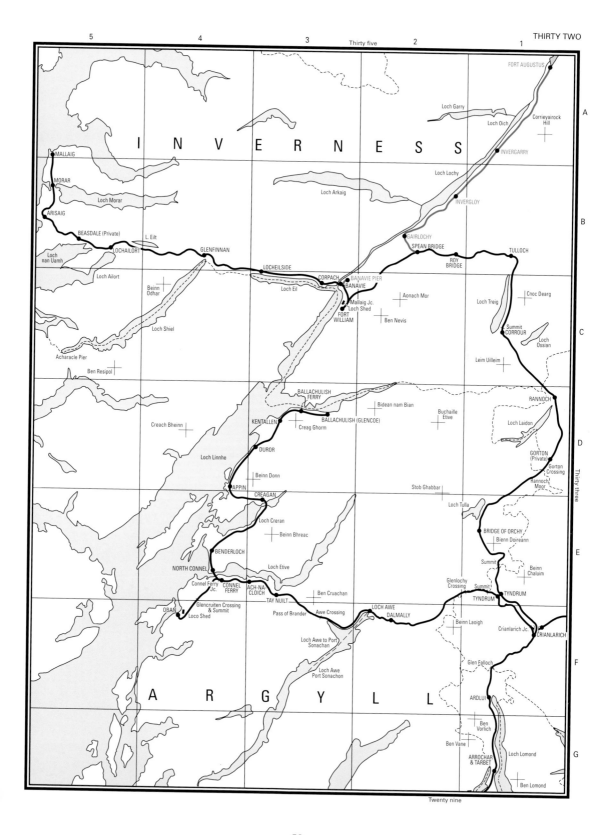

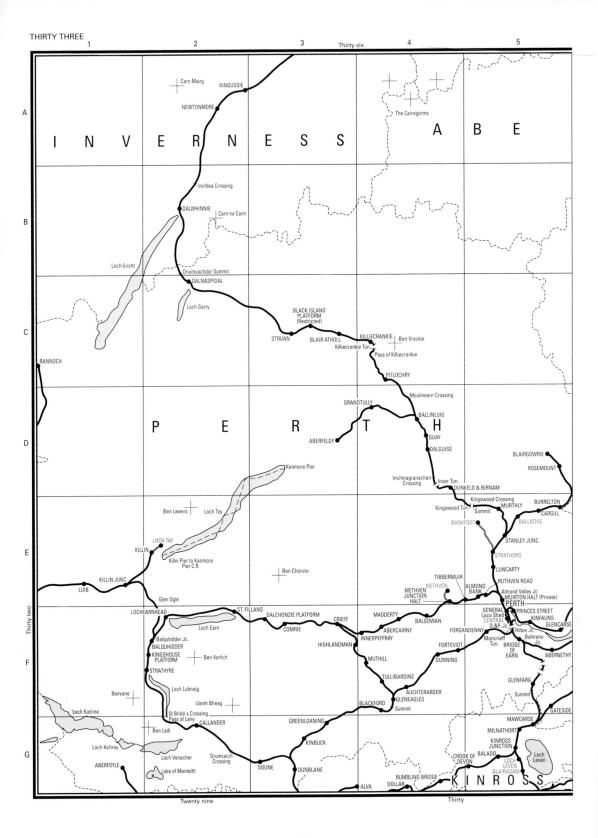

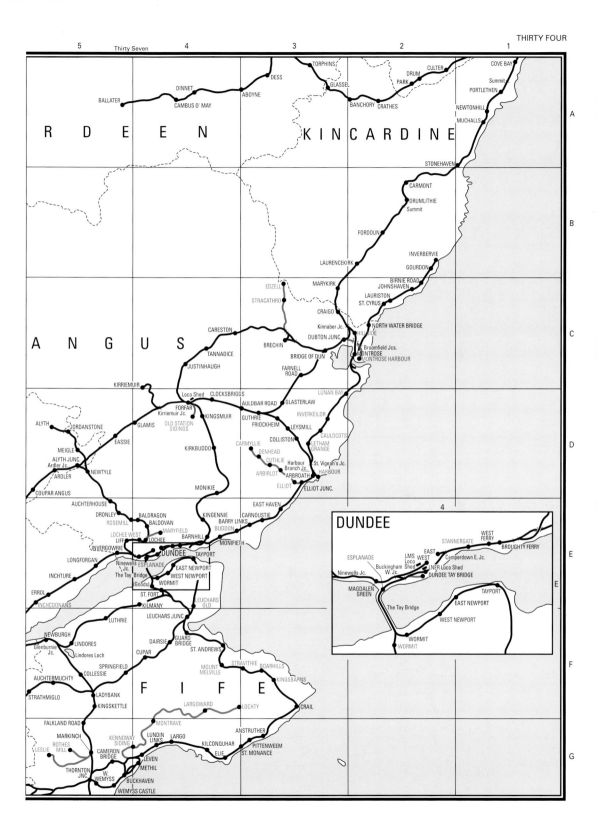

5   Thirty Seven   4   3   2   1

TORPHINS
GLASSEL
DESS
DRUM
CULTER
COVE BAY
DINNET
ABOYNE
PARK
Summit
PORTLETHEN
BALLATER
CAMBUS O' MAY
BANCHORY
CRATHES
NEWTONHILL

A

MUCHALLS

R D E E N   K I N C A R D I N E

STONEHAVEN

CARMONT

DRUMLITHIE

Summit

B

FORDOUN

INVERBERVIE

LAURENCEKIRK
GOURDON

MARYKIRK
BIRNIE ROAD
JOHNSHAVEN
LAURISTON
ST. CYRUS

EDZELL
CRAIGO
STRACATHRO
NORTH WATER BRIDGE

C

A N G U S

CARESTON
Kinnaber Jc.
HILLSIDE
Broomfield Jcs.
DUBTON JUNC.
MONTROSE
BRECHIN
MONTROSE HARBOUR
TANNADICE
BRIDGE OF DUN

JUSTINHAUGH
FARNELL
ROAD

KIRRIEMUIR

Loco Shed   CLOCKSBRIGGS
LUNAN BAY
FORFAR   AULDBAR ROAD   GLASTERLAW
Kirriemuir Jc.
KINGSMUIR
ALYTH
JORDANSTONE
GLAMIS
OLD STATION SIDINGS
GUTHRIE
FRIOCKHEIM
INVERKEILOR

D

MEIGLE
EASSIE
LEYSMILL
CARMYLLIE
COLLISTON
CAULDCOTS
ALYTH JUNC.
KIRKBUDDO
DENHEAD
LETHAM
GRANGE
Ardler Jc.
CUTHLIE
Harbour
St. Vigean's Jc.
ARDLER
ARBIRLOT
Branch Jc.
NEWTYLE
ARBROATH
HARBOUR
COUPAR ANGUS
MONIKIE
ELLIOT
ELLIOT JUNC.

AUCHTERHOUSE
EAST HAVEN

DRONLEY
KINGENNIE
CARNOUSTIE
ROSEMILL
BALDRAGON
BARRY LINKS
BALDOVAN
BUDDON

4

LOCHEE WEST
MARYFIELD
BUDDON

DUNDEE

LIFF
LOCHEE
BARNHILL
INVERGOWRIE
MONIFIETH

STANNERGATE
WEST
FERRY

LONGFORGAN
DUNDEE
TAYPORT
BROUGHTY FERRY

ESPLANADE
EAST
ESPLANADE
Camperdown E. Jc.
INCHTURE
Ninewells
EAST NEWPORT
LMS
WEST
Jc.
WEST NEWPORT
Loco
The Tay Bridge
Shed
LNER Loco Shed
WORMIT
Ninewells Jc.
Buckingham
DUNDEE TAY BRIDGE

E

ERROL
(Goods)
W. Jc.

ST. FORT
MAGDALEN
GREEN
TAYPORT

INCHCOONANS
LEUCHARS
OLD
The Tay Bridge
EAST NEWPORT

KILMANY
WEST NEWPORT

E

LUTHRIE
LEUCHARS JUNC.
WORMIT
WORMIT

NEWBURGH
DAIRSIE
GUARD
BRIDGE
LINDORES
CUPAR
ST. ANDREWS
Glenburnie
Jc.
Lindores Loch
SPRINGFIELD
STRAVITHIE
BOARHILLS

F

AUCHTERMUCHTY
COLLESSIE
MOUNT
MELVILLE
KINGSBARNS

STRATHMIGLO
F I F E
LADYBANK
CRAIL
KINGSKETTLE

FALKLAND ROAD
LARGOWARD
LOCHTY

MONTRAVE
MARKINCH
LUNDIN
LINKS
LARGO
ANSTRUTHER
LESLIE
KENNOWAY
SIDING
ROTHES
MILL
KILCONQUHAR
PITTENWEEM
CAMERON
BRIDGE
ELIE
ST. MONANCE

G

THORNTON
JNC.
W.
WEMYSS
LEVEN
METHIL
BUCKHAVEN
WEMYSS CASTLE

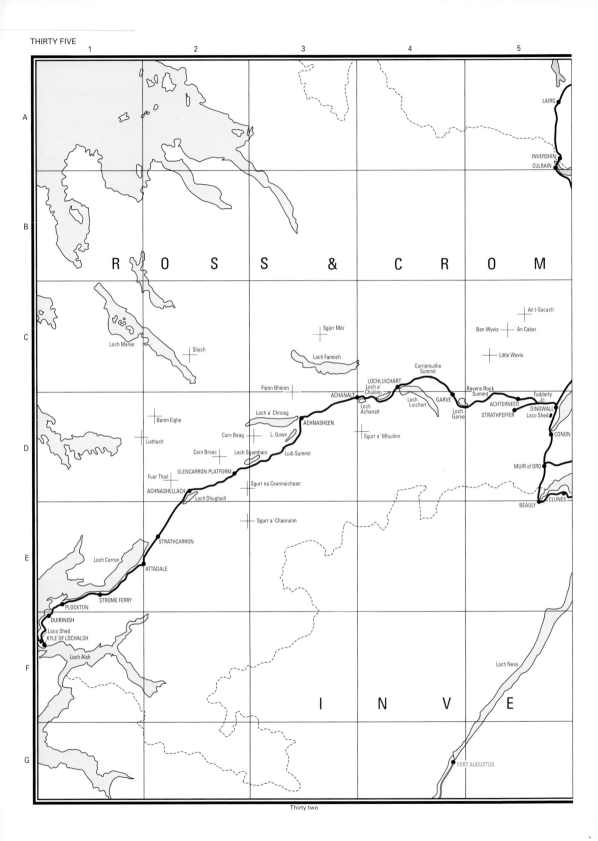

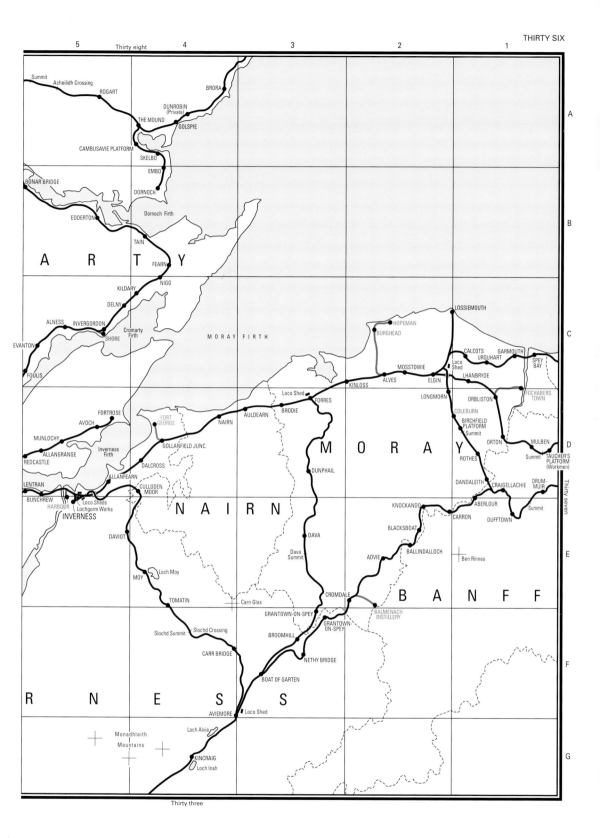

Thirty eight

5   4   3   2   1

A

B

A R T Y

FEARN

MORAY FIRTH

LOSSIEMOUTH

C

HOPEMAN
BURGHEAD

CALCOTS
URQUHART   GARMOUTH

SPEY
BAY

MOSSTOWIE

Loco
Shed

KINLOSS   ALVES   ELGIN
LHANBRYDE

Loco Shed
FORRES

LONGMORN   ORBLISTON

FOCHABERS
TOWN

TAUCHER'S
PLATFORM
(Workmen)

M O R A Y

COLEBURN
BIRCHFIELD
PLATFORM
Summit

BRODIE

NAIRN   AULDEARN

FORT
GEORGE

GOLLANFIELD JUNC.

ORTON

MULBEN

Summit

D

ROTHES

DANDALEITH   CRAIGELLACHIE

DRUM-
MUIR

Thirty seven

FORTROSE

AVOCH

MUNLOCHY

ALLANGRANGE
REDCASTLE

Inverness
Firth

DALCROSS

ALLANFEARN

N A I R N

DUNPHAIL

KNOCKANDO

ABERLOUR

CARRON

DUFFTOWN

Summit

LENTRAN
BUNCHREW
HARBOUR

Loco Sheds
Lochgorm Works

INVERNESS

CULLODEN
MOOR

DAVA

BLACKSBOAT

ADVIE   BALLINDALLOCH

Ben Rinnes

E

DAVIOT

DAVA
Summit

B A N F F

MOY   Loch Moy

TOMATIN

Carn Glas

CROMDALE

BALMENACH
DISTILLERY

R N E S S

GRANTOWN-ON-SPEY

Slochd Summit   Slochd Crossing

CARR BRIDGE

BROOMHILL

GRANTOWN-
ON-SPEY

NETHY BRIDGE

F

BOAT OF GARTEN

AVIEMORE   Loco Shed

Loch Alvie

Monadhliath
Mountains

KINCRAIG
Loch Insh

G

Thirty three

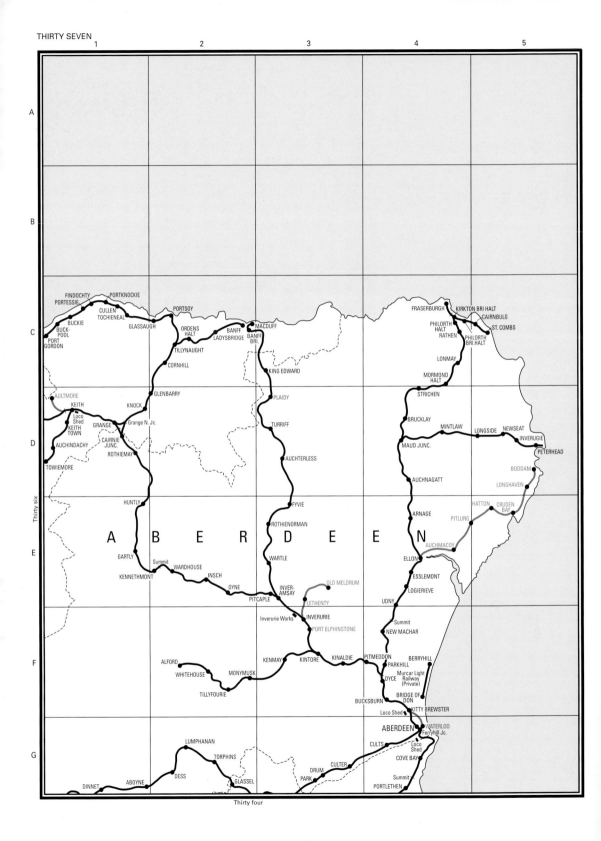

THIRTY SEVEN

A

B

C

THURSO

GEORGEMAS
JUNCTION
HOY   Loch
             Scarmdlett
HALKIRK   Georgemas
             Jc.   BOWER
SCOTSCALDER Loch   WATTEN   BILBSTER
             Watten

WICK

Loco Shed

THRUMSTER
WELSH'S CROSSING & HALT
County   Loch
March   Dubh   Loch Hempriggs
Summit   ALTNABREAC

FORSINARD   ULBSTER
                               MID CLYTH
C A I T H N E S S   ROSTER ROAD HALT
                               OCCUMSTER
Loch an Ruathair   PARKSIDE HALT
                               LYBSTER

KINBRACE
              ☩ Morwen

BORROBOL PLATFORM

KILDONAN   SALZCRAGGIE
              PLATFORM
              Loco Shed
           ☩ HELMSDALE
              Beinn Dobhrain

              LOTH

BRORA

DUNROBIN
(Private)

D

E

F

G

1   2   3   4   5

Reference Legend

1	Warwick Rd Jc.	11	KENSAL GREEN	28	WESTBOURNE PARK
2	West Street Jc.	12	BLACKFRIARS (S.R)	29	ROYAL OAK
3	SMITHFIELD G.W.	13	MANSION HOUSE	30	Junction Rd Jc.
4	WORSHIP STR	14	QUEEN'S PARK WEST	31	Highgate Rd Jc.
5	Minories Jc.	15	MONUMENT	32	CHALK FARM
6	ALDGATE EAST	16	MARK LANE	33	CAMDEN
7	HAYDON SQUARE	17	STEPNEY EAST	34	Hampstead Rd Jc.
8	GOODMAN'S YARD	18	WARWICK RD G.W.	35	Kentish Town Jc.
9	MINT STR. L.N.E.R (Goods)	19	WARWICK RD G.W.	36	CAMDEN TOWN
10	MINT STR. L.M.S (Goods)	20	Earls Court Jc.	37	Maiden Lane Jc.
		21	Goods Yard Jc.	38	St Pancras Jc. (West)
		22	West London Ext. Jc.	39	KENTISH TOWN WEST
		23	KEN. LILLIE BRI.	40	North London Jc.
		24	TURNHAM GREEN	41	North London Incline Jc.
		25	CHISWICK PARK	42	ST PANCRAS
		26	WEST END LANE	43	Copenhagen Jc,
		27	LADBROKE GROVE	44	Copenhagen Tun.

45	MAIDEN LANE
46	KINGS CROSS (SUBURBAN)
47	Campbell Road Jc.
48	Upper Abbey Mills Jc.
49	SPITALFIELDS
50	Bishopsgate Jc.
51	SPITALFIELDS (Coal)
52	Vallance Road Jc.
53	Borough Market Jc.
54	Metropolitan Jc.
55	Hampstead Tun.
56	St John's WoodTun
57	OLD OAK LANE HALT
58	WEST HAMPSTEAD
59	Primrose Hill Tuns

Map labels (selected): BELMONT, PINNER, HARROW & WEALDSTONE, KENTON, NORTH HARROW, WEST HARROW, RAYNER'S LANE, EASTCOTE, HARROW-ON-THE-HILL, KINGSBURY, PRESTON ROAD, SOUTH KENTON, NORTH WEMBLEY, SUDBURY HILL HARROW, SUDBURY & HARROW RD., WEMBLEY HILL, WEMBLEY STADIUM, WEMBLEY PARK, NEASDEN & K, DOLLIS HILL, CRICKLEWOOD, BRENT Jc., FINCHLEY (CHURCH END), CRANLEY GARDENS, EAST FINCHLEY, HIGHGATE, GOSPEL OAK, HAMPSTEAD HEATH, FINCHLEY RD & FROGNAL, WEST HAMPSTEAD, KILBURN BRON., FINCHLEY RD, SWISS COTTAGE, SOUTH HAMPSTEAD, KILBURN, NORTHOLT JUNC., NORTHOLT, GREENFORD, SOUTH GREENFORD HALT, SUDBURY HILL, SUDBURY TOWN, ALPERTON, PERIVALE HALT, STONEBRIDGE PARK, HARLESDEN, KENSAL RISE, WILLESDEN GREEN, BRONDESBURY, BRONDESBURY PARK, KENSAL GREEN Jc., WILLESDEN JUNC., WESTBOURNE PARK, ROYAL OAK, PADDINGTON, BISHOPS ROAD, CASTLE BAR PARK HALT, DRAYTON GREEN (EALING) HALT, BRENTHAM, NORTH EALING, EALING BROADWAY, ACTON, EALING COMMON, WEST EALING, HANWELL & ELTHORNE, SOUTHALL, MARYLEBONE, BAKER STREET, EDGWARE RD, PADDINGTON, PRAED STREET, BAYSWATER, GREAT PORTLAND ST, LORDS, NOTTING HILL GATE, LATIMER ROAD, SHEPHERDS BUSH, UXBRIDGE ROAD, HIGH ST KENSINGTON, ADDISON RD, GOLDHAWK RD., STAMFORD BROOK, RAVENSCOURT PARK, HAMMERSMITH, BARON'S COURT, WEST KENSINGTON, EARLS COURT, GLOUCESTER RD, VICTORIA, SLOANE SQUARE, STH. KENSINGTON, WEST BROMPTON, BROMPTON & FULHAM, WALHAM GREEN, CHELSEA & FULHAM, BATTERSEA, ACTON TOWN, SOUTH ACTON, ACTON CENTRAL, GUNNERSBURY, BRENTFORD, KEW BRIDGE, CHISWICK, KEW GARDENS, BARNES BRIDGE, BARNES, BOSTON MANOR, OSTERLEY, NORTHFIELDS, SOUTH EALING, HOUNSLOW EAST, HOUNSLOW CENTRAL, HOUNSLOW WEST, HOUNSLOW, RICHMOND, NORTH SHEEN, MORTLAKE, PUTNEY, WANDSWORTH TOWN, PARSONS GREEN, PUTNEY BRI., CHELSEA & FULHAM, BATTERSEA PARK, QUEENS ROAD, CLAPHAM JUNCTION, FALCON LANE, WANDSWORTH COMMON, EAST PUTNEY, SOUTHFIELDS, WIMBLEDON PARK, EARLSFIELD, BALHAM, HOUNSLOW Jc., FELTHAM Jc., WHITTON, TWICKENHAM, ST. MARGARETS, STRAWBERRY HILL, FULWELL, TEDDINGTON, HAMPTON, HAMPTON WICK, KINGSTON, NORBITON, KEMPTON PARK (RESTRICTED), CLAPHAM JUNCTION, BATTERSEA, LATCHMERE, QUEEN'S RD, SOUTH LAMBETH, STEWARTS LANE, WIMBLEDON, HAYDONS RD, TOOTING JUNC., RAYNES PARK, MALDEN, BERRYLANDS, SURBITON, HAMPTON COURT, THAMES DITTON, ESHER, MALDEN MANOR, MOTSPUR PARK, WORCESTER PARK, WIMBLEDON CHASE, MERTON PARK, SOUTH MERTON, MORDEN SOUTH, ST HELIER, SUTTON COMMON, MORDEN HALT, MERTON ABBEY, MITCHAM, MITCHAM JUNC., HACKBRIDGE

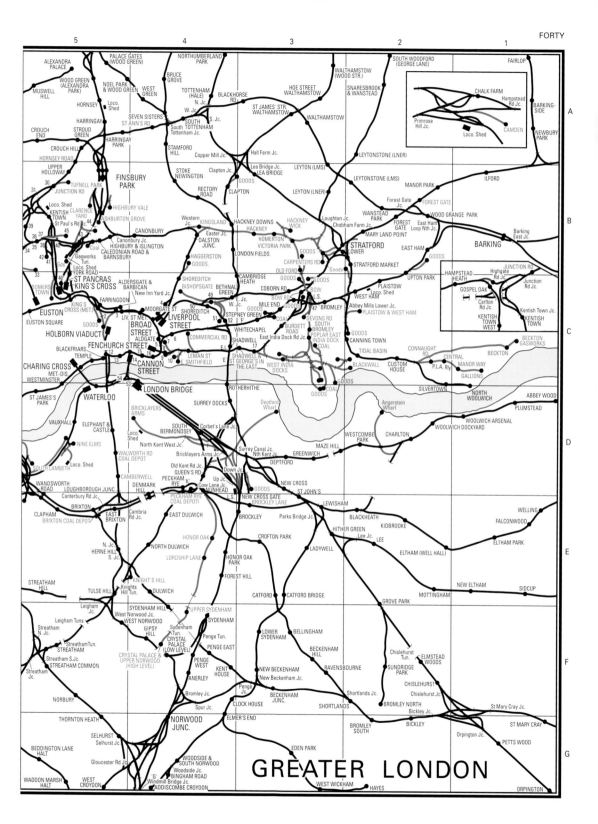

GREATER LONDON

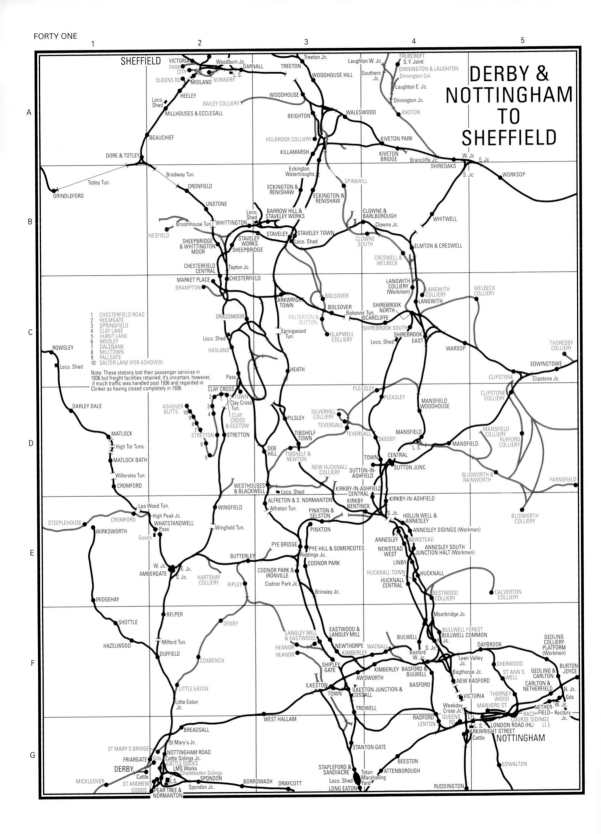

DERBY &
NOTTINGHAM
TO
SHEFFIELD

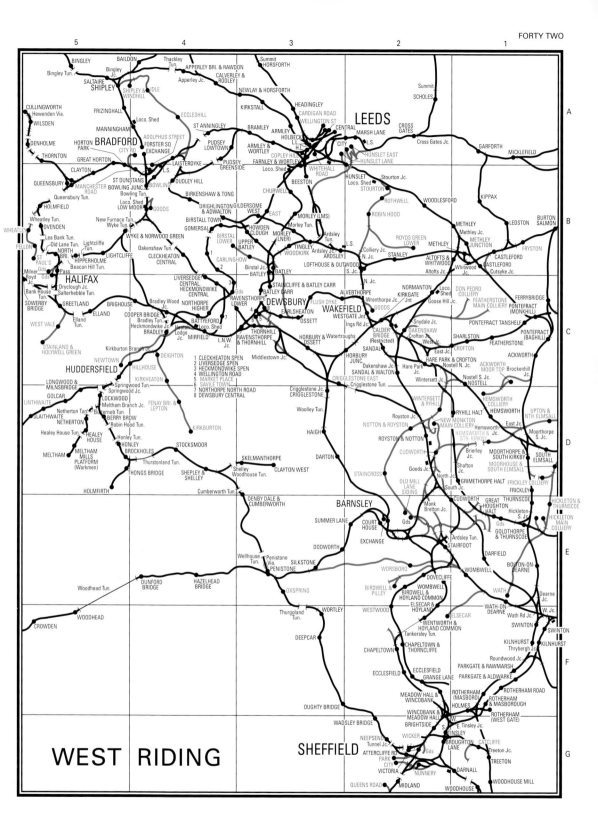

WEST RIDING

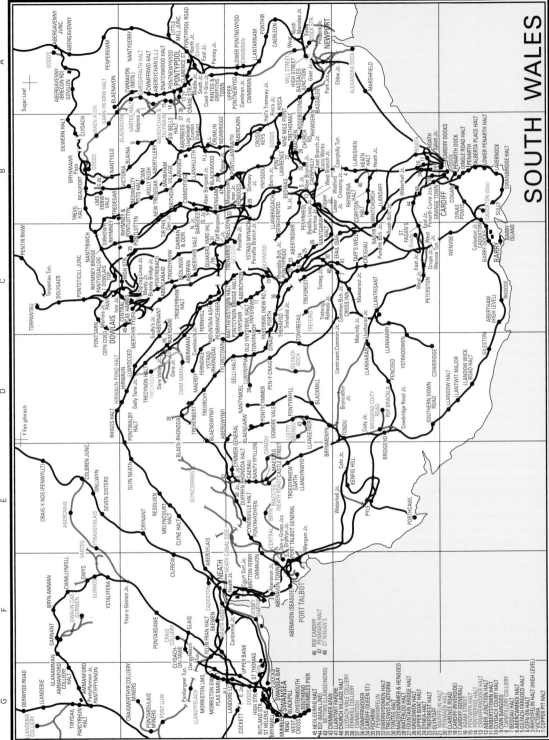

SOUTH WALES

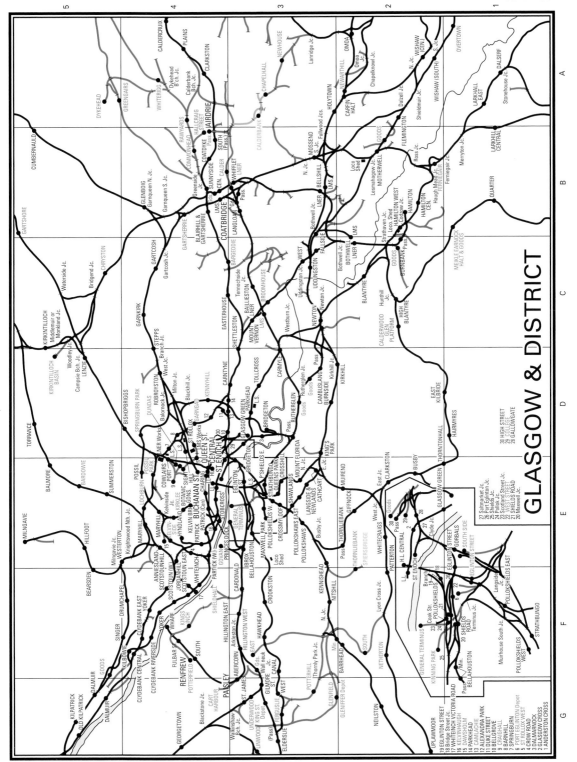

GLASGOW & DISTRICT

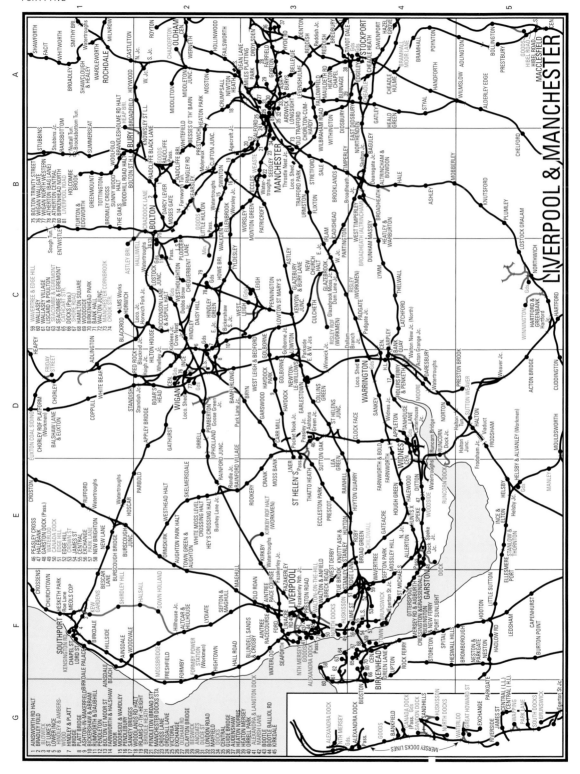

Liverpool & Manchester

1 AINSWORTH RD HALT
2 BRADLEY FOLD
3 BLOWICK
4 LOWER INCE
5 HINDLEY & AMBERS.
6 HINDLEY & PLATT BRIDGE
7 PLATT BRIDGE
8 ASHTON-IN-MAKERFIELD
9 BILLINGE
10 BICKERSHAW & ABRAM
11 RUMWORTH & DAUBHILL
12 PENDLETON
13 PENDLETON BROAD ST
14 BOLTON WITH & HALSHAW MOOR
15 MOORSIDE & WARDLEY
16 BOLTON TRINITY ST
17 SANKEY BRIDGES
18 WOODLANDS RD HALT
19 IRLAMS O'TH'HEIGHT
20 PENDLETON BROAD STA
21 MANCHESTER DOCKS STA
22 CROSS LANE
23 ORDSALL LANE
24 VICTORIA
25 EXCHANGE
26 CLAYTON BRIDGE
27 ARDWICK
28 BESWICK
29 ANCOATS
30 LONDON ROAD
31 MAYFIELD
32 DOCKS
33 CENTRAL
34 GUIDE BRIDGE
35 AUDENSHAW
36 HEATON NORRIS
37 ORRELL PARK
38 ALEXANDRA & LANGSTON DOCK
39 BOOTLE LANE
40 BOOTLE BALLIOL RD
41 KIRKDALE

46 PEASLEY CROSS
47 GARSTON DOCK (Pass.)
48 HALEBANK
49 GARSTON DOCK (Workmen)
50 WATERLOO
51 EDGE HILL
52 EDGE HILL
53 JAMES ST
54 CENTRAL
55 EXCHANGE
56 PARK LANE
57 ST MICHAELS
58 NEW LANE

59 WAVERTREE & EDGE HILL
60 WALLASEY
61 WALLASEY VILLAGE
62 SEACOMBE & EGREMONT
63 SEACOMBE (BGE LANE)
64 SHORE ROAD
65 OXTON & BIRKENHEAD
66 WOODSIDE
67 BIRKENHEAD PARK
68 HAMILTON SQUARE
69 BANK HALL
70 WALTON JUNC.
71 WALTON-ON-THE-HILL
72 WEST DERBY
73 KNOTTY ASH & STANLEY
74 HUYTON

75 BOLTON TRINITY STREET
76 WIGAN NORTH WESTERN
77 WIGAN WALLGATE
78 ATHERTON (BAG LANE)
79 ATHERTON (CENTRAL)
80 BIRKENHEAD NORTH
81 LIVERPOOL ROAD

72

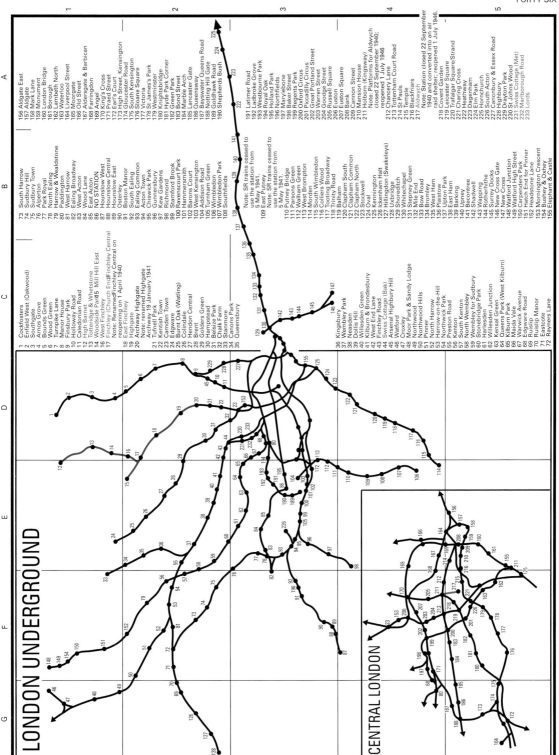

Alverstone	4F3
Alverthorpe	21E3/42C3
Alves	36C2
Alvescot	10E5
Alyth	34D5
Alyth Junction	34D5
Ambergate	16C5/41E2
Amberley	5F1
Amble	31F5
Ambrosden (Military)	10E3
Amersham	10F1
Amesbury	4C5
Amisfield	26A3
Amlwch	19C1/23G2
Ammanford	7A4/43G1
Ammanford Colliery Halt	7A4/43G1
Amotherby	22B5
Ampleforth	21A5
Ampthill	10C1/11D1
Ancaster	16C1/17C1
Anderston Cross	44E4
Andover Junction	4C4
Andover Town	4C4
Andoversford & Dowdeswell	9D4
Andoversford	9D4
Anerley	40F4
Angel	46E4
Angel Road	5A3
Angerstein Wharf	40D2
Angerton	27A4
Angling Club Cottage Platform (Private)	30E1
Angmering	5F2
Annan	26B2
Annan Shawhill	26B2
Annbank	29E4
Annesley	41E4
Annesley Sidings (Railwaymen)	41E4
Annesley South Junction Halt (Railwaymen)	41E4
Annfield Plain	27C5
Anniesland	44E4
Annitsford	27B5
Ansdell & Fairhaven	20A4/24E4
Anston	16A4/41A4
Anstruther	34G3
Apperley Bridge & Rawdon	21D2/42A4
Appin	32D4
Apple Pie Camp (Military)	4C1
Appleby	22F4
Appleby	27E2
Appledore	6E4
Appleford Halt	10F4
Appleton	45D4
Appley Bridge	20B3/24F3/45D2
Apsley	10E1/11F1
Arbirlot	34D3
Arbroath	34D3
Arbroath Harbour	34D3
Archway Highgate	46D2
Note: renamed Highgate Archway 19 January 1941	
Ardeer Works Platform (Workmen)	29E3
Arddleen	14A2
Ardingly	5E3
Ardleigh	12E4
Ardler	34D5
Ardley	10D4
Ardlui	32F1
Ardrossan South Beach	29D3
Ardrossan West Montgomerie Pier	29D3
Ardrossan Winton Pier	29D3
Ardsley	42B3

Ardwick	20B1/24F1/45A3
Arenig	19F4
Argoed Halt	8B4/43B2
Arisaig	32B5
Arkholme	24B2
Arksey	21F5
Arkwright Town	16B4/41C3
Arlesey & Henlow	11D2
Arley & Fillongley	16G5
Arley	9A2/15G2
Arley Colliery Sidings Workmen's Platform (Workmen)	16G5
Armadale	30C4
Armadale Colliery	30C4
Armathwaite	27D1
Armitage	15E5
Armley	21D3/42A3
Armley & Wortley	21D3/42A3
Arnage	37E4
Arncott (Military)	10E3
Arnos Grove	46D1
Arnside	24A3
Arpley	15A2/20C2/24G2/45C4
Arram	22D4
Arrochar & Tarbert	32G1
Arsenal Highbury Hill	46D2
Arthington	21D3
Arthog	13A5
Arundel	5F1
Ascot & Sunninghill	4A1/5B1
Ascott-under-Wychwood	10D5
Asfordby	16E3
Ash	4B1/5C1
Ash Town	6C2
Ash Vale	4B1
Ashbourne	15C5
Ashburton Grove	40B5
Ashburton	2C4
Ashbury	1B5
Ashburys	20B1/24F1/45A3
Ashby Magna	16G4
Ashby-de-la-Zouch	16E5
Ashchurch	9D3
Ashcott	3C2/8E2
Ashdon Halt	11D4
Ashey	4F3
Ashford (Middlesex)	5B2
Ashford	6D4
Ashington	27A5
Ashington Colliery (miners)	27A5
Ashley & Weston	16G2
Ashley Heath Halt	3E5
Ashley	15A3/20C1/24G1/45B4
Ashley Hill	8G1/9C1
Ashover Butts	41D2
Ashperton	9C2
Ashtead	5C2
Ashton	2C3
Ashton (Charlestown)	21A2
Ashton-in-Makerfield	45D3
Ashton Oldham Road	21A2
Ashton-under-Hill	9C4
Ashton-under-Lyne	21F1
Ashton Charlestown	21A2
Ashurst	5D4
Ashwater	1B5
Ashwell	16E2
Ashwell & Morden	11D2
Ashwellthorpe	12A3/18F3
Askam	24A5
Askern	21E5
Askrigg	21A1/27G3
Aslockton	16C2

Aspall & Thorndon	12C3
Aspatria	26D3
Aspley Guise Halt	10C1
Astley	20B2/24F2/45C3
Astley Bridge	20B2/24F2/45C1
Aston	13B4/15G4
Aston Botterell Siding	15G2
Aston Cantlow Halt	9B5
Note: Served by workmen's trains from Birmingham until 3 July 1944	
Aston Rowant	10F3
Aston-by-Stone	15D3/20F1
Astwood Halt	9B3
Aswarby & Sedringham	17D1
Athelney	3D1/8F3
Atherstone	16F5
Atherton Bag Lane	20B2/24F2/45C2
Atherton Central	20B2/24F2/45C2
Atherton Central	45B3
Attadale	35E2
Attenborough	16D4/41G4
Attercliffe Road	42G2
Attimore Hall Siding	11F2
Attleborough	12A4/18F4
Attlebridge	18E3
Auchendinny	30C2
Auchengray	30D4
Auchenheath	30D5
Auchenmade	29D3
Auchindachy	37D1
Auchinleck	29F5
Auchmacoy	37E4
Auchnagatt	37D4
Auchterarder	33F4
Auchterhouse	34E5
Auchterless	37D3
Auchtermuchty	34F5
Auchtertool	30A2
Audenshaw	21A2
Audenshaw	45A3
Audlem	15C2/20F2
Audley & Bignall End	15C3/20E1
Audley End	11E4
Aughton Park Halt	20B4/24F3/45E2
Auldbar Road	34D3
Auldearn	36C3
Auldgirth	26A4
Aultmore	37D1
Authorpe	17A3
Aviemore	36F4
Avoch	36D5
Avonbridge	30B4
Avoncliff Halt	3B4
Avonmouth Dock	3A2/8C2/9G1
Avonmouth Town	3A2/8C2/9G1
Avonside Wharf	3G1
Avonwick	2D4
Awre	8A1/9E2
Awsworth	16C4/41F3
Axbridge	3B1/8E3
Axminster	2B1
Aycliffe	28E5
Aylesbury	10E2
Aylesford	6C5
Aylsham	18D3
Aynho	10D4
Aynho Park Platform	10D4
Ayot	11F2
Ayr	29F3
Ayr Harbour	29F3
Aysgarth	21A1/27G4
Ayton	31C3

Backbarrow	24B4	Bankend Mine	30E5
Backrod	20B2/24F2/45C2	Bankfoot	33E5
Backworth	28B5	Bankhead	30D4
Bacton	14F1	Banknock	30B5
Bacup	20A1/24E1	Banks	20A4/24E4
Baddesley Colliery	125F5	Bannister Green Halt	11E5
Badminton	9G3	Bannockburn	30A5
Badnall Wharf	15E3/20F1	Banstead	5C3
Bagillt	20D5	Baptist End Halt	13C1
Bagshot	4B1/5C1	Barassie	29E3
Baguley	20C1/24G1/45B4	Barber's Bridge	9D2
Bagworth & Elliston	16E4	Barbon	24A2
Baildon	21D2/42A4	Barcombe Mills	5F4
Bailey Colliery	41A2	Barcombe	5F4
Bailey Gate	3E4	Bardney	17B1
Baillieston	44C3	Bardon Hill	16E4
Bainton	22C4	Bardon Mill	27B2
Baker Street	39C5/46F4	Bardowie	29B5/44E5
Bakewell	15B5	Bardsey	21D3
Bala	19F4	Bare Lane	24B3
Bala Junction	19F4	Bargeddie	29C5/44C3
Bala Lake Halt	19F4	Bargoed	8B4/43B2
Note: Only open on summer Sundays at closure		Barham	6C2
		Barking	5A4/40B1/46B3
Balado	30A3/33G5	Barkingside	40A1
Balchriston Siding	29F3	Barkston	16C1
Balcombe	5E3	Barlaston & Tittensor	15D3/20F1
Baldersby	21A3	Barleith	29E4
Balderton	20E4	Barlow	21D5
Baldock	11E2	Barmby	21E5
Baldovan	34E4	Barming	6C5
Baldragon	34E4	Barmouth	13A5
Balerno	30C3	Barmouth Junction	13A5
Balfron	29A4	Barnard Castle	27E4
Balgowan	33F4	Barnby Dun	21F5
Balgreen Halt	30B3	Barnby Moor & Sutton	16A3
Balham	5B3/39E5	Barnehurst	5B4
Balham (LUL)	46D4	Barnes	5B3/39E4
Ballabeg	23C2	Barnes Bridge	39D3
Ballachilsh (Glencoe)	32D3	Barnetby	22F3
Ballachulish Ferry	32D3	Barnham (Sussex)	5F1
Ballasalla	23C2	Barnham	12B5
Ballater	34A5	Barnhill	34E4
Ballathie	33E5	Barnhill	44D4
Ballaugh	23A2/25G4	Barnoldswick	21A1
Ballencrief	30B1	Barnsley Court House	21F3/42E2
Ballindalloch	36E2	Barnsley Exchange	42E2
Ballingham	9D1	Barnsley Old Mill Lane Siding	42E2
Ballinluig	33D4	Barnstaple	7F3
Balloch	29B2	Barnstaple Junction	7F3
Balloch Pier	29B2	Barnstaple Town	7F3
Balmenach Distillery	36E2	Barnstone	16D2
Balmore	29B5/44E5	Barnt Green	9A4
Balne	21E5	Barnton	30B3
Balne Moor	21E5	Barnwell	11A1/16G1/17G1
Balquhidder	33F2	Barnwell Junction	11C3
Balshaw Lane & Euxton	20A3/24E3/45D1	Baron's Court	39D4/46B3
Bamber Bridge	20A3/24E3	Baron's Lane Halt & Siding	12G5
Bamford	15A5	Barras	27F3
Bamfurlong	20B3/24F2/45D2	Barrasford	27B3
Bampton (Devon)	7G5	Barrhead	29C4/44F2
Banavie	32C3	Barrhead South	44F2
Banavie Pier	32C3	Barrhill	25A3
Banbury General	10C4	Barrmill	29D3
Banbury Merton Street	10C4	Barrow	15B1/20D3
Banchory	34A2	Barrow Central	24B5
Banff	37C2	Barrow Haven	22E3
Banff Bridge	37C2	Barrow Hill & Staveley Works	16A4/41B3
Bangor	19D2	Barrow Shipyard (Workmen)	24B5
Bangor-on-Dee	20F4	Barrow-on-Soar & Quorn	16E3
Note: Reopened 6 May 1946		Barry	8D4/43C5
Bank	46E5	Barry Docks	8D4/43C5
Bank Hall	45F3	Barry Island	8D4/43C5

Barry Links	34E3
Bartlow	11D4
Barton	22E4
Barton	27F5
Barton & Broughton	24D3
Barton & Walton	15E5
Barton Hill	22B5
Barton Stacey Halt (Military)	4C3
Barton-le-Street	22B5
Baschurch	14A1/20G4
Basford	16C4/41F4
Basford & Bulwell	41F4
Basingstoke	4B2
Bason Bridge	3B1/8E3
Bassaleg	8C4/43A3
Bassaleg Junction	43A3
Bassenthwaite Lake	26E2
Bath	3A3/8D1
Bathampton	3A3
Bathford Halt	3A4
Bathgate Lower	30C4
Bathgate Upper	30C4
Batley	21E3/42B3
Batley Carr	42C3
Battersby	28F4
Battersea Park	39D5
Battersea	5B4/39E5
Battle	6F5
Battlesbridge	6A5/11G5
Battyeford	42C4
Bathgate Lower	30C4
Bawdrip Halt	3C1/8E3
Bawtry	21G5
Baxenden	20A1/24E1
Bay Horse	24C3
Baynards	5D2
Bayswater Queens Road	39C5/46G5
Beaconsfield	5A1/10F1
Beag Fair Siding	13G12
Beal	31D4
Bealings	12D3
Beamish	27C5
Beanacre Halt	3A4
Bearley	9B5
Bearsden	29B4/44F5
Bearsted & Thurnham	6C5
Beasdale (Private)	32B5
Beattock	30G3
Beauchief	16A5/41A2
Beaufort	8A4/43B1
Beaulieu Road	4E4
Beauly	35E5
Beaumont's Halt	11F1
Beaver's Hill Halt	7D2
Bebington & New Ferry	20C4/24G4/45E4
Bebside	27A5
Beccles	12A2/18G2
Beckenham Hill	40F3
Beckenham Junction	40F3
Beckermet	26F3
Beckfoot	26F2
Beckford	9C4
Beckingham	22G5
Beckton	5B4/40C1
Becontree	46B3
Bedale	21A3/27G5
Beddau Halt	43C4
Beddington Lane Halt	40G5
Bedford Midland Road	10C1/11D1
Bedford St Johns	11D1
Bedhampton Halt	4E2
Bedlington	27A5
Bedlinog	8B5/43C2

Bedminster	3G1
Bedwas	8B4/43B3
Bedwellty Pits Halt	8A4/43B2
Bedworth	16G5
Bedwyn	4A5
Beechburn	27D5
Beeston	16D4/41G4
Beeston	21D3/42B3
Beeston Castle & Tarporley	15B1/20E3
Beighton	16A4/41A3
Beith	29D3
Beith North	29D3
Bekesbourne	6C2
Belasis Lane	28E4
Belford	31E4
Belgrave & Birtall	16E3
Bell Busk	21C1
Bellahouston	44E3
Bellevue	20C1/24G1/45A3
Bellgrove	44D4
Bellingham North Tyne	27A3
Bellingham	40F3
Bellshill	30C5/44B3
Belmont	39A2
Belmont	5C3
Belper	16C5/41F2
Belses	31E1
Belsize Park	46D2
Belting & Branbridges Halt	5D5
Belton & Burgh	18F1
Belton	22F5
Beluncle Halt	6B5
Belvedere	5B4
Bembridge	4F2
Bempton	22B3
Ben Rhydding	21C2
Benderloch	32E4
Benfleet	6A5
Bengeworth	9C4
Beningborough	21C4
Bensham	27C5/28B2
Bentham	24B2
Bentley	12D4
Bentley	4C1
Bentley Crossing (Workmen)	21F2
Benton	27B5
Bents	30C4
Benwick	11A3/17G3
Bere Alston	1D5
Bere Ferrers	1D5
Berkeley	8B1/9F2
Berkeley Road	8B1/9F2
Berkhamsted	10E1
Berkswell & Baswall Common	9A5
Berney Arms	18F1
Berrington & Eye	9B1
Berrington	15F1
Berry Brow	21E2/42D5
Berryhill	37F4
Berrylands	39G3
Berwick	31C3
Berwick	5F4
Berwyn	20F5
Bescar Lane	20A4/24E4/45F1
Bescot	13A3/15F4
Besses o'th' Barn	45B2
Bestwood Colliery	16C4/41E4
Beswick	45A3
Betchworth	5C2
Bethesda	19D2
Bethnal Green	40C4
Betley Road	15C2/20E2
Bettisfield	15D1/20F3

Bettws (Llangeindro)	7B5/43D3
Bettws-y-Coed	19E4
Bevercotes Colliery	16A3
Beverley	22D4
Bewdley	9A3
Bexhill (Eastern)	6F5
Bexhill Central	6F5
Bexley	5B4
Bexley Heath	5B4
Bicester	10D3
Bickershaw & Abram	45C2
Bickleigh	2D5
Bickley	40G2
Biddenden	6D4
Biddulph	15B3/20E1
Bideford	7F3
Bideford-on-Avon	9B5
Bidston	20C4/24G4/45G4
Biggar	30E3
Biggleswade	11D2
Bilbster	38D2
Billacombe	2E5
Note: Used by workmen's trains from 21 July
1941 to 3 November 1941 when passenger
services restored.
Billaford Platform	2D5
Billericay	5A5/11G5
Billing	10B2
Billingborough & Horbling	17D1
Billinge Green Halt	15B2/20D2
Billingham-on-Tees	28E4
Billingshurst	5E2
Bilson Junction	8A1/9E2
Bilsthorpe Colliery	16B3
Bilston	13A1/13A2/15F4
Binegar	3B3/8E1
Bingham	16C3
Bingham Road	16D3
Bingham Road	40G4
Bingley	21D2/42A5
Binton	9B5
Birch Vale	15A4/21G1
Birches & Bilbrook Halt	15F3
Birchfield Platform	36D1
Birchills	15F4
Birchington-on-Sea	6B2
Birdbrook	11D5
Birdingbury	10A4
Birdwell & Hoyland Common	21F3/42E2
Birdwell & Pilley	21F3/42E2
Birkdale Palace	20A4/24E4/45F1
Birkdale	20A4/24E4/45F1
Birkenhead Cathcart Street	45F4
Birkenhead Central	45F4
Birkenhead Docks	45F4
Birkenhead Hamilton Square	45F4
Birkenhead North	45F4
Birkenhead Park	45F4
Birkenhead Shore	45F4
Birkenhead Town	45F4
Birkenhead Woodside	20C4/24G4/45F4
Birkenshaw & Tong	21D2/42B4
Birmingham Central	13C4
Birmingham Curzon Street	13C4
Birmimgham Lawley Street	13C4
Birmingham Moor Street	13C4
Birmingham New Street	13C4/15G4
Birmingham Snow Hill	13C4/15G4
Birnie Road	34C2
Birstall Lower	21E2/42B4
Birstall Town	42B4
Birsthwith	21C3
Birtley	27C5

Bishop Auckland	27E5
Bishop's Cleeve	9D4
Bishop's Lydeard	8F4
Bishop's Nympton & Holland	7F4
Bishop's Stortford	11E3
Bishop's Waltham	4D3
Bishopbriggs	29C5/44D4
Bishopsbourne	6C2
Bishopsgate	40C4
Bishopstone	5G4
Bishopstone Beach Halt	5G4
Note: Summer only following opening of new
Bishopstone station on 26 September 1938
prior to closure
Bishopton	29C4
Bisley Camp (Military)	5C1
Bittaford Platform	2D5
Bitterley Siding	9A1
Bitterne	4E4
Bitton	3A3/8D1
Blaby	16F4
Black Bank	11A4/17G4
Black Bull	15C3/20E1
Black Dog Siding	3A5
Black Island Platform (Restricted)	33C3
Black Pill	43G3
Black Rock Halt	19F2
Blackburn	24D2
Blackburn King Street	24E2
Blackburn Taylor Street	24E2
Blackdyke Halt	26C3
Blackford Hill	30G2
Blackford	33F4
Blackfriars	40C5
Blackfriars (LUL)	46E5
Blackhall Colliery	28D4
Blackhall Rocks	28D4
Blackheath	5B4/40E2
Blackhill	27C4
Blackhorse Road	40A3
Blackmill	7C5/43D3
Blackpole Halt (Workmen)	9B3
Blackpool Central	24D4
Blackpool North	24D4
Blackpool South	24D4
Blackrod	20B2/24F2/45C2
Blacksboat	36E2
Blackthorn	10D3
Blackwall	5B4/40C2
Blackwater (Hants)	4B1
Blackwater (Isle of Wight)	4F3
Blackwell Mill (Staff)	15A5
Blackwell	9A4
Blackwood	30D5
Blackwood	8B4/43B2
Blacon	20D4
Blaenau Festiniog Central	19F3
Blaenavon	8A4/43A1
Blaengarw	7B5/43D3
Blaengwynfi	7B5/43D2
Blaenplwyf Halt	13E5
Blaenrhondda	7B5/43D2
Blagdon	3B2/8D2
Blaina	8A4/43B2
Blair Atholl	33C3
Blairadam	30A3/33G5
Blairgowrie	33D5
Blairhill & Gartsherrie	29C5/44B4
Blake Hall	11G4
Blake Street	15F5
Blakeney	8A1/9E2
Blakesley	10C3
Blanchland	27D4

Blandford	3E4	
Blanefield	29B4	
Blankney & Metheringham	16B1/17B1	
Blantyre	29C5/44C2	
Blaydon	27C5/28A3	
Bleadon & Uphill	3B1/8D3	
Bleasby	16C3	
Bledlow	10E2	
Bledlow Bridge Halt	10F2	
Blencow	26E1	
Blenheim & Woodstock	10E4	
Bletchington	10E4	
Bletchley	10D2	
Blidworth Colliery	41E5	
Blidworth & Railworth	16B3/41D5	
Blisworth	10B3	
Blockley	9C5	
Blodwell Junction	14A2/20G5	
Blowers Green	13B1	
Blowick	45F1	
Bloxham	10C4	
Bloxwich	15F4	
Blue Anchor	8E5	
Bluestone	18D3	
Blundell Sands & Crosby	20B4/24F4/45F3	
Blunham	11D1	
Bluntisham	11B3	
Blyth	28A5	
Blythe Bridge	15C4	
Blyton	22G5	
Bo'ness	30B4	
Boar's Head	20B3/24F3/45D2	
Boarhills	34F3	
Boat of Garten	36F3	
Boddam	37D5	
Bodfari	19D5	
Bodiam	6E5	
Bodmin	1D3	
Bodmin Road	1D3	
Bodorgan	19D1	
Bognor Regis	5G1	
Bogside	29E3	
Bogside (Fife)	30A4	
Bogston	29B3	
Bojea Siding	1D2	
Boldon	28C5	
Bolham Halt	2A3/7G5	
Bollington	15A3/20D1/45A5	
Bolsover	16B4/41C3	
Bolton	20B2/24F2/45B2	
Bolton Abbey	21C1	
Bolton Crook Street	45C2	
Bolton Great Moor Street	45C2	
Bolton Percy	21D4	
Bolton Trinity Street	45C2	
Bolton-le-Sands	24B3	
Bolton-on-Dearne	21F3/42E1	
Bonar Bridge	36B5	
Boncath	13F3	
Bond Street	46F5	
Bonhill	29B3	
Bonnington	30F2	
Bonny Bridge	30B5	
Bonnyrigg	30C2	
Bontnewydd	14A5/19G3	
Bonwm Halt	19F5	
Bookham	5C2	
Boosbeck	28E3	
Bootle	24A5/45F3	
Bootle	26G3	
Bootle Balliol Road	45F3	
Bordesley	13C4/15G5	
Bordon	4C1	

Borough	46E5	
Boroughbridge	21B4	
Borrobol Platform	38F5	
Borrowash	16D4/41G2	
Borth	13C5	
Borwick	24B3	
Boscombe	3F5	
Bosham	4E1	
Bosley	15B3/20D1	
Boston	17C3	
Boston Docks	17C3	
Boston Manor	39D2/46F3	
Botanic Garden	44E4	
Botanic Gardens	22A1	
Bothwell	29C5/44C2	
Botley	4E3	
Bott Lane Halt	21B1	
Bottesford	16D2	
Bottisham & Lode	11C4	
Boughrood & Llyswen	14F3	
Boughton	16B3	
Boughton Halt	9B3	
Bounds Green	46D2	
Bourne End	5A1/10G2	
Bourne	17E1	
Bournemouth Central	3F5	
Bournemouth West	3F5	
Bourton-on-the-Water	9D5	
Bovey	2C4	
Bovington Camp (Military)	3F4	
Bow Brickhill Halt	10D1	
Bow Road	40B3	
Note: Station reopened on 9 December 1946		
Bow Road (LUL)	46C3	
Bow Street	13C5	
Bow	2B4	
Bow	40B3	
Note: Station closed 15 May 1944 but bus replacement service operated until 23 April 1945		
Bowbridge Crossing Halt	9E3	
Bower	38C3	
Bowes	27F4	
Bowhouse	30B4	
Bowland	30D1	
Bowling	29B4	
Bowling	42B4	
Bowling Junction	42B4	
Box	3A4	
Box Mill Lane Halt	3A4	
Boxford	4A4	
Boxhill & Burford Bridge	5C2	
Boyces Bridge	17F4	
Braceborough Spa Halt	17E1	
Brackley	10C3	
Brackley Central	10C3	
Bracknell	4A1	
Bradbury	28E5	
Bradfield	12E4	
Bradford	21D2	
Bradford Adolphus Street	42A4	
Bradford City Road	42A4	
Bradford Exchange	42A4	
Bradford Forster Square	42A4	
Bradford on Avon	3B4	
Bradford Peverell & Stratton Halt	3F3	
Brading Junction	4F3	
Bradley	42C4	
Bradley Fold	20B2/24F1/45B2	
Bradnop	15C4	
Bradwell	10C2	
Brafferton	21B4	
Braidwood	30D5	

Braintree & Bocking	11E5	
Braithwaite	26E2	
Bramber	5F2	
Brambledown Halt	6B4	
Bramford	12D4	
Bramhall	15A3/20C1/45A4	
Bramhall Moor Lane	45A4	
Bramley	21D3/42A3	
Bramley	4B2	
Bramley CAD	4B2	
Bramley & Wonersh	5D1	
Brampford Speke Halt	2B3	
Brampton	12B2/18G2	
Brampton Junction	27C1	
Bramshot Halt	4B1	
Bramwith	21F5	
Brancepeth	27D5	
Brandlesham Road Halt	24B1/45B1	
Brandon	11A5/17G5	
Brandon & Wolston	10A5	
Brandon Colliery	27D5	
Bransford Road	9B3	
Branskome	3F5	
Branston	15E5	
Branston & Heighington	16B1/17B1	
Branthwaite	26E3	
Brasted	5C4	
Braughing	11E3	
Braunston	10B4	
Braunston & Willoughby	10B4	
Braunton	7F3	
Braystones	26F3	
Brayton	26D2	
Breadsall	16D5/41G2	
Breamore	4D5	
Brean Road Halt	3B1/8E3	
Brechin	34C3	
Breck Road	20C4/24G4/45F3	
Brecon Free Street	14F3	
Brecon Mount Street	14F3	
Brecon Watton	14G3	
Bredbury	21G1/45A3	
Bredon	9C3	
Breich	30C4	
Brent	2D4	
Brent	46E2	
Brent Knoll	3B1/8E3	
Brentford	5B2/39D2	
Brentham	39C2	
Brentor	1C5	
Brentwood & Warley	5A5	
Bretby	16E5	
Bretell Lane	15G3	
Bricket Wood	11G1	
Bricklayers Arms	40D4	
Bridestowe	2B5	
Bridge	6C3	
Bridge of Allan	30A5	
Bridge of Dee	26C5	
Bridge of Don	37F4	
Bridge of Dun	34C3	
Bridge of Earn	33F5	
Bridge of Orchy	32E1	
Bridge of Weir	29C3	
Bridgefoot	26E3	
Bridgend	7C5/43D4	
Bridgend Coity Road	7C5/43D4	
Bridgeness	30B4	
Bridgeton	44D3	
Bridgnorth	15F2	
Bridgwater	3C1/8F3	
Bridlington	22B3	
Bridport	3F1	

Brierfield	24D1
Brierley Hill	15G3
Briery Siding Halt	26E2
Brigg	22F4
Brigham	26E3
Brighouse	21E2/42C4
Brightlingsea	12F4
Brighton Central	5F3
Brighton Kemp Town	5F3
Brighton Road	13D4
Brightside	21G3/42G2
Brill & Ludgershall	10E3
Brimley Halt	2C3
Brimscombe	9F3
Brimscombe Bridge Halt	9F3
Brimsdown	5A3/11G3
Brindle Heath	45B3
Brindley Heath (Workmen)	15E4
Note: Opened 3 August 1939; became public	
station 26 August 1939	
Brinkburn	31G4
Brinklow	10A4/16G4
Brinkworth	9G4
Brinscall	20A2/24E2
Brislington	3A2/8D1
Bristol Cannon's Marsh	3G1
Bristol Road	3B1/8D3
Bristol St Philip's Marsh	3G1
Bristol St Philip's	3G1
Bristol Temple Meads	3A2/8C2
Britannia Halt (Naval college and workmen)	
	2D3
Britannia	20A1/24E1
Brithdir	8B4/43B2
Briton Ferry	7B4/43F3
Brixham	2D3
Brixton	5B3/40E5
Brixton Coal Depot	40E5
Brixton Road	2E5
Note: Used by workmen's trains from 21 July	
1941 to 3 November 1941 when passenger	
services restored.	
Brixworth	10A2
Brize Norton & Bampton	10E5
Note: renamed from Bampton 1 May 1940	
Broad Clyst	2B3
Broad Green	45E4
Broadfield	20B1/24F1/45A2
Broadheath	20C2/24G1/45B4
Broadley	20A1/24E1/45A1
Broadstairs	6B1
Broadstone (Dorset)	3F5
Broadstone	3A1/8D3
Broadway	9C4
Brock	24D3
Brockenhurst	4E4
Brocketsbrae	30D5
Brockford & Wetheringsett	12C4
Brockholes	21F2/42D5
Brocklesby	22E3
Brockley	40E3
Brockley Lane	40E3
Brockley Whins	28C5
Brockweir Halt	8B2/9F1
Brodie	36C3
Bromborough	20C4/45F5
Bromfield	9A1
Bromford Bridge	15G5
Bromham & Rowde Halt	3B5
Bromley Cross	20A2/24E2/44B1
Bromley	46C3
Bromley North	5B4/40F2
Bromley South	5B4/40G2

Bromley-by-Bow	40C3
Brompton	28G5
Brompton & Fulham	39D4
Brompton Camp (military)	27G5
Bromsgrove	9A4
Bromshall	15D4
Bromyard	9B2
Brondesbury	39B4
Brondesbury Park	39B4
Bronwydd Arms	13G4
Brookland	6E4
Brooklands	20C1/24G1/45B3
Brookmans Park	11G2
Brooksby	16E3
Brookwood	5C1
Brookwood Cemetery North	5C1
Brookwood Cemetery South	5C1
Broom Junction	9B4
Broome	14C1
Broomfleet	22E5
Broomhill	31G5
Broomhill	36F3
Broomhouse	29C5/44C3
Broomieknow	30C2
Broomielaw (Workmen)	27E4
Note: Became public station 9 June 1942	
Brora	36A4/38G5
Brotton	28E3
Brough	22E4
Broughton	16B3
Broughton	20D4
Broughton	30E3
Broughton & Bretton	20D4
Broughton Astley	16G4
Broughton Cross	26E3
Broughton Gifford Halt	3B4
Broughton Lane	42G2
Broughton-in-Furness	24A5
Broughty Ferry	34E4
Brownhills	15F4
Broxbourn Oil Works	30B3
Broxbourne & Hoddesdon	11F3
Broxton	15C1/20E3
Bruce Grove	40A4
Brucklay	37D4
Brundall	18F2
Brundall Gardens Halt	18F2
Brunswick	20C4/24G4/45E4
Bruton	3C3/8F1
Brymbo	20E4
Bryn	20B3/24F3/45D3
Bryn	7B5/43G3
Bryn Teify	13F4
Brynamman	7A4/43F1
Bryncelynog Halt	19F3
Brynglas	13B5
Bryngwyn	14A2
Brynkir	19F2
Brynmawr	8A4/43B1
Brynmill	43G3
Brynmenyn	7C5/43D3
Bubwith	21D5
Buchlyvie	29A4
Buckden	11C2
Buckenham	18F2
Buckfastleigh	2D4
Buckhaven	30A2/34G5
Buckie	37C1
Buckingham	10D3
Buckley (Old)	20D5
Buckley Junction	20E5
Bucknall & Northwood	15C3/20F1
Bucknell	14D1

Buckpool	37C1
Bucksburn	37F4
Buddon (Military)	34E4
Bude	1A4
Budleigh Salterton	2B2
Budworth Colliery	41E5
Bugle	1D2
Bugsworth	15A4
Buildwas	15F2
Builth Road	14E3
Builth Wells	14E3
Bulford	4C5
Bulford Camp	4C5
Bullgill	26D3
Bullo Cross Halt	8A1/9E2
Bullo Pill	8A1/9E2
Bulwell	16C4/41F4
Bulwell Common	16C4/1F44
Bulwell Forest	16C4/41F4
Bunchrew	36D5
Bungay	12A2/18G2
Bunham Beeches	10G1
Buntingford	11E3
Burbage	4A5
Burdale	22B5
Burdett Road	40C3
Bures	12E5
Burgess Hill	5E3
Burgh-by-Sands	26C1
Burghclere	4B3
Note: Station closed 4 August 1942 to	
8 March 1943	
Burghead	36C2
Burgh-le-Marsh	17B4
Burlescombe	8G5
Burley-in-Wharfedale	21C2
Burlington Road Halt	24D4
Burlish Halt	9A3
Burn Halt	2A3
Burn Naze Halt	24D4
Burnage	45A3
Burnbank	44C2
Burneside	27G1
Burngullow	1D2
Burnham (Bucks)	5A1/10G1
Burnham Market	18D5
Burnham on Crouch	6A4/12G5
Burnham-on-Sea	3B1/8E3
Burnley Bank Top	24D1
Burnley Barracks	24D1
Burnley Manchester Road	24D1
Burnley Towneley	24D1
Burnmouth	31C3
Burnside	29C5/44D3
Burnt House	11A3/17G3
Burnt Mill	11F3
Burnt Oak (Watling)	46E2
Burntisland	30A2
Burrator Halt	2D5
Burrelton	33E5
Burrington	3B2/8D2
Burry Port	7B2
Burscough Bridge	20B4/24F3/45E1
Burscough Junction	20B4/24F3/45E1
Bursledon	4E3
Burslem	15C3/20E1
Burston	12B3
Burton & Holme	24A3
Burton Agnes	22B3
Burton Dassett Halt (Military)	10B5
Burton Joyce	16C3/41F5
Burton Latimer	10A2
Burton Point	20D4/45F5

Burton Salmon	21D4/42B1	Camberley	4B1	Carlisle Citadel	26C1
Burton-on-Trent	15D5	Camberwell	40E5	Carlisle Crown Street	26D1
Burwarton	15G2	Camborne	1E5	Carlisle Dentonholme	26D2
Burwell	11C4	Cambridge	11C3	Carlisle London Road	26D1
Burwell (Goods)	11B4	Cambridge Heath	40C4	Carlisle Petteril Bridge	26D1
Bury Bolton Street	20B1/24F1/45B1	Cambridge Mill Road Wharf	11C3	Carlisle St Nicholas Wharf	26D1
Bury Knowsley Street	20B1/24F1/45B2	Cambridge Station	11C3	Carlisle Viaduct	26D1
Bury St Edmunds	12C5	Cambridge Upper Yard	11C3	Carlton	28E5
Busby	29C5/44E2	Cambus	30A5	Carlton & Netherfield	16C3/41F5
Bush Hill Park	5A3/11G3	Cambus O'May	34A4	Carlton Towers	21E5
Bushbury	15F3	Cambusavie Platform	36A4	Carlton-on-Trent	16B2
Bushey & Oxhey	5A2/11G1/46F1	Cambuslang	29C5/44D3	Carluke	30D5
Butterknowle	27E5	Camden	40B5	Carmarthen Junction	7A2/13G4
Butterley	16C5/41E2	Camden Town	40B5	Carmarthen Town	13G4
Butterwell	27A5	Camden Town (LU)	46D3/46F4	Carmont	34B2
Buttington	14A2	Camel's Head Halt	1A1	Carmyle	29C5/44D3
Buxted	5E4	Camelford	1B3	Carmyllie	34D3
Buxton	15A4	Cameron Bridge	30A2/34G5	Carn Brae	1E5
Buxton Lammas	18E3	Camerton	26E3	Carnaby	22B3
Byers Green	27D5	Camerton	3B3/8D1	Carnforth	24B3
Byfield	10B4	Camlachie	44D4	Carno	14B4
Byfleet	5C1	Camp Hill	13C4	Carnoustie	34E3
Byker	28A1	Campfield (Military)	6A4	Carntyne	29C5/44D3
Bynea	7B3	Campden	9C5	Carnwath	30D4
		Campsie Glen	29B5	Carpenders Park	46F1
Cadbury Road	3A1/8C3	Canley Halt	10A5	Carpenters Road	40B3
Cadeleigh	2A3	Canning Town	40C2	Carr Bridge	36F4
Cadishead	20C2/24G2/45C3	Cannock	15E4	Carr Mill	45D3
Cadoxton	8D4/43B5	Cannock Wood Colliery (Miners)	15E4	Carrog	20F5
Cadoxton	43F2	Cannon Street (LU)	46E5	Carron	36E2
Caerau	7B5/43E3	Canonbie	26B1	Carronbridge	30G4
Caergwrle Castle & Wells	20E4	Canonbury	40B4	Carshalton	5C3
Caerleon	8B3/43A3	Canonbury & Essex Road	46D3	Carstairs	30D4
Caernarvon	19D2	Canons Park	46E2	Cart Harbour	44G4
Caerphilly	8C4/43B3	Canterbury East	6C3	Carter's Siding	3E5
Caersws	14C3	Canterbury South	6C3	Carterton	10E5
Caersws (Van)	14C3	Canterbury West	6C3	Cartsdyke	29B3
Caerwent (RNPF)	8B2/9F1	Cantilever (Military)	1A1	Carville	28B5
Caerwys	20D5	Cantley	18F2	Carway Colliery Siding (Miners)	7A2
Cairn Point	25B2	Capel	12D4	Cassilis	29F3
Cairnbulg	37C5	Capel Bangor	13C5	Castle Ashby & Earl's Barton	10B2
Cairneyhill	30A3	*Note: Summer only passenger service*		Castle Bar Park Halt	39C2
Cairnie Junction (Exchange)	37D1	*withdrawn 31 August 1939; station reopened*		Castle Bromwich	15G5
Cairnryan (Military)	25B2	*23 July 1945*		Castle Bytham	16E1/17E1
Caister Camp Halt	18E1	Capel Celyn Halt	19F4	Castle Caereinion	14B2
Caister-on-Sea	18E1	Capenhurst	20D4/45F5	Castle Cary	3C3/8F1
Calbourne & Shalfleet	4F4	Caradog Falls Halt	14D5	Castle Donington & Shardlow	16D4
Calcots	36C1	Carbean	1D2	Castle Douglas	26C5
Caldarvan	29B4	Carbis Bay	1E4	Castle Eden	28D5
Calder	44B4	Carbis	1D2	Castle Howard	22B5
Calderbank	30C5/44A3	Carcroft & Adwick-le-Street	21F4	Castle Kennedy	25C2
Calderwood Glen Platform		Cardenden	30A2	Castlecary	30B5
(Excursions)	44C2	Cardiff Adam Street	43B4	Castleford	21E4/42B1
Caldercruix	30C5/44A4	Cardiff Clarence Road	43B4	Castlehill	30D5
Caldon Low	15C4	Cardiff Docks	8C4/43B5	Castlethorpe	10C2
Caldwell	29D4	Cardiff General	8B4/43B4	Castleton	20B1/24F1/45A1
Caldy	20C5/24G5	Cardiff Queen Street	8C4/43B5	Castleton	28F3
Caledonian Road	46D2	Cardiff Riverside	43B4	Castletown	23C2
Caledonian Road & Barnsbury	40B5	Cardigan	13E2	Castor	11A1/17F1
California Halt	18E1	Cardington	11D1	Catcliffe	21G4/42G1
Callander	33G2	Cardonald	44F3	Caterham	5C3
Callerton	27B5	Cardrona	30D2	Catfield	18E2
Callington	1C5	Cardross	29B3	Catford	40E3
Calne	3A5	Careston	34C4	Catford Bridge	40E3
Calshot Spit (Military)	4E3	Carfin Halt	44A2	Cathcart	29C5/44E3
Calstock	1C5	Cargill	33E5	Caton	24B3
Calthwaite	27D1	Cargo Fleet	28E4	Catrine	29E5
Calveley	15B1/20E3	Carham	31D2	Cattal	21C4
Calverley & Rodley	21D2/42A4	Carisbrooke	4F3	Catterick	27F5
Calvert	10D3	Cark & Cartmel	24B4	Catterick Camp (Military)	27G5
Calverton Colliery	41E5	Carlinghow	42B3	Cattewater Harbour	1A2
Cam	8B1/9F2	Carlisle Bog	26D1	Cauldcots	34D3
Camber	6E4	Carlisle Canal	26D2	Causeland	1D4

Causewayend	30B4
Causewayhead	30A5
Cavendish	11D5
Cawood	21D5
Cawston	18E3
Caythorpe	16C1
Cayton	22A3
Cefn	20F4
Cefn Coed	8A5/43C1
Cefn-On Halt	43B4
Cefn-y-Bedd	20E4
Cement Mills Halt (Workmen)	4F3
Cemmaes	14B4
Cemmaes Road	14B5
Central	40C2
Central Office (Military)	1A1
Cerist	14C4
Chacewater	1E1/1E5
Chadderton	45A2
Chalcombe Road Halt	10C4
Chalfont & Latimer	10F1/11G1
Chalford	9F3
Chalk Farm	39B5/46D2
Challow	10F5
Chancery Lane	46F4
Chandler's Ford	4D4
Chapel Lane	14A1
Chapel-en-le-Frith	15A4
Chapelhall	30C5/44A3
Chapelton	7F3
Chapeltown	21F3/42F2
Chapeltown & Thorncliffe	42F2
Chappel & Wakes Colne	12E5
Chard	2A1/3E1
Chard Junction	3E1
Chard Town	2A1/3E1
Charfield	8B1/9F2
Charing	44E4
Charing	6C4
Charing Cross (LU)	46F5
Charlbury	10D5
Charlesfield Halt (Workmen)	31E1
Charlestown	30A3
Charlton	5B4/40D2
Charlton Kings	9D4
Charlton Mackrell	3D2/8F2
Chartham	6C3
Chartley	15D4
Charwelton	10B4
Chatburn	24D1
Chatham	6B5
Chatham Dockyard	6B5
Chathill	31E5
Chattenden	6B5
Chatteris	11A3/17G3
Chatterley	15C3/20E1
Cheadle	15C4
Cheadle	45A4
Cheadle Hulme	15A3/20C1/24G1/45A4
Cheam	5C3
Checker House	16A3
Cheddar	3B2/8E2
Cheddington	10E1
Cheddleton	15C4
Chedworth	9E4
Chelford	15A3/20D1/45B5
Chellaston & Swarkstone	16D5
Chelmsford	11F5
Chelsea & Fulham	5B4/39D5
Chelsea Basin	39D5
Chelsfield	5C4
Cheltenham Lansdown	9D4
Cheltenham Malvern Road	9D4
Cheltenham Racecourse (Restricted)	9D4
Cheltenham South & Leckhampton	9D4
Cheltenham St James	9D4
Chepstow	8B2/9F1
Chequerbent	45C2
Cherry Burton	22D4
Cherry Hinton	11C3
Cherry Tree	20A2/24E2
Chertsey	5B1
Chesham	10F1
Cheshunt	11G3
Chessington North	5C2
Chessington South	5C2
Chester General	20D4
Chester le Street	27C5
Chester Northgate	20D4
Chester Road	15F5
Chesterfield	16B5/41C2
Chesterfield Brampton	16B5/41C2
Chesterfield Central	16B5/41C2
Chesterfield Market Place	16B5/412C2
Chesterfield Road	41D2
Chestfield & Swalecliffe Halt	6B3
Chettisham	11B4
Chevening Halt	5C4
Chevington	31G5
Chichester	4E1
Chigwell Lane	5A4/11G3
Chigwell	5A4
Chilcompton	3B3/8E1
Childwall	20C4/24G3/45E4
Chilham	6C3
Chilmark (Military)	3C4
Chilsworthy	1C5
Chiltern Green	11F1
Chilton Halt & Siding	9A2
Chilvers Coton	16G5
Chilworth & Albury	5D1
Chingford	5A4/11G3
Chinley	15A4
Chinnor	10F2
Chippenham	3A4
Chipping Norton	10D5
Chipping Sodbury	8C1/9G2
Chipstead	5C3
Chirk	20F4
Chirnside	31C3
Chiseldon	9G5
Chislehurst	5B4/40F2
Chislet Colliery Halt	6C2
Chiswick	39D3
Chiswick Park	39D3/46E3
Chittening Platform (Workmen)	8C2/9G1
Chollerton	27B3
Cholsey & Moulsford	10G4
Choppington	27A5
Chorley	20A3/24E2/45D1
Chorley Friday Street	20A3/24E2/45D1
Chorley ROF Platform (Workmen)	20A3/24E2/45D1
Chorleywood & Chenies	5A1/10F1/11G1
Chorlton-cum-Hardy	20C1/24G1/45B3
Christchurch	4F5
Christian Malford Halt	3A5/9G4
Christon Bank	31E5
Christow	2B4
Christs Hospital (West Horsham)	5E2
Chryston	44C5
Chudleigh	2C3
Chudleigh Knighton Halt	2C3
Church & Oswaldtwistle	24E1
Church Fenton	21D4
Church Road	8B4/43B3
Church Stretton	14B1/15F1
Church Village Halt	8C5/43C3
Churchdown	D3
Churchill & Blakedown	9A3
Churchtown	20A4/24E4/45F1
Churn	10G4
Churston	2D3
Churwell	21D3/42B3
Chwilog	19F1
Cilfrew	7B4/43F2
Cilfynydd	8B5/43C3
Ciliau Aeron Halt	13E4
Cilmery	14E3
Cinderford	8A1/9E2
Cirencester Town	9F4
Cirencester Watermoor	9F4
Clackmannan & Kennet	30A4
Clacton-on-Sea & Holland-on-Sea	12F3
Clandon	5C1
Clapham	24B1
Clapham	40E5
Clapham Common	46D4
Clapham Junction	5B3/39E5
Clapham North	46D4
Clapham South	46D4
Clapton	40B4
Clapton Road	3A1/8C3/9G1
Clarbeston Road	13G1
Clare	11D5
Clarence Park	30B5
Clarkston	29C5/44E2
Clarkston	30C5/44A4
Clatford	4C4
Claverdon	9B5
Claxby & Usselby	22G3
Clay Cross	16B5/41C2
Clay Cross & Egstow	41D2
Clay Cross Town	16B5/41D2
Claydon	10D3
Clay Lane	41D2
Claydon	12D4
Claygate	5C2
Claypole	16C2
Clayton	21D2/42B5
Clayton Bridge	45A3
Clayton West	21F3/42D3
Clearbrook Halt	2D5
Cleator Moor	26F3
Cleator Moor East	26F3
Note: Used by workmen's trains 11 March 1940 to 8 April 1940	
Cleckheaton Central	21E2/42B4
Cleckheaton Spen	21E2/42B4
Cledford Bridge Halt	15B2/20D2
Clee Hill	9A1
Cleethorpes	22F2
Cleeve	9D3
Cleghorn	30D4
Clenchwarton	17E4
Cleobury Mortimer	9A2
Cleobury North Crossing	15G2
Cleobury Town Halt & Siding	9A2
Clevedon	3A1/8D3
Clevdon (All Saints)	3A1/8C3
Clevedon East	3A1/8D3
Cliburn	27E1
Cliff Common	21D5
Cliffe	6B5
Clifford	14E2
Clifton	15C5
Clifton & Lowther	27E1
Clifton Bridge Halt	3A2
Clifton Down	3A2/8C2

Clifton Junction	20B1/24F1/45B2
Clifton Mill	10A4
Clifton Moor	27E1
Clifton-on-Trent	16B2
Climpy Colliery	30C4
Clipston & Oxendon	10A3/16G3
Clipstone	16B3/41C5
Clipstone Colliery	41D5
Clitheroe	24D1
Clock Face	20C3/24G3/45D4
Clock House	40F4
Clocksbriggs	34D4
Closeburn	26A4
Clough Fold	20A1/24E1
Cloughton	28G1
Clovenfords	30E1
Clowne & Barlborough	16A4/41B4
Clowne South	16A4/41B4
Cloy Halt	20F4
Note: Reopened 6 May 1946	
Clunes	35D5
Clutton	3B3/8D1
Clydach	8A4/43B1
Clydach Court Halt	43E3
Clydach-on-Tawe	7B4/43F2
Clydebank	29C4/44F4
Clydebank Central	44F4
Clydebank East	44F4
Clydebank Riverside	44F4
Clynderwen	13G2
Clyne Halt	43E2
Clyst St Mary & Digby Halt	2B3
Coal Pit Heath	8C1/9G2
Coalbrookdale	15F2
Coalburn	30E5
Coaley	8B1/9F2
Coalport	15F2
Coalville	16E4
Coalville East	16E4
Coanwood	27C2
Coatbridge	30C5/44B4
Coatbridge Central	44B4
Coatdyke	44B4
Coates (Glos)	9F4
Cobbinshaw	30C4
Cobham	5C2
Coborn Road	40C3
Cobridge	15C3/20E1
Cockburnspath	31B2
Cockermouth	26E3
Cockett	7B3/43G3
Cockfield	12C5
Cockfield Fell	27E4
Cockfosters	11G2/46D1
Cocking	4D1
Codford	3C5
Codnor Park	16C4/41E3
Codnor Park & Ironville	16C4/41E3
Codsall	15F3
Coed Poeth	20E5
Coed Talon	20E5
Cogan	8C4/43B5
Colbren Junction	7A5/43E1
Colby	23C2
Colchester	12E4
Colchester St Botolph's	12E4
Cold Meece (workmen)	15E3/20F1
Cold Norton	12G5
Coldham	17F3
Coldharbour Lane	2A2
Coldstream	31D3
Cole Green	11F2
Cole	3C3/8F1

Coleburn	36D1
Coleford	8A2/9E1
Colehouse Lane	3A1/8D3
Coleshill	15G5
Colfin	25C2
Colindale	46E2
Colinton	30C2
College	44D3
Collessie	34F5
Colliers Wood	46D4
Collingham	16B2
Collingham Bridge	21C4
Collingbourne	4B5
Collingbourne Kingston Halt	4B5
Collington Halt	6F5
Collins Green	20C3/24G3/45D3
Colliston	34D3
Colnbrook	5B1/10G1
Colne	21B1
Coltishall	18E3
Colwall	9C2
Colwich	15E4
Colwyn Bay	19D4
Colyford	2B1
Colyton	2B1
Colzium	30B5
Combpyne	2B1
Commercial Road	40C4
Commondale	28F3
Commondyke	29F5
Commonhead	44B4
Compton	10G4
Comrie	33F3
Comrie Colliery	30A4
Condover	15F1
Congleton	15B3/20E1
Congleton Brunswick	
Street Wharf	15B3/20D1
Congresbury	3A1/8D3
Coningsby	17C2
Conisborough	21F4
Coniston	26G1
Connah's Quay	20D4
Connah's Quay & Shotton	20D4
Connaught Road	40C2
Connel Ferry	32E4
Conon	35D5
Cononley	21C1
Consall	15C4
Consett	27C4
Constable Burton	21A2/27G5
Conway	19D3
Conwil	13G4
Cooden Beach	6F5
Cookham	5A1/10G2
Cooksbridge	5F4
Coombe	1D4
Coombe Lane	5C3
Cooper Bridge	42C4
Cop Lane Halt	20A3/24E3
Note: Renamed Penwortham Cop Lane	
30 March 1940	
Copgrove	21B3
Copley Hill	21C2/42A3
Copmanthorpe	21C5
Copper Pit Halt	43G2
Copplestone	2A4
Coppull	20A3/24E3/45D1
Corbridge	27C4
Corby & Weldon	16F1
Corby (Lincs)	16D1/17E1
Corfe Castle	3G5
Corkickle	26E4

Cornhill	37C2
Cornwood	2D5
Corpach	32C3
Corpusty & Saxthorpe	18D4
Corringham (Workmen)	6A5
Corris	14B5
Corrour	32C1
Corsham	3A4
Corstorphine	30B3
Corton	12A1/18F1
Corwen	19F5
Coryates Halt	3F3
Coryton Halt Glamorgan	8C4/43B4
Coryton	1C5
Coryton (Workmen)	6A5
Cosford Aerodrome Halt	15F3
Note: renamed Cosford 28 October 1940	
Cosham	4E2
Cossington	3C1/8E3
Cotehill	27C1
Cotham	16C2
Cotherstone	27E4
Cottam	16A2
Cottesmore	16E1
Cottingham	22D3
Cottingwith	21D5
Coughton	9B4
Coulsdon & Cane Hill	5C3
Coulsdon	5C3
Coulter	30E4
Cound Halt	15F1
Coundon	27E5
Coundon Road	10A5
Counter Drain	17E2
Countesthorpe	16F3
County School	18E4
Coupar Angus	34D5
Cove Bay	34A1/37B2
Cove Halt	7G5
Covent Garden	46F5
Coventry	10A5
Cowbit	17E2
Cowbridge	8C5/43D4
Cowden	5D4
Cowdenbeath New	30A3
Cowdenbeath Old	30A3
Cowes	4F3
Cowlairs Port	44E4
Cowley	5A2/10G1
Cowton	28F5
Cox Green	28C5
Coxbench	16C5/41F2
Coxhoe	28D5
Coxhoe Bridge	28D5
Coxlodge	27B5
Coxwold	21A4
Craddock Lane	45B2
Cradley Heath	15G4
Cradoc	14F3
Craigellachie	36D1
Craigendoran	29B2
Craighall	44E4
Craigleith	30F3
Craiglockhart	30G2
Craiglon Bridge Halt	7A2
Craigmerthyr Colliery (Miners)	43G2
Craigo	34C3
Craig-y-Nos (Penwyllt)	7A5/43E1
Crail	34F3
Crakehall	21A3/27G5
Cramlington	27B5
Cranbrook	6D5
Crane Street	8B4/43A2

Cranford	10A1
Crank	20B3/24F3/45E3
Note: Became Crank Halt 1940	
Cranleigh	5D2
Cranley Gardens	39A5
Cranmer Pond (Military)	4D1
Cranmore	3C3/8E1
Cransley	10A2
Cranwell (RAF)	16C1/17C1
Crathes	34A2
Craven Arms & Stokesay	14C1
Crawford	30F4
Crawley	5D3
Cray	14G4
Crayford	5B4
Creagan	32E3
Credenhill	9C1/14F1
Crediton	2B4
Creech St Michael Halt	8F4
Creekmoor Halt	3F5
Creetown	25C4
Creigiau	8C5/43C4
Cressage	15F1
Cressing	11F5
Cressington & Grassendale	20C4/45E4
Cresswell	15D4
Creswell & Welbeck	16A4/41B4
Crew Green	14A1
Crewe	15C2/20E2
Crewe Cumberland Wharf	15B2/20E2
Crewkerne	3E1
Crews Hill	11G2
Criagendoran	29B3
Crianlarich	32F1
Criccieth	19F2
Cricklade	9F5
Cricklewood	5A3/39B4
Crieff	33F3
Criggion	14A2
Crigglestone	42D3
Crigglestone East	21E3/42C3
Crouch Hill	40A5
Croesor	19F3
Croft	16F4
Croft Depot	28F5
Croft Spa	28F5
Crofton	21E3/42C1
Crofton Park	40E3
Crofton (Private)	26C2
Cromdale	36E2
Cromer	18D3
Cromer Beach	18D3
Cromer Links Halt	18D3
Cromford	16B5/41D1
Cronberry	29F5
Crook	27D5
Crook of Devon	30A4/33G5
Crookston	29C4/44F3
Cropredy	10C4
Crosby Garrett	27F2
Crosby	23B2
Cross Hands	7A3
Cross House	29E4
Cross Inn	8C5/43C4
Cross Keys	8B4/43B3
Cross Lane	45B3
Crossens	20A4/24E4/45F1
Crossfield	26F3
Crossford	26A4
Crossgates	21D3/42A2
Crosshill	44E3
Crosshouse	29E4
Crossmichael	26B5

Crossmyloof	29C5/44E3
Crossways Halt	13E4
Croston	20A3/24E3/45E1
Crouch End	40A5
Crouch Hill	40A5
Crow Park	16B2
Crow Road	44E4
Crowborough & Jarvis Brook	5E4
Crowcombe	8F4
Crowden	21F2/42F5
Crowhurst	6F5
Crowle	22E5
Crowle Central	22F5
Crowthorne	4B1
Croxall	15E5
Croxdale	27D5
Croxley	11G1/46G1
Croxley Green	5A2/11G1
Croy	30B5
Cruckton	14A1
Cruden Bay	37E5
Crudgington	15E2
Crumlin High Level	8B4/43B2
Crumlin Low Level	8B4/43B2
Crumpsall	20B1/24F1/45A2
Crymmych Arms	13F2
Crynant	7A5/43E2
Crystal Palace (High Level) &	
Upper Norwood	40F4
Note: Station reopened 4 March 1946	
Crystal Palace (Low Level)	5B3/40F4
Cuddington	15B1/20D2/45D5
Cudworth	21F4/42D2
Cudworth	42E1
Cuffley & Goff's Oak	11G2
Culcheth	20C2/24G2/45C3
Culgaith	27E1
Culham	10F4
Culkerton	9F3
Cullen	37C1
Cullercoats	28B5
Cullingworth	21D2/42A5
Culloden Moor	36D4
Cullompton	2A2
Culmstock	2A2/8G5
Culrain	35A5
Culross	30A4
Culter	34A2/37G3
Cults	37G4
Culworth	10C4
Cumbernauld	30B5/44B5
Cummersdale	26C1
Cummertrees	26B3
Cumnock	29F5
Cumwhinton	26C1
Cunninghamhead	29D3
Cupar	34F4
Currie Hill	30C3
Currie	30C3
Curthwaite	26C1
Custom House	40C2
Cuthlie	34D3
Cutler's Green	11E4
Cutnall Green	9A3
Cuxton	6B5
Cwm	8A4/43B2
Cwm Aman	8B5/43D2
Cwm Avon	7B4/43F3
Cwm Blawd (Miners)	7A3
Cwm Mawr	7A3
Cwm Prysor	19F4
Cwm-y-Glo	19E2
Cwmavon (Mon)	8A4/43A2

Cwmbran	8B3/43A3
Cwmdu	7B5/43E3
Cwmffrrwd Halt	43A2
Cwmffrwdoer Halt	43A2
Cwmllynfell	7A4/43F1
Cwmmer Afan	43E3
Cwmmer General	7B5/43E3
Cwmntddu	43B2
Cwmsyfiog	43B2
Cymtillery Colliery	43B2
Cyfronydd	14B3
Cynghordy	14F5
Cynheidre (Miners)	7A3
Cynonville Halt	43E2
Cynwyd	19F5
Dacre	21B2
Dagenham	5A4/46A3
Dagenham Dock	5A4
Daggons Road	3E5
Dailly	29G3
Daimler Halt (Workmen)	10A5
Dairsie	34F4
Dairycoats	22A2
Daisy Bank & Bradley	13A1/15F4
Daisy Hill	45C2
Daisyfield	24D2
Dalbeattie	26D4
Dalchonzie Platform	33F3
Dalcross	36D4
Dalderse Depot	30B5
Dalebank	41D2
Dalguise	33D4
Dalhousie	30C2
Dalkeith	30C2
Dallow Lane Wharf	15D5
Dalmally	32F2
Dalmarnock	44D3
Dalmellington	29G4
Dalmeny	30B3
Dalmuir	29C4/44G5
Dalnaspidal	33C2
Dalreoch	29B3
Dalry	29D3
Dalry Road	30G2
Dalrymple	29F3
Dalrymple Junction	29F3
Dalserf	30D5/44A1
Dalston	26C1
Dalston Junction	40B4
Dalton	24B5
Dalwhinnie	33B2
Damems	21D1
Danby	28F3
Danby Wiske	28G5
Dandaleith	36D1
Dan-y-Graig	7B4
Danzey	9A5
Darby End Halt	13C1
Darcy Lever	45B2
Daresbury	15A1/20C3/45D4
Darfield	21F4/42E1
Darlaston	13A2/15F4
Darley	21C2
Darley Dale	16B5/41D1
Darlington Bank Top	28F5
Darlington North Road	28E5
Darnall	16A5/21G4/41A2/42G1
Darran & Deri	8B4/43C2
Darras Hall	27B5
Darsham	12B2
Dartford	5B5
Darton	21F3/42D3

Darvel	29E5
Darwen	20A2/24E2
Datchet	5B1/10G1
Dauntsey	9G4
Dava	36E3
Davenport	15A3/20C1/21G1/45A4
Daventry	10B3
Davidsons Mains	30B2
Daviot	36E5
Dawlish	2C3
Dawlish Warren	2C3
Dawsholm	44E4
Daybrook	16C3/41F5
Dduallt	19F3
Deadwater	27A1/31G1
Deal	6C1
Dean	4D5
Dean Hill (RNAD)	4D5
Dean Lane	
(Newton Heath)	20B1/24F1/45A2
Dearham Bridge	26D3
Deepcar	21F3/42F3
Deepdale Street	24D3
Deepdene	5C2
Deepfields	13A1/15F4
Deepings St James	17F2
Defford	9C3
Deganwy	19C3
Deighton	21E242C4
Delabole	1B3
Delamere	15B1/20D3
Delny	36C5
Delph	21F1
Denaby Halt	21F4
Denbigh	19D5
Denby	16C5/41F2
Denby Dale & Cumberworth	21F2/42E3
Denham	5A1/10G1
Denham Golf Club Platform	5A1/10G1
Denhead	34D3
Denholme	21D2/42A5
Denmark Hill	40E4
Denny	30B5
Dennyloanhead	30B5
Denstone	15C5
Dent	24A1
Denton	20C1/21G1/45A3
Denton Halt	5B5
Denton Siding	16D2
Denver	11A4/17F4
Deptford	40D3
Deptford Wharf	40D3
Derby	16D5/41G2
Derby Cattle Docks	41G1
Derby Chaddesden Sidings	41G1
Derby Friargate	16D5/41G1
Derby Road	12D3
Derby St Andrews	16D5/41G1
Derby St Mary's Bridge	41G1
Dereham	18E4
Derry Ormond	13E5
Dersingham	17D5
Derwen	19E5
Derwydd Road	7A3/13G5/43G1
Desborough & Rothwell	10A2/16G2
Desford	16F4
Dess	34A3/37G2
Detton Ford Siding	9A2
Devil's Bridge	14C5

Note: Summer only passenger service withdrawn 31 August 1939; station reopened 23 July 1945

Devizes	3B5
Devonport	1D5
Devons Road	40C3
Devynock & Sennybridge	14F4
Dewsbury	21E3/42C3
Dewsbury Central	42C3
Dewsbury Market Place	42C3
Dewsbury Savile Town	42C3
Dewsbury Wellington Road	42C3
Dicconson Lane &	
Aspull Halt	20B2/24F2/45C2
Didcot	10F4
Didsbury	20C1/24G1/45A3
Digby	17C1
Diggle	21F1
Dilton Marsh Halt	3B4
Dinas	19E2
Dinas (Rhondda)	8B5/43D3
Dinas Mawddy	14A4
Dinas Powis	8C4/43B5
Dingestow	8A2/9E1
Dingle Road Halt	43B5
Dingwall	35D5
Dinmore	9B1
Dinnet	34A4/37G1
Dinnington Colliery	41A4
Dinnington & Laughton	16A4/21G5/41A4
Dinsdale	28F5
Dinting	21G1
Dinton	3C5
Dinwoodie	26A3
Dipple Siding	29G3
Dirleton	31B1
Disley	15A4
Diss	12B4
Distington	26E3
Ditchford	10A1

Note: Used by railwaymen until 1952.

Ditchingham	12A2/18G2
Ditton Priors Halt	15G1
Ditton	15A1/20C3/24G3/45E4
Docking	17D5
Dockyard Halt	1A1
Doddington & Harby	16B2
Dodworth	21F3/42E3
Doe Hill	16B4/41D3
Dogdyke	17C2
Dolau	14D3
Doldowlod	14D4
Dolgelly	14A5
Dolgoch	13B5
Dollar	30A4/33G4
Dollis Hill	39B4/46E2
Dolphinton	30D3
Dolserau Halt	14A5/19G3
Dolwen	14C3
Dolwyddelen	19E3
Dolygaer	8A5/43C1
Dolyhir	14E2
Don Pedro Colliery	42C1
Doncaster	21F5
Doncaster Cherry Tree Lane	21G2
Doncaster Marsh Gate	21G2
Doncaster York Road	21G2
Donibristle Halt (Workmen)	30B2
Donington Road	17D2
Donington-on-Bain	17A2
Donisthorpe	16E5
Donlow Halt	15B5
Donnington	15E2
Dorchester	3F3
Dore & Totley	16A5/41A1
Dorking North	5C2
Dorking Town	5C2

Dormans	5D4
Dornoch	36B4
Dorrington	14B1/15F1
Dorstone	14F1
Dorton Halt	10E3
Doublebois	1D4
Douglas	23C3
Douglas West	30E5
Doune	29A5/33G3
Doura	29D3
Dousland	2C5
Dove Holes	15A4
Dovecliffe	42E2
Dover Priory	6D2
Dover Town	6D2
Dovercourt Bay	12E3
Dovey Junction	14B5
Dowlais	8A5/43C1
Dowlais Top	8A5/43C1
Dowlais Cae Harris	43C2
Dowlais Central	43C2
Dowlais High Street	43C2
Downfield Crossing Halt	9E3
Downham	17F4
Downholland	20B4/24F4/45F2
Downton	4D5
Drax Abbey	21E5
Drax Hales	21E5
Draycott	16D4/41G3

Note: Station renamed Draycott & Breaston 9 August 1939

Draycott	3B2/8E2
Drayton Green (Ealing) Halt	39C2
Drayton	18E3
Drayton	4E1/5F1
Drayton Park	46D2
Dreghorn	29E3
Drem	30B1
Driffield	22C4
Drigg	26G3
Drighlington & Adwalton	42B4
Drinnick Mill	1D2
Droitwich Road	9B3
Droitwich Spa	9B3
Dronfield	16A5/41B2
Drongan	29F4
Dronley	34E5
Droxford	4D3
Droylsden	21F1/45A3
Drum	34A2/37G3
Drumburgh	26C2
Drumchapel	44F4
Drumclog	29E5
Drumlithie	34B2
Drummuir	36D1
Drumshoreland	30B3
Drybridge	29E3
Drybrook Road	8A1/9E2
Drymen	29B4
Drypool	22A1
Dryslwyn	7A3/13G5
Drys-y-Nant	14A5/19G4
Dubton Junction	34C3
Dudbridge	9E3
Dudding Hill	39B4
Duddingston	30G1
Dudley	13B1/15G4
Dudley Castle	13B1
Dudley Hill	21D2/42B4
Dudley Port (High Level)	13B2/15F4
Dudley Port (Low Level)	13B2/15F4
Duffield	16C5/41F2
Duffryn Rhondda Halt	43E3

Dufftown	36E1
Duirinish	35F1
Duke Street	44D4
Dukeries Junction	16B2
Dukinfield & Ashton	21A2
Dukinfield	21A2
Dullatur	30B5
Dullingham	11C4
Dulverton	7F5
Dulwich	40E4
Dumbarton East	29B4
Dumbarton	29B3
Dumbuck Siding	29B4
Dumfries	26B3
Dumfries House	29F4
Dumfries St Mary's	26B3
Dumgoyne	29B4
Dumpton Park	6B1
Dunball	3C1/8E3
Dunbar	31B1
Dunblane	30A5/33G3
Dunbridge	4D4
Dunchurch	10A4
Dundas	44E4
Dundee	34E4
Dundee East	34E2
Dundee Esplanade	34E4
Note: requisitioned by the War Department 1939	
Dundee Tay Bridge	34E2
Dundee West	34E2
Dunduff Quarry	30£5
Dunfermline Lower	30A3
Dunfermline Netherton	30A3
Dunfermline Upper	30A3
Dunford Bridge	21F2/42E4
Dungeness	6E3
Dunham	18E5
Dunham Hill	15A1/20D3
Dunham Massey	15A2/20C2/24G2/45B4
Dunkeld & Birnam	33D4
Dunlop	29D4
Dunmere Halt	1C3
Dunmow	11E4
Dunning	33F4
Dunnington	21C5
Dunphail	36C3
Dunragit	25C2
Dunrobin (Private)	36A4/38G5
Duns	31C2
Dunsbear Halt	1A5/7G3
Dunscore	26A4
Dunsford Halt	2B4
Dunsland Cross	1A5
Dunstable	10D1/11E1
Dunstable London Road	10D1/11E1
Dunstable Town	10D1/11E1
Dunstall Park	15F3
Dunster	8E5
Dunston Staithes	28A2
Dunston-on-Tyne	28B2
Dunsyre	30D3
Dunton Green	5C4
Dunure	29F3
Dunvant	7B3
Durham	27D5
Durham Elvet	28D5
Durham Gilesgate	28D5
Duror	32D3
Dursley	8B1/9F2
Durston	3D1/8F3
Dyce	37F4
Dyffryn-on-Sea	13A5/19G2

Dykehead	30B5/44A5
Dymchurch	6E3
Dynea Halt	43C3
Dymock	9D2
Dysart	30A2
Dyserth	19D5
Eaglehurst Camp	4E3
Eaglescliffe	28F5
Ealing Broadway	5B2/39C2/46F3
Ealing Common	39C3/46E3
Earby	21B1/21C1
Eardington	15G2
Eardisley	14E2
Earith Bridge	11B3
Earlestown	20C3/24G2/45D3
Earley	4A2
Earls Colne	12E5
Earl's Court	39D5/46G5
Earlsfield	5B3/39E5
Earlsheaton	42C3
Earlston	31D1
Earlswood Lakes	9A5
Earlswood	5D3
Earsham	12A2/18G2
Earswick	21C5
Easington	28D5
Easingwold	21B4
Eassie	34D5
East Acton	39C4/46E3
East Anstey	7F5
East Barkwith	17A2
East Boldon	28C5
East Brixton	40E5
East Budleigh	2B2
East Calder	30C3
East Croydon	5C3
East Dulwich	40E4
East Farleigh	6C5
East Finchley	5A3/39A5/46D2
Note: Transferred to the Northern Line 3 July 1939	
East Fortune	31B1
East Garston	4A4/10G5
East Grange	30A4
East Grinstead High Level	5D4
East Grinstead Low Level	5D4
East Halton	22E3
East Ham	40B2/46B3
East Haven	34E3
East Horndon	5A5
East India Docks	40D1
East Kilbride	29D5/44D1
East Langton	16G3
East Leake	16D4
East Linton	31B1
East Minster-on-Sea	6B4
East Newport	34E4
East Norton	16F2
East Pilton	30F2
East Putney	39E4/46E4
Note: SR platforms closed 5 May 1941	
East Rudham	18D5
East Smithfield	40C4
East Southsea	4E2
East Tilbury Halt	5B5
East Ville	17C3
East Winch	17E5
Eastbourne	5G5
Eastbury Halt	4A4/10G5
Eastchurch	6B4
Eastcote	39B1/46F2
Easter Road	30F2

Easterhouse	44C4
Eastgate	27D3
Easthope Halt	15F1
Eastleigh	4D3
Eastoft	22E5
Easton	3G3
Easton Court	9A1
Easton Lodge	11E4
Eastriggs	26B2
Eastry	6C2
Eastry South	6C2
Eastwood	21E1
Eastwood & Langley Mill	16C4/41F3
Ebberston	22A4
Ebbw Vale	8B4/43B1
Ebchester	27C4
Ebdon Lane	3A1/8D3
Ebley Crossing Halt	9E3
Ecclefechan	26B2
Eccles	45B3
Eccles Road	12A4/18G4
Ecclesfield	21G3/42F2
Eccleshill	21D2/42A4
Eccleston Park	20C3/24G3/45E3
Eckington	9C3
Eckington & Renishaw	16A4/41B3
Edale	15A5
Edderton	36B5
Eddleston	30D2
Eden Park	5B4/40G3
Edenbridge	5D4
Edenbridge Town	5D4
Edge Hill	45F4
Edge Lane	45F4
Edgebold	14A1/15E1
Edgware	5A2/46E1
Edgware Road	39C5/46D3/46G4
Edinburgh Haymarket	30F2
Edinburgh Lothian Road	30F2
Edinburgh Princes Street	30B2/30G2
Edinburgh St Leonard's	30F2
Edinburgh Waverley	30B2/30G2
Edington Junction	3C1/8E3
Edington & Bratton	3B4
Edlingham	31F4
Edington	21G2
Edmondthorpe & Wymondham	16E2
Edrom	31C2
Edwalton	16D3/41G5
Edwinstowe	16B3/41C5
Edzell	34C3
Efail Isaf	8C5/43C4
Effingham Junction	5C2
Eggesford	2A5/7G4
Eggington	16D5
Note: Platforms on line to Derby Friargate closed 4 December 1939	
Egham	5B1
Eglinton Street	44E3
Egloskerry	1B4
Egremont	26F3
Note: Used by workmen's trains after 11 March 1940	
Egton	28F2
Elburton Cross	2E5
Note: Used by workmen's trains from 21 July 1941 to 3 November 1941 when passenger services restored.	
Elderslie	29C4/44G3
Elephant & Castle	40E5
Elephant & Castle (LU)	46E5
Elford	15E5
Elgin	36C2

Elham	6D2	Eskmeals	26G3	Farnham	4C1
Elie	30A1/34G4	Essendine	16E1/17E1	Farnley & Wortley	21C1/42A3
Elland	21E2/42C5	Esslemont	37E4	Farnsfield	16B3/41D5
Ellenbrook	45B2	Eston	28E4	Farnworth	45D4
Ellerby	22D3	Etchingham	6E5	Farnworth & Bold	15A1/20C3/24G3/45D4
Ellerdine Halt	15E2	Etherley	27E5	Farnworth &	
Ellesmere Port	20D4/45E5	Etruria	15C3/20F1	Halshaw Moor	20B2/24F1/45B2
Ellesmere	20F4	Ettington	10C5	Farringdon	40C5/46F4
Ellingham	12A2/18G2	Ettingshall Road & Bilston	15F4	Farrington Gurney Halt	3B3/8D1
Ellington (miners)	28A5	Etwall	16D5	Farrington Halt	4C2
Elliot	34D3	Euston (LU)	46F4	Farthinghoe	10C4
Elliot Junction	34D3	Euston Square	39C5/46F4	Faslane Platform (Military)	29A3
Ellon	37E4	Euxton Coal Siding	45D1	Faslane Port (Military)	29A3
Elm Bridge	17F4	Evanton	36C5	Fauldhouse & Crofthead	30C4
Elm Park	46A3	Evenwood	27E5	Fauldhouse	30C4
Elms Bridge Halt	8A2	Evercreech (New)	3C3/8E1	Faversham	6C3
Elmers End	5B4/40G4	Evercreech Junction	3C3/8F1	Faversham Docks	6C3
Elmesthorpe	16F4	Everingham	22D5	Fawkham	5B5
Elmstead Woods	40F2	Evershot	3E2	Fawley	9D1
Elmswell	42F2	Evesham	9C4	Fawley	4E3
Elmton & Creswell	16A4/41B4	Ewell	5C3	Faygate	5D3
Elrington	27C3	Ewesley	27A4/31G4	Fazackerley	20B4/24F4/45F3
Elsecar	42F2	Ewood Bridge & Edenfield	20A1/24E1	Fearn	36B4
Elsecar & Hoyland	21F342F2	Exeter Central	2B3	Featherstone	21E4/42C1
Elsenham	11E4	Exeter St David's	2B3	Featherstone Main Colliery	42C1
Elsham	22F4	Exeter St Thomas's	2B3	Featherstone Park	27C2
Elslack	21A1/21C1	Exminster	2B3	Feering Halt	12F5
Elson Halt	20F4	Exmouth	2B3	Felin Fach	13E5
Note: Reopened 6 May 1946		Exning Road Halt	11C4	Felin Foel	7B3
Elsted	4D1	Extension (Military)	1A1	Felin Fran Halt	7B4/43F2
Elston & Orston	16C2	Eyarth	19E5/20E5	Felin Hen Halt	19D2
Elstree	5A2/11G2	Eydon Road Halt	10C4	Felixstowe Beach	12E3
Elswick	28A2	Eye	12B3	Felixstowe Pier	12E3
Eltham (Well Hall)	5B4/40E2	Eye Green	17F2	Felixstowe Town	12E2
Eltham Park	40E1	Eyemouth	31C3	Felling	28A1
Elton	11A1/17G1	Eynsford	5C5	Felmingham	18D3
Elvanfoot	30F4	Eynsham	10E4	Felstead	11E5
Elvington	21C5	Eythorne	6C2	Feltham	5B2
Elvington	6C2			Fen Ditton Halt	11C3
Ely	11B4	Facit	20A1/24E1/45A1	Fenay Bridge & Lepton	21E2/42D4
Ely (Main Line)	8C4/43B4	Failsworth	20B1/45A2	Fencehouses	28C5
Embleton	26E2	Fairbourne	13A5	Fencote	9B1
Embo	36B4	Fairfield Siding	29A5	Feniscowles	20A2/24E2
Embsay	21C1	Fairfield	45A3	Fenn's Bank	15D1/20F3
Emerson Park Halt	5A5	Fairford	9F5	Fenny Bentley	15C5
Emneth	17F4	Fairlie	29D2	Fenny Compton	10B4
Emswell	12C4	Fairlie	29D4	Fenny Compton West	10B4
Emsworth	4E2	Fairlie Pier	29D2	Fenny Stratford	10D2
Enderby	16F4	Fairlop	5A4/40A1	Fenton	15C3/20F1
Endon	15C4	Fakenham	18D5	Fenton Manor	15C3/20F1
Enfield Chase	11G2	Falcon Lane	39E5	Ferguslie	44G3
Enfield Lock	11G3	Falconwood	40E1	Ferndale	8B5/43D2
Enfield Town	11G2	Falkirk Camelon	30B5	Fernhill	43C2
Enfield West	11G2	Falkirk Grahamstown	30B4	Fernhill Colliery	43D2
Enfield West (Oakwood)	46D1	Falkirk High	30B4	Fernhill Heath	9B3
Enthorpe	22C4	Falkland Road	34G5	Ferniegair	30D5/44B2
Entwistle	20A2/24E2/44B1	Fallgate	41D2	Ferriby	22E4
Epping	11G3	Fallowfield	20C1/24G1/45A3	Ferry Hill	28D5
Epsom	5C2	Fallside	44B3	Ferry	17E3
Epsom Downs	5C3	Falmer	5F3	Ferrybridge	21E4/42C1
Epworth	22F5	Falmouth	1F1	Ferryside	7A2
Erdington	15F5	Falstone	27A2	Festiniog	19F3
Eridge	5D5	Fambridge	6A4/12G5	Ffairfach	13G5
Erith	5B4	Fangfoss	22C5	Ffridd Gate	14B5
Errol	34E5	Fareham	4E3	Ffrith	20E4
Erwood	14F3	Faringdon	10F5	Fidlers Ferry &	
Eryholme	28F5	Faringham Road & Sutton-at-Home	5B5	Penketh	15A1/20C3/24G3/45D4
Escrick	21D5	Farington	20A3/24E3	Fighting Cocks	28F5
Esgairgeiliog	14B5	Farleigh Down	3A4	Filey	22A3
Esher	5B2/39G1	Farlington Siding	4E2	Filleigh	7F4
Esholt	21D2	Farnborough	4B1	Filton Junction	3A2/8C1/9G1
Eskbank	30C2	Farnborough North	4B1	Finchley	5A3
Eskdale Green	26F2	Farnell Road	34C3	Finchley (Church End)	39A5/46D2

Geldeston	12A2/18G2	Glenfield	44G3	Gosberton	17D2
Gelli Halt	43D3	Glenfinnan	32B4	Gosford Green	10A5
Georgemas Junction	38C3	Glengarnock	29D3	Gospel Oak	39B5
Georgetown	29C4/44G4	Glengarnock High	29D3	Gosport	4E2
Gerrards Cross	5A1/10F1	Gleniffer	44G3	Gosport Pier	4E3
Gidea Park	5A4	Glenluce	25C3	Goswick	31D4
Giffen	29D3	Glenside	29F3	Gotham	16D4
Giffnock	29C5/44E2	Glenwhilly	25B3	Gotherington	9D4
Gifford	31C1	Glodwick Road	21F1	*Note: Renamed Gotherington Halt 1 January*
Giggleswick	24B1	Glogue	13F3	*1941*
Gildersome	21D3	Glossop Central	21G1	Goudhurst	6D5
Gildersome East	42B3	Gloucester	9E3	Gourdon	34B2
Gildersome West	42B3	Gloucester Docks	9E3	Gourock	29B3
Gileston	8D5/43D5	Gloucester Road	39D5/46G5	Govan	29C4/44E4
Gilfach Fargoed Halt	43B2	Glyn Abbey	7A2	Govilon	8A4/43A1
Gilfach Goch	8B5/43D3	*Note: Renamed Glyn Abbey Halt 3 May 1943*		Gowerton	7B3
Gillett's Crossing Halt	24D4	Glyn Neath	7A5/43E2	Goxhill	22E3
Gilling	21A5	Glyncorrwg	43E2	Grafham	11B1
Gillingham (Dorset)	3D4	Glynde	5F4	Grafton & Burbage	4B5
Gillingham	6B5	Glyndyfrdwy	20F5	Graig Colliery	43F2
Gilmerton	30C2	Glynhebog Colliery Siding (Miners)	7A3	Grain Crossing Halt	6B4
Gilnockie	26B1	Glyntaff	43C3	Grainsby Halt	22F2
Gilsland	27B1	Gnosall	15E3/20G1	Grampound Road	1E2
Gilwern Halt	8A4/43B1	Goathland	28F2	Grandtully	33D4
Gipsy Hill	40F4	Gobowen	20F4	Grane Road	20A1/24E1
Girtford Halt & Siding	11D1	Godalming	5D1	Grange	37D1
Girvan	29G3	Godalming Old	5D1	Grange Court	8A1/9E2
Girvan Old	29G3	Godley	21G1	Grange Lane	42F2
Gisburn	24C1	Godmanchester	11B2	Grange Park	11G2
Glais	7B4/43F2	Godshill Halt	4G3	Grange Road	5D3
Glaisdale	28F2	Godstone	5D3	Grangemouth	30B4
Glamis	34D4	Godwin's Halt	10E1/11F1	Grange-over-Sands	24A3
Glan Conway	19D4	Gogar	30B3	Grangetown	8C4/43B4
Glanammam	7A4/43F1	Gogarth Halt	13B5	Grangetown	28E4
Glandyfi	14B5	Golant Halt	1D3	Grantham	16D1
Glanrafon	13C5	*Note: station closed 1 January 1940 to*		Granton	30B2
Note: Summer only passenger service		*9 February 1942, 24 August 1942 to 3 October*		Granton East	30F2
withdrawn 31 August 1939; station reopened		*1942 and 2 May 1944 to 2 October 1944.*		Granton Road	30F2
23 July 1945		Golborne	20B2/24F2/45D3	Grantown-on-Spey	36F4
Glanrhyd	14G5	Golcar	21E2/42D5	Grantshouse	31C2
Glanton	31F4	Golden Grove	13G5	Grassington & Threshfield	21B1
Glan-yr-Afon Halt	14C4	Golden Hill Platform	7D2	Grassmoor	16B5/41C2
Glanyrafon	14A2/20G5	Golders Green	46E2	Grateley	4C5
Glapwell Colliery	16B4/41C3	Goldhawk Road	39D4/46E3	Gravelly Hill	15G5
Glasbury-on-Wye	14F2	Goldsborough	21C4	Graveney Siding	6C3
Glasgow Buchanan Street	29C5/44E4	Goldthorpe & Thurnscoe	42E1	Gravesend	5B5
Glasgow Central	29C5/44E4	Golf Links	6E4	Grayrigg	27G1
Glasgow Cross	44E2	Gollanfield Junction	36D4	Grays	5B5
Glasgow General Terminus	44E3	Golspie	36A4	Great Alne	9B5
Glasgow Green	44E4	Gomer Halt	4E3	*Note: served by workmen's trains from*
Glasgow Queen Street	29C5/44E4	Gomersal	21D2/42B4	*Birmingham until 3 July 1944*
Glasgow St Enoch	29C5/44E4	Gomshall & Shere	5D2	Great Ayton	28F4
Glassaugh	37C2	Goodge Street	46F4	Great Barr	13B3/15F4
Glassel	34A3/37G2	Goodman's Yard	40C4	Great Bentley	12E4
Glassford	29D5	Goole	22E5	Great Bridge	13B2
Glasson Dock	24C3	Goole Docks	22E5	Great Bridgeford	15D3/20G1
Glasterlaw	34D3	Goonbell Halt	1E1	Great Chesterford	11D4
Glastonbury & Street	3C2/8E2	Goonhavern Halt	1D1	Great Coates	22F2
Glazebrook	20C2/24G2/45C3	Goostrey	15B3/20D1	Great Dalby	16E2
Glazebury & Bury Lane	20B2/24F2/45C3	Gorbals	44E1	Great Glen	16F3
Glemsford	12D5	Gordon Hill	11G2	Great Harwood	24D1
Glenbarry	37D2	Gordon	31D1	Great Haywood	15E4
Glenboig	30C5/44B4	Gorebridge	30C2	Great Horton	21D2/42A5
Glenbuck	30E5	Gorgie	30F3	Great Houghton Halt	42E1
Glencarron Platform	35D2	Gorgie West	30F3	Great Linford	10C2
Glencarse	33F5	Goring & Streatley	10G3	Great Longstone	15B5
Glencorse	30C2	Goring-by-Sea	5F2	Great Malvern	9C3
Glencraig Colliery	30A3	Gorleston Links Halt	18F1	Great Missenden	10F2
Glendon & Rushton	10A2/16G2	Gorleston North	18F1	Great Ormesby	18E1
Gleneagles	33F4	Gorleston-on-Sea	18F1	Great Ponton	16D1
Glenesk	30C2	Gorseinon	7B3	Great Portland Street	39C5/46F4
Glenfarg	33F5	Gorton	45A3	Great Shefford	4A4/10G5
Glenfield	16F4	Gorton (Private)	32D1	Greatham	28E4

Greatstone Halt	6E3
Greatstone-on-Sea	6E3
Gree Depot	29D4
Green Mount	20A1/24E1/45B1
Green Park	46F5
Green Road	24A5
Green's Siding	14F2
Green's Wharf	16F5
Greenfield	21F1
Greenford	5A2/39B1
Greengairs	30C5/44A5
Greenham Castle	29F3
Greenhead	27B2
Greenhill	30B5
Greenhithe	5B5
Greenlaw	31D2
Greenloaning	33G3
Greenock Central	29B2
Greenock Princes Pier	29B2
Greenock West	29B3
Greenodd	24A4

Note: passenger services reintroduced 3 June 1946

Greenway Halt	9D2
Greenwich	5B4/40D3
Greetland	21E2/42C5
Gresford	20E4
Gresley	16E5
Gregson Lane Halt	20A3/24E3
Gretna	26B1
Gretna Green	26B1
Gretton Halt	9D4
Gretton	16F2
Griffiths Siding	19D2
Grimes Hill & Wythall	9A5
Grimethorpe Halt	21F4/42D1
Grimoldby	17A3/22G1
Grimsargh (Hospital)	24D2
Grimsby Docks	22F2
Grimsby Pasture Street	22F2
Grimsby Pier	22F2
Grimsby Town	22F2
Grimston	16E3
Grimston Road	17E5
Grimstone & Frampton	3F3
Grindleford	16A5/41B1
Grindley	15D4
Grindley Brook Halt	15C1/20F3
Grinkle	28E3
Gristhorpe	22A3
Groeslen	19E2
Grogley Halt	1D2
Groombridge	5D4
Groeswen Halt	43C3
Grosefordd Halt	14G3
Grosmont	28F2
Grotton & Springhead	21F1
Grove Ferry	6C2
Grove Park	5B4/40E2
Guard Bridge	34F4
Guay	33D4
Guestwick	18D4
Guide Bridge	21F1/45A3
Guildford	5C1
Guisborough	28E3
Guiseley	21D2
Gullane	30B1
Gunheath	1D2
Gunhouse Wharf	22F5
Gunnersbury	39D3/46E3

Note: Also used by LMS passenger services.

Gunness & Burringham	22F5
Gunnislake	1C5

Gunton	18D3
Gurnos	7A4/43F1
Guthrie	34D3
Guyhirne	17F3
Gwaun-cae-Gurwen	43F2
Gwddelwern Halt	19F5
Gwernydomen Halt	43B3
Gwersyllt	20E4
Gwinear Road	1E4
Gwys	7A4/43F1
Habrough	22E3
Hacheston Halt	12C2
Hackbridge	39G5
Hackney	40B3

Note: Station closed 15 May 1944 but bus replacement service operated until 23 April 1945

Hackney Downs	5A4/40B4
Hackney Wick	40B3
Haddenham	10E3
Haddenham	11B3
Haddington	30B1
Haddiscoe (High Level)	12A1/18F1
Haddiscoe (Low Level)	12A1/18F1
Hadfield	21G1
Hadham	11F3
Hadleigh	12D4
Hadley	15E2
Hadley Wood	11G2
Hadlow Road	20D4/45F5
Hadnall	15E1/20G3
Haggerston	40B4
Hagley	9A3
Hagley Road	13C3
Haigh	21F3/42D3
Hailes Halt	30C2
Hailsham	5F5
Hainton Street Halt	22F2
Hairmyres	29D5/44D1
Halbeath	30A3
Halberton Halt	2A3/8G5
Hale	15A3/20C1/24G1/45B4
Halebank	15A1/20C3/45E4
Halesowen	9A4/15G4
Halesworth	12B2
Halewood	15A1/20C3/24G3/45E4
Halifax	21E2/42B5
Halifax North Bridge	21E2/42C5
Halkirk	38D3
Hall Green	9A5/15G5
Hall Hills	17C3
Hall Norton Junction	9B3
Hall Road	20B4/24F4/45F2
Hallaton	16F2
Hallatrow	3B3/8D1
Hallcraig	30D5
Halliford Halt	5B2

Note: Station opened 1 May 1944; renamed Upper Halliford Halt 22 May 1944

Halling	6C5
Hallington	17A2/22G2
Halliwell	45C2
Halmerend	15C3/20E1
Halsall	20B4/24F4/45F2
Halstead	11E5
Halton	15A1/20D3/24B3/45D5
Halton	24B3
Halton Holgate	17B3
Haltwhistle	27C2
Halwill	1A5
Ham Bridge Halt	5F2
Ham Lane	3A1/8D3

Ham Mill Crossing Halt	9F3
Ham Street & Orlestone	6D4
Hambleton	21D5
Hamilton	44B2
Hamilton Central	30D5/44B2
Hamilton West	44B2
Hammersmith	39D4/46E3
Hammersmith & Chiswick	39D3
Hammerton	21C4
Hammerwich	15E4
Hampden Park	5F5
Hampole	21F4
Hampstead	46D2
Hampstead Heath	39B5
Hampstead Norris	4A3/10G4

Note: Station closed 4 August 1942 to 8 March 1943

Hampsthwaite	21C3
Hampton	5B2/39F1
Hampton	9A5
Hampton Court	5B2/39G2
Hampton in Arden	9A5/15G5
Hampton Loade	15G2
Hampton Wick	39F2
Hampton-in-Arden	9A5
Hamworthy	3F5
Hamworthy Junction	3F5
Handborough	10E4
Handforth	15A3/20C1/45A4
Handsworth & Smethwick	13B3
Handsworth Wood	13B3
Hanington	9F5
Hanley	15C3/20E1
Hanwell & Elthorne	5B2/39C2
Hanwood	14A1
Happendon	30E5
Hapton	24D1
Harborne	9A4/13C3/15G4
Harbrough	22E3
Harburn	30C3
Harby & Stathern	16D2
Hardingham	18F4
Hardwick Road Siding	17E5
Hare Park & Crofton	21E3/42C2
Harecastle	15C3/20E1
Haresfield	9E3
Harker	26C1

Note: Also used by workmen from 1936 to 1941 and from 1 March 1943 to postwar.

Harlech	19F2
Harlesden	39B3/46E2
Harlesford	12C2
Harleston	12B3/18G3
Harling Road	12A4/18G4
Harlington	10D1/11E1
Harlington Halt	21F4
Harlow	11F3
Harmston	16B1
Harold Wood	5A5
Harpenden	11F1
Harperley	27D4
Harrietsham	6C4
Harringay	40A5
Harringay Park	40A5
Harrington	26E3
Harringworth	16F1
Harrogate	21C3
Harrow & Wealdstone	5A2/39A2/46F2
Harrow-on-the-Hill	5A2/39A2/46F2
Harston	11D3
Hart	28D4
Hartfield	5D4
Hartford	15B2/20D2/45C5

Hartford & Greenbank	15A2/20D2/45C5
Hartington	15B5
Hartlebury	9A3
Hartlepool	28D4
Hartley	28B5
Harton Road	14C1/15G1
Harts Hill	15G4
Hartshay Colliery	41E2
Hartwood	30C5
Hartwood Hill	30C5
Harty Road Halt	6B3
Harvington	9C4
Harwich Town	12E3
Hasland	16B5/41C2
Haslemere	4C1/5D1
Haslingden	20A1/24E1
Hassall Green	15B3/20E1
Hassendean	31F1
Hassockrigg Colliery	30C5
Hassocks	5F3
Hassop	15B5
Hastings	6F5
Haswell	28D5
Hatch	3D1/8G3
Hatch End for Pinner	5A2/46F1
Hatfield	11F2
Hatfield Moor Depot	22F5
Hatfield Peverel	11F5
Hatherleigh	2A5
Hathern	16E4
Hathersage	20D4
Hatton	9B5
Hatton	37E5
Haughley	12C4
Haughton Halt	20G4
Haughton	15E3/20G1
Havant	4E2
Haven Street	4F3
Havenhouse	17B4
Haverfordwest	7C2
Haverhill North	11D5
Haverhill South	11D5
Haverthwaite	24A4

Note: passenger services reintroduced 3 June 1946

Haverton Hill	28E4
Hawarden	20D4
Hawes	24A1/27G3
Hawick	31F1
Hawkesbury Lane	16G5
Hawkhead	44F3
Hawkhurst	6E5
Hawkmoor Halt	2C4
Hawkser	28F2
Haworth	21D1
Hawsham	22F3
Hawthorn Tower Halt (Workmen)	28D5
Haxby	21C5
Haxey & Epworth	22G5
Haxey Junction	22F5
Haxey Town	22F5
Hay	14F2
Hayburn Wyke	28G1
Haydock	20B3/24F3/45D3
Haydock Park	45D3
Haydon Bridge	27B3
Haydon Square	40C4
Haydons Road	39F5
Hayes	5C2
Hayes	5B2/40G2
Hayfield	15A4/21G1
Hayle	1E4
Hayle Wharf	1E4

Hayles Abbey Halt	9D4
Hayling Island	4E2
Haywards Heath	5E3
Haywood	30C4
Hazel Grove	15A3/20C1/21G1/45A4
Hazelhead Bridge	21F2/42E4
Hazelwell	9A4
Hazelwood	16C5/41F1
Heacham	17D5
Headcorn	6D5
Headingley	21D3/42A3
Heads Nook	27C1
Heads of Ayr	29F3
Headstone Lane	46F2

Note: Also used by LMS passenger services.

Heald Green	15A3/20C1/24G1/45A4
Healey House	21F2/42D5
Healing	22F2
Heanor	16C4/41F3
Heap Bridge	20B1/24F1/45A1
Heapey	20A2/24E2/45D1
Heath	16B4/41C3
Heath Halt	43B4
Heath Park Halt	10E1/11F1
Heather & Ibstock	16E5
Heathfield	2C4
Heathfield	5E5
Heathway	46A3
Heatley & Warburton	15A2/20C2/24G2/45B4
Heaton Chapel	45A3
Heaton Mersey	20C1/24G1/45A4
Heaton Norris	45A4
Heaton Park	20B1/24F1/45B2
Heaton	28A1
Hebburn	28B5
Hebden Bridge	21E1
Heck	21E5
Heckington	17C2
Heckmondwike Central	21E2/42C4
Heckmondwike Spen	21E2/42C4
Heddon-on-the-Wall	27B5
Hedgeley	31F4
Hednesford	15E4
Hednesford (Miners)	15E4
Hedon	22E3
Heeley	16A5/41A2
Heighington	27E5
Heighington ROF Demons Bridge (Workmen)	28E5
Heighington ROF Simpasture (Workmen)	27E5
Hele & Bradninch	2A3
Helensburgh	29B3
Helensburgh Upper	29B3
Hellaby	21G4
Hellesdon	18E3
Hellifield	24C1
Hellingly	5F5
Helmdon	10C4
Helmsdale	38F4
Helmshore	20A1/24E1
Helmsley	21A5
Helpringham	17D1
Helpston	17F1
Helsby	15A1/20D3/45E5
Helsby & Alvanley	15A1/20D3/45E5

Note: Used by workmen's trains from September 1939

Helston	1F5
Hemel Hempstead	10E1/11F1
Hemel Hempstead & Boxmoor	10E1/11F1
Hemingborough	21D5

Hemsby	18E1
Hemsworth	42D1
Hemsworth & South Kirkby	42D1
Hemsworth Colliery	42D1
Hemyock	2A2/8G4
Henbury	8C2/9G1
Hendford Halt	3D2/8G2
Hendon	5A3/39A4
Hendon Central	46E2
Henfield	5F2
Hengoed	8B4/43B3
Henham Halt	11E4
Heniarth	14B3
Henley-in-Arden	9B5
Henley-on-Thames	10G2
Henllan	13F4
Henlow Camp	11E1
Hensall	21E5
Henstridge	3D3/8G1
Henwick	9B3
Heolgerrig Halt	43C2
Hepscott	27A5
Hereford Barrs Court	9C1
Hereford Barton	9C1
Hereford Moorfields	9C1
Heriot	30C1
Hermitage	4A3

Note: Station closed 4 August 1942 to 8 March 1943

Herne Bay	6B2
Herne Hill	5B3/40E5
Hersham	5B2
Hertford East	11F2
Hertford North	11F2
Hertingfordbury	11F2
Hesketh Bank	20A3/24E3
Hesketh Park	20A4/24E4/45F1
Hesleden	28D5
Heslerton	22A4
Hessay	21C4
Hessle	22E4
Hest Bank	24B3
Heswall	20C5
Heswall Hills	20C4/45F4
Hethersett	18F3
Hetton	28D5
Hever	5D4
Heversham	24A3
Hexham	27B3
Hey's Crossing Halt	20B3/24F3/45E2
Heyford	10D4
Heysham Harbour	24C4
Heytesbury	3C4
Heywood	20B1/24F1/45A2
Hickleton & Thurnscoe	21F4/42E1
Hickleton Main Colliery	42E1
High Barnet	5A3/11G2/46E1

Note: Transferred to Northern Line and electrified on 14 April 1940.

High Blantyre	29C5/44C2
High Brooms	5D5
High Field	22D5
High Halden Road	6D4
High Halstow Halt	6B5
High Harrington	26E3
High Lane	15A4/21G1
High Rocks Halt	5D5
High Shields	28B5
High Street Kensington	39D5/46G5
High Street	44D4
High Town Halt	20E4

Note: Reopened 6 May 1946

High Westwood	27C5

High Wycombe 10F2
Higham 11C5
Higham 6B5
Higham Ferrers 10A1
Highams Park & Hale End 5A4
Highbridge 3B1/8E3
Highbury 46D2
Highbury & Islington 40B5
Highbury Vale 40B5
Highclere 4B3
Note: Station closed 4 August 1942 to 8 March 1943
Higher Buxton 15A4
Highgate 5A3/39A5/46D2
Note: Low Level (Northern Line platforms used as air raid shelters from September 1940 with services being operated from 19 January 1941.
Highlandman 33F3
Highley 9A2/15G2
Hightown 20B4/24F4/45F2
Highworth 9F5
Hildenborough 5D5
Hilgay 11A4/17F4
Hill End 11F2
Hillfoot 29B5/44E5
Hillhouse 21E2/42C4
Hillingdon (Swakeleys) 46G2
Hillington 17E5
Hillington East 44F3
Hillington West 44F3
Hillside 34C2
Hillside 45F1
Hilsea Halt (Workmen) 4E2
Note: Became public station on 2 November 1941
Hilton House 20B2/24F2/45C2
Himley 15G3
Hinckley 16F4
Hinderwell 28E2
Hindley 20B2/24F2/45C2
Hindley & Amberswood 45C2
Hindley & Platt Bridge 45C2
Hindley Green 45C2
Hindlow 15B4
Hindolvestone 18D4
Hinton Admiral 4F5
Hinton 9C4
Hipperholme 42C5
Hirwaun 8A5/43D2
Histon 11C3
Hitchin 11E2
Hither Green 40E3
Hixon 15D4
Hockerill Halt 11E4
Hockley 13C3/15G4
Hockley 6A5
Hodbarrow 24A5
Hoddlesden 20A2/24E2
Hodnet 15D2/20G2
Hoe Street Walthamstow 40A3
Hoghton 20A2/24E2
Holbeach 17E3
Holbeck High Level 21D2/42A3
Holbeck Low Level 21D2/42A3
Holborn (Kingsway) 46F4
Note: Platforms for Aldwych closed 22 September 1940; reopened 1 July 1946
Holbrook Colliery 41A3
Holcombe Brook 20A1/24E1/45B1
Hole 1A5
Holehouse 29F4
Holkham 18C5
Holland Arms 19D1
Holland Park 46E3
Holland Road Halt 5F3
Hollin Well & Annesley 41E4
Hollingbourne 6C5
Hollingswood 15E2
Hollins 20A2/24E2
Hollins (Workmen) 21F1
Hollinwood 45A2
Holloway Road 46D2
Holly Bush 8A4/43B2
Hollybush 29F4
Holme Hale 18F5
Holme Lacy 9C1
Holme Moor 22D5
Holme 11A2/17G2
Holmes Chapel 15B3/20D1
Holmfield 21D2/42C5
Holmfirth 21F2/42D5
Holmgate 3F4
Holmsley 4E5
Holmwood 5D2
Holsworthy 1A4
Holt 18D4
Holt Junction 3B4
Holtby 21C5
Holton le Clay 22F2
Holton Heath 3F4
Holton Village Halt 22F2
Holton-le-Moor 22F3
Holwell Junction 16E3
Holygate 30B3
Holyhead 19B2
Holymegate 22E2
Holytown 30C5/44A3
Holywell 28B5
Holywell Junction 20D5
Holywell Town 20D5
Holywood 26A4
Homersfield 12A3/18G3
Homerton 40B3
Note: Station closed 15 May 1944 but bus replacement service operated until 23 April 1945
Honeybourne 9C5
Honing 18D2
Honington 16C1
Honiton 2A2
Honley 21F2/42D5
Honor Oak Park 40E4
Honor Oak 40E4
Note: reopened 4 March 1946
Hook 4B2
Hook Colliery 7C2
Hook Norton 10D5
Hookagate & Red Hill 14B1/15E1
Hoole 20A3/24E3
Hooton 20D4/45F5
Hope 15A5
Hope & Penyffordd 20E4
Hope Villaage 21E4
Hopeman 36C2
Hopperton 21C4
Hopton Heath 14C1
Hopton-on-Sea 18F1
Horbury & Ossett 21E3/42C3
Horbury Junction 42C2
Horden 28D4
Horeb (Miners) 7A3
Horfield 3A3/8C1
Horham 12B3
Horley 5D3
Hornby 24B2
Horncastle 17B2
Hornchurch 5A4/46A2
Horninglow 15C5
Horninglow Wharf 15D5
Hornsea Bridge 22C2
Hornsea 22C2
Hornsey 40A5
Hornsey Road 40A5
Horrabridge 1C5
Horringford 4F3
Horrocksford 24D1
Horsebridge 4C4
Horsehay 15F2
Horsforth 21D3/42A3
Horsham 5E2
Horsley 5C2
Horsmonden 6D5
Horspath Halt 10E4
Horsted Keynes 5E3
Horton in Ribblesdale 24B1
Horton Park 21D2/42B5
Horwich 20B2/24F2/45C1
Hoscar 20B3/24F3/45E1
Hothfield Halt 6D4
Hough Green 15A1/20C3/24G3/45E4
Hougham 16C1
Hounslow 5B2/39E1
Hounslow Central 39D1/46F3
Hounslow East 5B2/39D1/46F3
Hounslow West 5B2/39D1/46F4
House O'Hill Halt 30B2
Houston 29C4
Hove 5F3
Hovingham Spa 21A5
How Mill 27C1
Howden Clough 42B3
Howdon-on-Tyne 28B5
Howe Bridge 20B2/24F2/45C2
Howsham 22F3
Howwood 29C4
Hoy 38C3
Hoylake 20C/24G5
Hubbert's Bridge 17C2
Hucknall 16C4/41E4
Hucknall Central 16C4/41E4
Hucknall Town 16C4/41E4
Note: Used by railwaymen
Huddersfield 21E2/42C5
Huddersfield Hillhouse 42C3
Huddersfield Newtown 21E2/42C5
Hugglescote 16E4
Hulands (Workmen) 27F4
Hull Burleigh Street 22A1
Hull Cannon Street 22A1
Hull Kingston Street 22A1
Hull Neptune Street 22A1
Hull Paragon 22A1/22E3
Hullavington 9G3
Humberstone 16F3
Humberstone Road 16F3
Humbie 30C1
Humshaugh 27B3
Huncoat 24D1
Hundred End 20A4/24E3
Hungerford 4A4
Hunmanby 22B3
Hunnington 9A4/15G4
Note: Used by workmen's services
Hunslet 21D3/42A2
Hunslet East 42A2
Hunslet Lane 21C2/42A2
Hunstanton 17D5
Huntingdon East 11B2

Huntingdon North	11B2
Huntly	37E1
Hunts Cross	20C4/45E4
Hunwick	27D5
Hurdlow	15B5
Hurlford	29E4
Hurst Green Halt	5C4
Hurst Lane	41D2
Hurstbourne	4B4
Hurworth Burn	28D5
Husbourne Crawley Halt	10C1
Husthwaite Gate	21B4
Hutton Cranswick	22C4
Hutton Gate	28E3
Huttons Ambo	22B5
Huyton	20C3/24G3/45E4
Huyton Quarry	20C3/24G3/45E4
Hyde	21G1
Hyde Junction	21G1
Hyde Park Corner	46F5
Hyde Road	45A3
Hykeham	16B1
Hylton Lane	28C5
Hylton	28C5
Hyndland	44E4
Hythe (Hants)	4E4
Hythe	12E4
Hythe	6D3
Ibrox	29C4/44E3
Ickenham Halt	46G2
Ide	2B3
Idle	21D2/42A4
Idmiston Halt	4C5
Idridgehay	16C5/41E1
Ifield Halt	5D3
Ilderton	31E4
Ilford	5A4/40B1
Ilfracombe	7E3
Ilkeston	16C4/41F3
Ilkeston Junction & Cossall	16C4/41F3
Ilkeston Town	41F3
Ilkley	21C2
Ilminster	3D1/8G3
Ilton Halt	3D1/8G3
Immingham Docks	22E2
Ince	45D2
Ince & Elton	15A1/20D3/45E5
Ingleby	28F4
Inch Green	29B3
Inchcoonans	34E5
Inches	30E5
Inchgreen	29B2
Inchture	34E5
Ingatestone	11G4
Ingersby	16F3
Note: Station renamed Ingarsby 25 September 1939	
Ingestre	15D4
Ingham	12B5
Ingleton	24B2
Ingliston	30B5
Ingrator Halt	2C5
Ingrow	21D1
Innerleithen	30E2
Innermessan (Military)	25C2
Innerpeffray	33F4
Innerwick	31B2
Insch	37E2
Instow	7F3
Inveramsay	37E3
Inverbervie	34B2
Inveresk	30B2

Invergarry	32A1
Invergloy	32B2
Invergordon	36C5
Invergordon Shore	36C5
Invergowrie	34E5
Inverkeilor	34D3
Inverkeithing	30B3
Inverkip	29C2
Inverness	36E5
Inverness Harbour	36E5
Invershin	35A5
Inverugie	37D5
Inverurie	37F3
Inworth	12F5
Ipstones	15C4
Ipswich	12D3
Irchester	10B1
Irlam	20C2/24G2/45C3
Irlams-o'-th'-Height	45B2˙
Iron Acton	8C1/9G2
Iron Bridge & Broseley	15F2
Irongray	26A4
Irthlingborough	10A1
Irton Road	26F3
Irvine	29E3
Irvine Harbour	29E3
Isfield	5F4
Isleham	11B4
Isleworth	39D2
Islip	10E4
Itchen Abbas	4C3
Ivybridge	2D5
Jackfield Halt	15F2
Jamestown	29B3
Jarrow	28B5
Jedburgh	31E1
Jedfoot	31E1
Jefferstone Lane	6E3
Jerry Halt (Military)	4G5
Jersey Marine	7B4/43F3
Jervaulx	21A2/27G5
Jesmond	27B5/28A1
John O'Gaunt	16E2
Johnshaven	34C2
Johnston (Pem.)	7C1
Johnstone	29C4
Johnstone North	29C4
Johnstown & Hafod	20F4
Jones' Drove	11A3/17G3
Joppa	30G1
Jordanhill	44E4
Jordanston Halt	13F1
Jordanstone	34D5
Junction Bridge	30F2
Junction Road	40B5
Junction Road Halt	6E5
Juniper Green	30C3
Justinhaugh	34C4
Keadby	22F5
Kearsley	20B2/24F1/45B2
Kearsney	6D2
Keekle Colliers' Platform (Workmen)	26E3
Keele	15C3/20F1
Kegworth	16D4
Keighley	21D1
Keinton Mandeville	3D2/8F2
Keith	37D1
Keith Town	37D1
Kelmarsh	10A2
Kelmscott & Langford Platform	9E5
Kelso	31E3

Kelston	3A3/8D1
Kelty	30A3
Kelvedon	12F5
Kelvedon Low Level	12F5
Kelvin Bridge	44E4
Kelvinhaugh	44E4
Kelvinside	44E4
Kemble Junction	9F4
Kempston & Elstow Halt	10C1/11D1
Kempston Hardwick Halt	10C1/11D1
Kempton Park (Restricted)	39F1
Kemsing	5C5
Kendal	24A3/27G1
Kenfig Hill	7C5/43E4
Kenilworth	10A5
Kenley	5C3
Kenmay	37F3
Kennett	11C5
Kennethmont	37E2
Kennington	46D3
Kennishead	44E3
Kennoway Siding	34G5
Kennyhill	44D4
Kensal Green	46E3
Kensal Rise	39B4
Kensington Lillie Bridge	39D4
Kent House	40F4
Kent's Bank	24B4
Kentallen	32D3
Kentish Town	5A3/40B5
Kentish Town West	40B5
Kentish Town (LU)	46D2
Kenton Bank	27B5
Kenton	12C3
Kenton	39A2/46F2
Note: Also used by LMS passenger services.	
Kenyon Junction	20C2/24G2/45C3
Kerne Bridge	8A2/9D1
Kerry	14C2
Kershopefoot	27A1
Keswick	26E2
Ketley	15E2
Kettering	10A2
Kettlesness	28E2
Ketton & Collyweston	16F1/17F1
Kew Bridge	39D3
Kew Gardens	20A4/24E4/45F1
Kew Gardens	39D3/46E3
Keyham	1D5
Keyingham	22E2
Keynsham & Somerdale	3A3/8D1
Kibworth	16F3
Kidbrooke	40E2
Kidderminster	9A3
Kidlington	10E4
Kidsgrove Halt	15C2/20E1
Kidsgrove Liverpool Road	15C2/20E1
Note: 'Liverpool Road added 2 October 1944	
Kidwelly	7A2
Kidwelly Flats Halt	7A2
Kielder	27A2/31G1
Kikintilloch	29B5/44C5
Kilbagie	30A4
Kilbarchan	29C4
Kilbirnie	29D3
Kilbowie	29C4/44F4
Kilburn	39B5
Kilburn Brondesbury	39B4
Kilburn Park	46E3
Kilburn & Brondesbury	46E3
Kilconquhar	30A1/34G4
Kildale	28F3
Kildary	36C4

Kildonan	38F5	
Kildwick & Crosshills	21C1	
Kilgerran	13F3	
Kilgetty	7D3	
Kilkerran	29G3	
Killamarsh	16A4/41A3	
Killay	7B3	
Killearn	29B4	
Killiecrankie	33C4	
Killin	33E2	
Killin Junction	33E1	
Killingholme Admiralty		
Platform (Military)	22E3	
Killingholme	22E3	
Killingworth	27B5	
Killochan	29G3	
Killywhan	26B4	
Kilmacolm	29C3	
Kilmany	34E4	
Kilmarnock	29E4	
Kilmaurs	29D4	
Kilnhurst	21F4/42F1	
Kilnsea Fort (Workmen)	22E1	
Kilnwick Gate	22C4	
Kilpatrick	29B4/44G5	
Kilsby & Crick	10A4	
Kilsyth	29B5	
Kilwinning	29D3	
Kimberley Park	18F4	
Kimberley	16C4/41F4	
Kimbolton	11B1	
Kinaldie	37F3	
Kinbrace	38E5	
Kinbuck	33G3	
Kincardine	30A4	
Kincraig	36G4	
Kineton	10B5	
Kinfauns	33F5	
King Edward	37C3	
King George Dock	22E3	
King Street Depot	44G3	
King Tor Halt	2C5	
King William	20A2/24E2/45B1	
King's Cross (LU)	40C5/46F4	
Kings Cross (LU – Met)	46F4	
Note station closed 16 October 1940 to		
14 March 1941 as a result of bomb damage.		
King's Cross Suburban	40C5	
King's Langley &		
Abbot's Langley	10F1/11G1	
King's Lynn	17E4	
King's Park	44D3	
Kingsbury	46E2	
Kingennie	34E4	
Kingham	9D5	
Kinghorn	30A2	
Kinglassie Colliery	30A2	
King's Cliffe	11A1/16F1/17F1	
Kings Heath	9A4/15G4	
Kings Inch	44F4	
Kings Norton	9A4	
King's Sutton	10C4	
Kingsbarns	34F3	
Kingsbridge	2E4	
Kingsbury	15F5	
Kingsbury	39A3/46E2	
Kingscote	5D3	
Kingshouse Platform	33F2	
Kingskerswell	2D3	
Kingskettle	34F5	
Kingsknowe	30B2	
Kingsland	14D1	
Kingsley & Froghall	15C4	
Kingsley Halt	4C1	
Kingsmuir	34D4	
Kingsnorth	6B5	
Kingston Crossing Halt	10F3	
Kingston Road	3A1/8D3	
Kingston	5B2/39F2	
Kingston-on-Sea	5F3	
Kingswear	2D3	
Kingswood & Burgh Heath	5C3	
Kingsworthy	4C3	
Note: Station closed 4 August 1942 to		
* 8 March 1943*		
Kingthorpe	17B1	
Kington	14E2	
Kingussie	33A2	
Kinloss	36C2	
Kinmel Bay Halt	19C5	
Kinnerley Halt (Military)	14A1	
Kinnerley Junction	14A1/20G4	
Kinnersley	14E1	
Kinnerton	20E4	
Kinning Park	44F2	
Kinross	30A3	
Kinross Junction	33G5	
Kintbury	4A4	
Kintore	37F3	
Kipling Cotes	22D4	
Kippax	21D4/42B1	
Kippen	29A5	
Kirby Cross	12E3	
Kirby Moorside	21A5	
Kirby Muxloe	16F4	
Kirby Park	20C5/24G5	
Kirby (Black Bull)	22A5	
Kirk Michael	23B2/25G4	
Kirk Smeaton	21E4	
Kirkandrews	26C1	
Kirkbank	31E2	
Kirkbride	26C2	
Kirkbuddo	34D4	
Kirkburton	21E2/42D4	
Kirkby	20B4/24F3/45E3	
Kirkby	24A5	
Kirkby Bentinck	41E4	
Kirkby Lonsdale	24A2	
Kirkby ROF Halt (Workmen)	45E3	
Kirkby Stephen	27F2	
Kirkby Thore	27E2	
Kirkby-in-Ashfield Central	41E4	
Kirkby-in-Ashfield	16C4/41E4	
Kirkcaldy	30A2	
Kirkcaldy Harbour	30A2	
Kirkconnel	30F5	
Kirkcowan	25C3	
Kirkcudbright	26C5	
Kirkdale	45F3	
Kirkgunzeon	26B4	
Kirkham & Wesham & Wyre	24D3	
Kirkham Abbey	22B5	
Kirkheaton	21E2/42C4	
Kirkhill	29C5/44D2	
Kirkinner	25C4	
Kirkintilloch	44D5	
Kirkintilloch Basin	44D5	
Kirkland	26A5	
Kirklee	44E4	
Kirkliston	30B3	
Kirknewton	31E4	
Kirkpatrick	26B2	
Kirkstall	21D3/42A3	
Kirkton Bridge Halt	37C4	
Kirlington & Edingley	16B3	
Kirriemuir	34C4	
Kirtlebridge	26B2	
Kirton Lindsey	22F4	
Kirton	17D3	
Kittybrewster	37F4	
Kiveton Bridge	41A4	
Kiveton Park	16A4/41A4	
Knapton	22B4	
Knaresborough	21C3	
Knebworth	11E2	
Knight's Hill	40E4	
Knighton	14D2	
Knightsbridge	46F5	
Knightwick	9B2	
Knitsley	27C5	
Knock	37D1	
Knockando	36E2	
Knockholt	5C4	
Knott End	24C4	
Knottingley	21E4	
Knotty Ash & Stanley	45E3	
Knowesgate	27A4	
Knoweside	29F3	
Knowle & Dorridge	9A5	
Knowlton	6C2	
Knucklas	14D2	
Knutsford	15A2/20D2/45B5	
Kuddington	22E5	
Kyle of Lochalsh	35F1	
Lacock Halt	3A4	
Ladbroke Grove	39C4/46E3	
Lade Halt	6E3	
Ladmanlow	15B4	
Lady Helen Colliery	30A2	
Ladybank	34F5	
Ladylands Siding	29A5	
Ladysbridge	37C2	
Ladywell	40E3	
Laindon	5A5	
Lairg	35A5	
Laisterdyke	21D2/42A4	
Lakenheath	11A5/17G5	
Lambeth North	46F5	
Lambley	27C2	
Lambourn	4A4/10G5	
Lamesley	27C5	
Lamington	30E4	
Lampeter	13E5	
Lamphey	7D2	
Lamplugh	26E3	
Lamport	10A2	
Lanark	30D4	
Lancaster Castle	24C3	
Lancaster Gate	46G5	
Lancaster Green Ayre	24B3	
Lanchester	27D5	
Lancing	5F2	
Lando Platform	7B2	
Lando ROF	7A2/7B2	
Note: Three stations.		
Landore	7B4/43G2	
Lane End	27D4	
Langbank	29B3	
Langford & Ulting	12F5	
Langford	3B2/8D2	
Langford	3C5	
Langho	24D2	
Langholm	26A1	
Langley	27C3	
Langley	5B1/10G1	
Langley Green & Rood End	13C2/15G4	
Langley Mill & Eastwood	41F3	
Langloan	44B3	

Langport East	3D1/8F3	Leek	15B4	Linacre Road	45A3
Langport West	3D1/8F3	Leek Brook Halt (Workmen)	15C4	Linby	16C4/41E4
Langrick	17C2	Leeming Bar	21A3/28G5	Lincoln (LMS)	16B1
Langside & Newlands	44E3	Lees	21F1	Lincoln (LNER)	16B1
Langston	4E2	Leffnoll North (Military)	25B2	Lincoln Bracebridge	16B1
Langwathby	27D1	Legacy	20E4	Lincoln East	16A1
Langwith	16B4/41C4	Legbourne Road	17A3	Lincoln Peham Street	17B1
Langwith Colliery	41C4	Leicester Belgrave Road	16F3	Lincoln West	16A1
Langwith Colliery (Workmen)	41C4	Leicester Central	16F3	Lindal	24B4
Langworth	16A1/17A1	Leicester London Road	16F3	Lindean	30E1
Lansalson	1D2	Leicester Square	46F5	Lindores	34F5
Lapford	2A4	Leicester West Bridge	16F3	Lingdale Mine	28F3
Lapworth	9A5	Leigh	15D4	Lingfield	5D4
Larbert	30B5	Leigh	20B2/24F2/45C3	Lingwood	18F2
Largo	34G4	Leigh-on-Sea	6A5	Linley	15F2
Largoward	34F4	Leight Court	9B3	Linlithgow	30B4
Largs	29C2	Leighton Buzzard	10D1	Linthwaite	21E2/42D5
Larkhall Central	30D5/44B1	Leire Halt	16G4	Linton (Miners)	27A5
Larkhall East	30D5/44A1	Leiston	12C2	Linton	11D4
Larkhill Camp (Military)	4C5	Leith	30B2/30F2	Lintz Green	27C5
Lartington	27E4	Leith Central	30F2	Linwood	29C4/44G3
Lasswade	30C2	Leith East	30F1	Lion's Holt Halt	2B3
Latchford	15A2/20C2/24G2/45C4	Leith Rosebank	30F2	Liphook	4D1
Latchley	1C5	Leith Walk	30F2	Lipson Vale Halt	1A2
Latimer Road	39C4/46E3	Lelant	1E4	Liscard & Poulton	45F4
Lauder	31D1	Leluncle Halt	6B5	Liskeard	1D4
Launceston	1B4	Leman Street	40C4	Lidd	4D1
Launton	10D3	Lemington	27B5/28A3	Liss (Military)	4D1
Laurencekirk	34B2	Lemsford Road Halt	11F2	Liss Forest Road (Military)	4D1
Lauriston	34C2	Lenham	6C4	Lissens	29D3
Lavant	4E1	Lennoxtown	29B5	Litchfield (Hants)	4B3
Lavenham	12D5	Lenton	16D4/41G4	*Note: Station closed 4 August 1942 to*	
Lavernock	8D4/43B5	Lentran	36D5	*8 March 1943*	
Laverton Halt	9C4	Lenwade	18E4	Little Bytham	16E1/17E1
Lavington	3B5	Lenzie	29B5/44D5	Little Drayton Halt	15D2/20F2
Law	30D5	Leominster	9B1	Little Eaton	16C5/41F2
Lawhead	30D4	Leslie	30A2/34G5	Little Hulton	45B2
Lawley Bank	15E2	Lesmahagow	30D5	Little Kimble	10E2
Lawrence Hill	3G1	Letchworth	11E2	Little Mill	31F5
Lawton	15C2/20E1	Letham Grange	34D3	Little Mill Junction	8B3/43A2
Laxey	23B3	Lethans No 2 Colliery	30A3	Little Ormesby Halt	18E1
Laxfield	12B3	Lethenty	37E3	Little Salkeld	27D1
Layerthorpe	21C5	Letterston	13F1	Little Somerford	9G4
Layton	24D4	Leuchars Junction	34F4	Little Steeping	17B3
Lazonby & Kirk Oswald	27D1	Leuchars Old	34E4	Little Stretton Halt	14C1
Lea Bridge	40B3	Leven	30A1/34G4	*Note: reopened on 6 May 1946*	
Lea Green	20C3/24G3/45D3	Levenshulme	20C1/24G1/45A3	Little Sutton	20D4/45F5
Lea Hall	15G5	Leverton	16A2	Little Weighton	22D4
Leadburn	30C2	Levisham	22A5/28G2	Littleborough	21E1
Leadenham	16C1	Lewes	5F4	Littlegate Colliery	30D5
Leadgate	27C5	Lewes Road	5F3	Littleham	2C2
Leagrave	10D1/11E1	Lewisham	40E3	Littlehampton	5G1
Lealholm	28F3	Lewknor Bridge Halt	10F3	Littlehaven Halt	5E2
Leamington Spa	10B5	Leyburn	21A2/27G5	Littlemore	10E4
Leamington Spa Avenue	10B5	Leycett	15C3/20F1	Littleport	11A4/17G4
Leamside	28D5	Leyland	20A3/24E3	Littlestone Holiday Camp	6E3
Leasowe	20C5/24G4	Leysdown	6B3	Littleton & Badsey	9C4
Leatherhead	5C2	Leysmill	34D3	Littleworth	17E2
Leaton	14A1/15E1	Leyton	40B3	Liverpool Alexandra Dock	45F3
Lechlade	9F5	Leytonstone	40B2	Liverpool Bankfield	45G4
Ledbury	9C2	Leytonstone	5A4/40A2	Liverpool Canada Dock	45F3
Ledbury Town Halt	9C2	Lezayre	23A3/25G4	Liverpool Central	20C4/24G4/45F4
Ledsham	20D4/45F5	Lhanbryde	36C1	Liverpool Crown Street	45F4
Ledston	21D4/42B1	Lichfield City	15E5	Liverpool Exchange	20C4/24G4/45F4
Lee	5B4/40E2	Lichfield Trent Valley	15E5	Liverpool Great Howard Street	45G4
Leebotwood	14B1/15F1	Lidlington	10C1	Liverpool Huskisson	45F3
Leeds Cardigan Road	42A3	Liff	34E5	Liverpool James Street	45F5
Leeds Central	21B2/42A3	Lifford	9A4	Liverpool Lime Street	20C4/24G4/45F4
Leeds City	21D3/42A3	Lifton	1B5	Liverpool North Docks	45F3
Leeds Marsh Lane	21D3/42A2	Lightcliffe	21E2/42B5	Liverpool North Mersey	45F3
Leeds Wellington Street	21D3/42A3	Lightmoor Platform	15F2	Liverpool Park Lane	45F4
Leeds Whitehall Road	21C2/42A3	Lilborne	10A4	Liverpool Riverside	45G3
Leegate	26D2	Limpley Stoke	3B3	Liverpool Road	20D4

Liverpool Sandon Dock	45G4	
Liverpool South Docks	45G5	
Liverpool Street (LU)	46E5	
Liverpool Wapping	45G5	
Liverpool Waterloo	45F3	
Liversedge Central	21E2/42C4	
Liversedge Spen	21E2/42B4	
Livingstone	30C4	
Llafar Halt	19F3	
Llanaber Halt	13A5	
Llanarthney	13G5	
Llanbadarn	13C5	

Note: Summer only passenger service withdrawn 31 August 1939; station reopened 23 July 1945

Llanbedr & Pensarn	19G2	
Llanberis	19E2	
Llanbister Road	14D2	
Llanbradach	8B4/43B3	
Llanbrynmair	14B4	
Llandaff	8C4/43B4	
Llandanwg Halt	19G2	
Llandderfel	19F5	
Llandebie	7A3/43G1	
Llandebie Colliery	7A3/43G1	
Llandecwyn Halt	19F2	
Llandenny	8A3	
Llandilo	13G5	
Llandilo Bridge	13G5	
Llandinam	14C3	
Llandogo Halt	8B2/9E1	
Llandovery	14F5	
Llandow Halt	43D5	
Llandow Wick Road Halt	43D5	
Llandre	13C5	
Llandrillo	19F5	
Llandrindod Wells	14E3	
Llandrinio Road	14A2	
Llandudno	19C3	
Llandudno Junction	19D4	
Llandulas	19D4	
Llandyssul	13F4	
Llanelly	7B3	
Llanelly Abert Road	7B3	
Llanelly Docks	7B3	
Llanelly Gas Works	7B3	
Llanerch-Ayron Halt	13D4	
Llanerchymedd	19C1/23G1	
Llanfair Caereinion	14B3	
Llanfair PG	19D2	
Llanfairfechan	19D3	
Llanfalteg	13G2	
Llanfaredd Halt	14E3	
Llanfechain	14A2/20G5	
Llanfyllin	14A3	
Llanfynydd	20E4	
Llanfyrnach	13F3	
Llangadock	14G5	
Llangammarch Wells	14E4	
Llangedwyn	14A2/20G5	
Llangefni	19D1	
Llangeinor	7B5/43D3	
Llangelynin Halt	13B5	
Llangennech	7B3	
Llanglydwen	13G2	
Llangollen	20F5	
Llangorse Lake Halt	14F3	
Llangunllo	14D2	
Llangwyllog	19C1	
Llangwynwyd	7B5/43E3	
Llangybi	13E5	
Llangybi	19F1	
Llangyfelach	7B4/43G2	

Llangynog	19G5	
Llanharan	8C5/43D4	
Llanharry	8C5/43C4	
Llanhilleth	8B4/43B2	
Llanidloes	14C4	
Llanilar	13D5	
Llanishen	8C4/43B4	
Llanmorlais	7B3	
Llanpumpsaint	13F4	
Llanrhaiadr Mochnant	14A3/20G5	
Llanrhaiadr	19E5	
Llanrhystyd Road	13C5	
Llanrwst & Trefriw	19D3	
Llansantffraid	14A2	
Llansilin Road	14A2/20G5	
Llanstephan Halt	14F3	
Llantarnam	8B3/43A3	
Llantrisant	8C5/43C4	
Llantwit Fardre	8C5/43C4	
Llantwit Major	8D5/43D5	
Llanuwchllyn	19G4	
Llanvihangel (Monmouth)	8A3/14G2	
Llanwern	8B3	
Llanwnda	19E3	
Llanwrda	14F5	
Llanwrtyd Wells	14E4	
Llanyblodwell	14A2/20G5	
Llanybyther	13F5	
Llan-y-Cefn	13G2	
Llanymynech	14A2/20G5	
Lletty Brongu	7B5/43D3	
Llong	20E5	
Llwydcoed	8A5/43D2	
Llwyn Gwern	14B5	
Llwyngwril	13A5	
Llwynypia	8B5/43D3	
Llydach Vale Colliery	43D3	
Llynclys Junction	20G4	
Llynclys	14A2/20G4	
Llys Halt	19G4	
Loanhead	30C2	
Loch Awe	32F2	
Loch Leven	30A3/33G5	
Loch Tay	33E2	
Lochailort	32B5	
Lochanhead	26B4	
Locharbriggs	26B3	
Lochburn	44E4	
Lochearnhead	33F2	
Lochee	34E4	
Lochee West	34E4	
Locheilside	32B3	
Lochgelly	30A3	
Lochluichart	35C4	
Lochmaben	26A3	
Lochmill	30B4	
Lochside	29C3	
Lochty	34F3	
Lochwinnoch	29C3	
Lockerbie	26A3	
Lockerley Sidings	44D4	
Lockington	22C4	
Lockwood	21E2/42D5	
Loddington	10A2	
Loddiswell	2E4	
Lodge Hill	3B2/8E2	
Lodge Hill (Military)	6B5	
Lofthouse & Outwood	21E3/42B2	
Loftus	28E3	
Logierieve	37E4	
Login	13G2	
Londesborough	22D5	
London Bridge (LU)	46E5	

London Broad Street	5A3/40C4	
London Charing Cross	5B3/40C5	
London Euston	5A3/40C5	
London Fenchurch Street	5A3/40C4	
London Fields	40B4	
London Holborn Viaduct	5B3/40C5	
London King's Cross	5A3/40C5	
London Liverpool Street	5A3/40C4	
London London Bridge	5B3/40D4	
London Marylebone	5A3/39C5	
London Paddington	5A3/39C5	
London St Pancras	5A3/40C5	
London Road	5F3	
London Road	29C2	
London Road, Guildford	5C1	
London Victoria	5B3/39D5	
London Waterloo	5B3/40D5	
London & Thames Haven Oil Wharves (Workmen)	6A5	
Long Ashton	3A2/8D2	
Long Buckby	10B3	
Long Clawson & Hose	16D2	
Long Eaton	16D4/41G3	
Long Marston	9C5	
Long Marton	27E2	
Long Melford	12D5	
Long Padeswood	20E4	
Long Parish	4C4	
Long Preston	24C1	
Long Stanton	11C3	
Long Stow	11B1	
Long Sutton & Pitney	3D1/8F2	
Long Sutton	17E3	
Long Witton	27A4	
Longcliffe	15B5	
Longcross Halt	5B1	

Note: Station opened c1940 for military use and to public on 21 September 1942

Longdon Halt	15E2	
Longdon Road	9C5	
Longdown	2B3	
Longford & Exhall	10A5/16G5	
Longforgan	34E5	
Longhaven	37D5	
Longhirst	27A5	
Longhope	8A1/9D2	
Longhoughton	31F5	
Longmoor Down (Military)	4D1	
Longmorn	36D2	
Longniddry	30B1	
Longport	15C3/20E1	
Longridge	24D2	
Longriggend	30C5	
Longside	37D5	
Longsight	45A3	
Longton Bridge	20A3/24E3	
Longton	15C3/20F1	
Longtown	26B1	
Longville	15F1	
Longwood & Milnsbridge	21E2/42D5	
Lonmay	37C4	
Looe	1D4	
Lords	46D3	
Lords Bridge	11C3	
Lordship Lane	40E4	

Note: Station reopened 4 March 1946

Lossiemouth	36C1	
Lostock Gralam	15A2/20D2/45C5	
Lostock Hall	20A3/24E3	
Lostock Junction	20B2/24F2/45C2	
Lostwithiel	1D3	
Loth	38G4	
Loudonhill	29E5	

Station	Ref
Loudwater	5A1/10F2
Loughborough	16D4
Loughborough Central	16D4
Loughborough Derby Road	16D4
Loughborough Junction	40E5
Loughor	7B3
Loughton	5A4/11G3
Louth	17A3/22G2
Low Bentham	24B2
Low Fell	27C5/28B1
Low Gill	27G1
Low Moor	21D242B4
Low Row	27C1
Low Street	5B5
Lowca	26E3
Lowdham	16C3
Lower Darwen	20A2/24E2
Lower Edmonton	5A3/11G3

Note: Low Level platform closed 11 September 1939

Station	Ref
Lower Ince	45D2
Lower Penarth Halt	8D4/43B5
Lower Pontnewydd	8B3/43A3
Lower Sydenham	40F3
Lowesby	16F3
Lowestoft Central	12A1/18G1
Lowestoft Kirkley	12A1/18G1
Lowestoft North	12A1/18F1
Lowthorpe	22C3
Lowton St Mary's	45C3
Lowton	20C2/24G2/45D3
Lubenham	16G3
Lucas Terrace Halt	1A2
Lucker	31E4
Luckett	1C5
Ludborough	22G2
Luddenden Foot	21E1
Luddington	22E5
Ludgershall	4B5
Ludlow	9A1
Luffenham	16F1
Lugar	29F5
Luib	33E1
Lumphanan	37G2
Lunan Bay	34D3
Luncarty	33E5
Lundin Links	34G4
Lustleigh	2C4
Luthrie	34F5
Lutnor	6B5
Luton	11E1
Luton Hoo	11F1
Lutterworth	10A4/16G4
Luxulyan	1D3
Lybster	38D2
Lydbrook Junction	8A2/9E1
Lydd Town	6E3
Lydd-on-Sea	6E3
Lydford	1C5
Lydiate	20B4/24F4/45F2
Lydney Junction	8B1/9E2
Lydney Town	8A1/9E2
Lydstep Halt	7D2
Lye	9A3/15G3
Lyghe Halt	5D5
Lyme Regis	3F1
Lyminge	6D3

Note: Station reopened 7 October 1946

Station	Ref
Lymington Pier	4F4
Lymington Town	4F4
Lymm	15A2/20C2//24G2/45C4
Lympstone	2B3
Lyndhurst Road	4E4

Station	Ref
Lyne	30D2
Lynedoch	29B3
Lyneside	26C1
Lyng Halt	3D1/8F3
Lyonshall	14E1
Lytham	20A4/24E4
Mabblethorpe	17A4
Macclesfield Central	15A3/20D1/45E5
Macclesfield Hibel Road	15A3/20D1/45E5
Macduff	37C2
Machen	8B4/43B3
Machynlleth	14B5
Machynlleth (Corris)	14B5
Macmerry	30B1
Maddaford Moor Halt	1B5
Madderty	33F4
Madeley	15C3/20F1
Madeley (Salop)	15F2
Madeley Market	15F2
Madeley Road	15C3/20F1
Maenclochog	13G2
Maentwrog Halt	19F3
Maerdy	8B5/43D2
Maesbrook	14A2/20G4
Maesteg	7B5
Maesteg (Neath Road)	43E3
Maesteg Castle Street	43E3
Maesycrugiau	13F4
Maesycwmmer & Hengoed	43B3
Magdalen Bridge	34E2
Magdalen Green	34E4
Magdalen Road	17E4
Maghull	20B4/24F4/45F2
Magor	8C3
Maida Vale	46D3
Maiden Lane	40B5
Maiden Newton	3F2
Maidenhead	4A1/5B1/10G2
Maidens	29G3
Maidstone Barracks	6C5
Maidstone East	6C5
Maidstone Tovil	6C5
Maidstone West	6C5
Malden	5F3/39F4
Malden Manor	39G3
Maldon East & Heybridge	12F5
Maldon West	12F5
Malins Lee	15E2
Mallaig	32A5
Malling	6C5
Malmesbury	9F3
Malpas	15C1/20E3
Malswick Halt	9D2
Maltby	21G5
Malton	22B5
Malvern Link	9C3
Malvern Wells (GW)	9C3
Malvern Wells (LMS)	9C3
Manchester Ancoats	45A3
Manchester Central	20B1/24F1/45A3
Manchester Cornbrook	45B3
Manchester Docks (Pass)	45B3
Manchester Docks	45B3
Manchester Ducie Street	45A3
Manchester Exchange	20B1/24F1/45A3
Manchester London Road	20B1/24F1/45A3
Manchester Mayfield	45A3
Manchester Oldham Road	45A3
Manchester Victoria	20B1/24F1/45A3
Manea	11A4/17G3
Mangotsfield	3A3/8C1/9G2

Station	Ref
Manley	15B1/20D3/45E5
Manningham	21D2/42A4
Manningtree	12E4
Manod	19F3
Manor House	46D2
Manor Park	40B2
Manor Road	20B5/24G5
Manor Way	40C1
Manorbier	7D2
Manors East	28A1
Manors North	28A1
Mansfield	16B4/41D4
Mansfield Colliery	16B3/41D5
Mansfield Woodhouse	16B4/41D4
Mansion House	40C5/46E3
Manton	16F2
Manuel	30B4
Marazion	1F4
Marble Arch	46F5
March	11A3/17F3
Marchington	15D5
Marchmont	31D2
Marchwiel	20E4

Note: Reopened 6 May 1946

Station	Ref
Marchwood	4E4
Marden	6D5
Mardock	11F3
Marfleet	22D3
Margate East	6B1
Margate	6B1
Marishes Road	22A5
Mark Lane	40C4/46E5
Market Bosworth	16F5
Market Drayton	15D2/20F2
Market Harborough	16G2
Market Rasen	17A1/22G3
Market Weighton	22D5
Markham Village	43B2

Note: Renamed Markham Village Halt 5 May 1941

Station	Ref
Markinch	30A2/34G5
Marks Tey	12E5
Marlborough High Level	4A5
Marlborough Low Level	4A5
Marlborough Road	39A3/46D3
Marlesford	12C2
Marlow	10G2
Marple	21G1
Marsden Cottage Halt	28B5
Marsden	21F1
Marsden	28B5
Marylebone (LU)	46F4
Marsh Brook	14C1
Marsh Gibbon & Poundon	10D3
Marsh Lane	42A2
Marsh Lane & Strand Road	45F3

Note: Station closed as a consequence of war damage 19 May 1941 to 12 July 1943

Station	Ref
Marsh Mills	2D5
Marshfield	8C4/43A4
Marske	28E3
Marston Gate	10E2
Marston Green	15G5
Marston Magna	3D2/8G1
Marston Moor	21C4
Marteg Halt	14D4
Martham	18E1
Martin Mill	6D1
Martock	3D2/8G2
Marton	10A5
Mary Tavy & Blackdown	1C5
Maryfield	34E4
Maryhill	29C5/44E4

Marykirk	34C3	Merton Abbey	39F5	Milton of Campsie	29B5
Maryland Point	40B2	Merton Park	39F4	Milton Range Halt (Military)	5B5
Maryport	26D3	Methil	30A2/34G4	Milton Road	3B1/8D3
Maryport Docks	26D3	Methley	42B1	Milverton	8F4
Masbury Halt	3C2/8E1	Methley Junction	21E4/42B1	Mindrum	31E4
Masham	21A3	Methven	33E4	Minehead	8E5
Massingham	18E5	Methven Junction Halt	33F3	Minera	20E5
Mathry Road	13F1	Mexborough	21F4	Minety & Ashton Keynes	9F4
Matlock	16B5/41D1	Micheldever	4C3	Minffordd	19F2
Matlock Bath	16B5/41D1	Mickle Trafford	15B1/20D3	Minshull Vernon	15B2/20E2
Matthewstown Halt	43C3	Micklefield	21D4/42A1	Minster	6C2
Mauchline	29E4	Micklehurst	21F1	Minsterley	14B1
Maud Junction	37D4	Mickleover	16D5/41G1	Minster-on-Sea	6B4
Mauldeth Road	45A3	Mickleton Halt	9C5	Mint Steeet LMS	40C4
Mawcarse	33G5	Mickleton	27E4	Mint Steeet LNER	40C4
Maxton	31E1	Mid Clyth	38D2	Mintlaw	37D4
Maxwell Park	44E3	Midcalder	30C3	Mirfield	21E2/42C4
Maxwelltown	26B4	Middle Drove	17F4	Mislingford	4E3
Maybole	29F3	Middle Stoke Halt	6B5	Misson Siding	21G5
Mayes Crossing Halt	5A5	Middlesbrough	28E4	Misterton	22G5
Mayfield	5E5	Middleton	20B1/24F1/45A2	Mistley	12E4
Maze Hill	40D3	Middleton Junction	20B1/24F1/45A2	Mitcham	5B3/39G5
Meadow Hall & Wincobank	42F2	Middleton North	27A4	Mitcham Junction	39G5
Mealsgate	26D2	Middleton Road	24C3	Mitcheldean Road	9D2
Measham	16E5	Middleton Towers	17E5	Mitchell & Newlyn Halt	1D1
Medge Hall	22F5	Middleton-in-Teesdale	27E3	Mithian Halt	1D1
Medina Wharf	4F3	Middleton-on-Lune	24A2/27G1	Mitre Bridge	39C4
Medstead & Four Marks	4C2	Middleton-on-the-Wolds	22C4	Moat Lane Junction	14C3
Meeth Halt	2A5	Middletown	14A2	Mobberley	15A3/20C1/45B4
Meickle Earnock Halt & Goods	29D5/44B1	Middlewich	15B2/20D2	Model Room Platform (Military)	4G5
Meigle	34D5	Middlewood	15A4	Moffat	30G3
Meir	15C4	Midford	3B3/8D1	Moira	16E5
Melangoose Mill	1D2	Midge Hall	20A3/24E3	Mold	20D5
Melbourne	16D5	Midgham	4A3	Mollington	20D4
Note: Used by troops from 10 November 1939 until 1 January 1945		Midhurst	4D1	Moniaive	26A5
		Midsomer Norton & Welton	3B3/8E1	Monifieth	34E4
Melcombe Regis	3G3	Midville	17C3	Monikie	34D4
Meldon	27A5	Milborne Port	3D3/8G1	Monk Fryston	21D4
Meldon Quarry Halt (Workmen)	2B5	Milcote	9B5	Monk Moors Halt (Workmen)	26G3
Meldreth & Melbourn	11D3	Mildenhall	11B5	Monks Lane Halt	5C4
Meledor Mill	1D2	Mile End	40C3	Monks Risborough & Whiteleaf Halt	10E2
Meliden	19C5	Mile End (LU)	46C3	Monkseaton	28B5
Melin Court Halt	43E2	Mileage Yard	39C5	Monkton	29E3
Melksham	3A4	Miles Platting	20B1/24F1/45A3	Monkton & Came (Golf Links) Halt	3F3
Melling	24B2	Milford	5D1	Monkton Combe	3B3/8D1
Mellis	12B4	Milford & Brocton	15E4	Monkwearmouth	28C5
Mells Road	3B3/8E1	Milford Haven	7D1	Monmouth May Hill	8A2/9E1
Melmerby	21A3	Milkwall	8A2/9E1	Monmouth Troy	8A2/9E1
Melmerby MOS	21B3	Mill Hill	20A2/24E2	Monsal Dale	15A5
Melrose	31E1	Mill Hill	4F3	Montacute	3D2/8G2
Meltham	21F2/42D5	Mill Hill	5A3	Montgomery	14B2
Melton	12D3	Mill Hill East	5A3/46E2	Montgreenan	29D3
Melton Constable	18D4	*Note: LNER service withdrawn 11 September 1939 and LPTB electric service commenced 18 May 1941*		Monton Green	45B3
Melton Crossing Halt (Workmen)	22E4			Montpelier	3F1/3G1
Melton Mowbray	16E2			Montrave	34G4
Melverley	14A1	Mill Hill the Hale	5A3	Montrose	34C2
Menai Bridge	19D2	Millbrook	10C1/11D1	Montrose Harbour	34C2
Mendlesham	12C4	Millbrook	4E4	Monument	40C4/46E5
Menheniot	1D4	Miller's Dale	15A5	Monument Lane	13C3
Menston	21D2	Millerhill	30B2	Monymusk	37F2
Menstrie	30A5	Millfield	28C5	Moor Park & Sandy Lodge	5A2/11G1/46G1
Menthorpe Gate	21D5	Millhouses & Ecclesall	16A5/41A2	Moor Row	26F3
Meole Brace	14B1/15E1	Milliken Park	29C4	*Note: Used by workmen's trains from 11 March 1940*	
Meols	20C5/24G5	Millisle	24D4		
Meols Cop	20E4/24E4/45F1	Millom	25A5	Moor Street Wharf	15D5
Meopham	5B5	Milltown	41D2	Moore	15A1/20C3/45D4
Merchiston	30G2	Millway (Workmen)	15C3/20E1	*Note: Used by railwaymen post closure on 1 February 1943*	
Mersey Road & Augburth	45F4	Milnathort	33G5		
Merstham	5C3	Milngavie	29B5/44E5	Moorgate	46E5
Merstone	4F3	Milnrow	20B1/21F1/45A1	Moorhampton	14E1
Merthyr	8A5/43C2	Milnthorpe	24A3	Moorhouse & South Elmsall	21F4/42D1
Merthyr Tydfil	43C2	Milton	15C3/20E1	Moorside & Wardley	45B2
Merthyr Vale	8B5/43C2	Milton Halt	10C4	Moorswater	1D4

Moorthorpe & South Kirkby	21F4/42D1
Moortown	22F3
Morar	32B5
Morchard Road	2A4
Morcott	16F1
Morden Halt	39F5
Morden	46E4
Morden South	39G4
Morebath Junction Halt	7F5
Morebath	8F5
Morecambe Euston Road	24B3
Morecambe Promenade	24B3
Moresby Junction Halt (Workmen)	26E3
Morseby Park	26E3
Moreton	20C5/24G4
Moreton	3F3
Moretonhampstead	2B4
Moreton-in-Marsh	9D5
Moreton-on-Lugg	9C1
Moreton-on-Lugg US Army Depot	9C1
Morice Yard (Military)	1A1
Morley	21E3/42B3
Mormond Halt	37C4
Morningside	30C5
Morningside Road	30G2
Mornington Crescent	46F4
Morpeth	27A5
Morris Cowley	10E4
Morriston	7B4/43G2
Mortehoe	7E3
Mortimer	4A2
Mortlake	5B2/39E3
Morton Pinkney	10C4
Morton Road	17E1
Moseley	9A4/15G4
Moses Gate	45B2
Moss	21E5
Moss & Pentre	20E4
Moss Bank	20B3/24F3/45D3
Moss Side	24D4
Mossend	30C5/44B3
Mossley	21F1
Mossley Hill	20C4/24G4/45E4
Mosstowie	36C2
Moston	20B1/24F1/45A2
Mostyn	20C5
Motherwell Central	30C5/44B2
Motspur Park	39G4
Mottingham	5B4/40E2
Mottisfont	4D4
Mottram	21G1
Mottram Yard Halt (Railwaymen)	21G1
Mouldsworth	15B1/20D3/45D5
Moulton	17E3
Moulton	27F5
Mount Florida	44E3
Mount Hawke Halt	1E1
Mount Melville	34F4
Mount Vernon	29C5/44C3
Mountain Ash	8B5
Mountfield Halt	6E5
Mow Cop & Scholar Green	15B2/20E1
Moy	36E4
Much Wenlock	15F2
Muchalls	34A1
Muir of Ord	35D5
Muiredge Colliery	30A2
Muirend	29C5/44E2
Muirkirk	29E5
Muirton Halt (Private)	33E5
Mulben	36D1
Mulberry Halt (Military)	4E4
Mumbles Pier	7B3/43G3

Mumbles Road	7B3/43G3
Mumby Road	17A4
Mundesley-on-Sea	18D2
Munlochy	36D5
Murrayfield	30F2
Murrow	17F3
Murthly	33E5
Murton Junction	28C5
Murton Lane	21C5
Musgrave	27F2
Musselburgh	30B2
Muswell Hill	5A3/40A5
Muthill	33F4
Mynydd-y-Garreg	7A2
Mytholmroyd	21E1
Naburn	21C5
Nafferton	22C3
Nailsea & Backwell	3A2/8D2
Nailsworth	9F3
Nairn	36D4
Nancegollan	1F5
Nannerch	20D5
Nanstallon Halt	1D3
Nantclwyd	19E5
Nantgaredig	13G4
Nantgarw Halt (High Level)	43C3
Nantlle	19E2
Nantmawr	20G5
Nantwich	15C2/20E5
Nantybwch	8A4/43C1
Nantyderry	8A3/43B1
Nantyffyllon	7B5/43E3
Nantyglo	8A4/43B1
Nantymoel	7B5/43D3
Nantyronen	14C5
Note: Summer only passenger service
withdrawn 31 August 1939; station reopened
23 July 1945
Napsbury	11G1
Napton & Stockton	10B4
Narberth	7C3
Narborough	16F4
Narborough & Pentney	17E5
Nassington	11A1/16F1/17F1
Nast Hyde Halt	11F2
Nateby	24C3
Navenby	16B1/17C1
Naworth	27C1
Nawton	21A5
Neasden	5A2/39B4/46E2
Note: Temporary platforms erected on LNER
line to Marylebone in use from early October
1940, following temporary closure due to
bombing of line to Marylebone on 5 October;
ceased use on 26 November 1940
Neath	7B4
Neath Abbey	7B4
Neath Canal Side	43F3
Needham	12C4
Neen Sollars	9A2
Neepsend	21G3/42G2
Neilston	29C4/44G2
Nelson	21B1/24D1
Nesfield	16A5/41B2
Nesscliff & Pentre	14A1
Nesscliff Halt (Military)	14A1
Netherhope Halt	8B2/9F1
Neston	20D4/45F5
Neston & Parkgate	45F5
Netherburn	30D5
Nethercleugh	26A3
Netherfield	16D3/41F5

Netherseal Colliery	16E1
Netherton	13B1/15G4
Netherton	21E2/42D5
Netherton	29C4/44F2
Nethertown	26F3
Nethy Bridge	36F3
Netley	4E3
Netley Docks	4E3
Netley Victoria Hospital (Military)	4E3
New Barnet	5A3/11G2
New Basford	41F4
New Beckenham	40F3
New Biggin	27E1
New Bolingbroke	17C3
New Brighton	20C4/24G4/45F3
New Church Halt	45C3
New Clee	22F2
New Cross	40D3/46C3
New Cross Gate	40D3/46C3
New Cumnock	29F5
New Eltham	5B4/40E1
New Galloway	26B5
New Hailes	30B2
New Hall Bridge Halt	24D1
New Hey	21F1
New Holland	22E3
New Hucknall Colliery	41D3
New Hythe	6C5
New Lane	20A4/24E3/45E1
New Longton & Hutton	20A3/24E3
New Luce	25C3
New Machar	37F4
New Mills	15A4
New Milton	4F5
New Monkton Main Colliery	42D2
New Moor (Miners)	27A5
New Radnor	14E2
New Ranges (Military)	6A4
New Romney & Littlestone-on-Sea	6E3
New Romney	6E3
New Southgate & Friern Barnet	5A3
New Tredegar	8A4/43B2
New Wandsworth	30F2
Newark	16C2
Newarthill	44A2
Newbiggin-by-the-Sea	28A5
Newbigging	30D4
Newbridge	43B2
Newbridge-on-Wye	14E3
Newburgh	34F5
Newburn	27B5/28A3
Newbury	4A3
Newbury (Westfields) Halt	4A3
Newbury Park	40A1
Newbury Racecourse (Restricted)	4A3
Newby Bridge	24A4
Newby Wiske	21A3/28G5
Newcastle Central	27B5/28A1
Newcastle Emlyn	13F3
Newcastle Quay	28A1
Newcastle under Lyme	15C3/20F1
Newcastleton	27A1
Newchapel & Golden Hill	15C3/20E1
Newchurch	4F3
Newent	9D2
Newham	31E4
Newhaven	30F2
Newhaven Harbour	5G5
Newhaven Town	5F4
Newhouse	30C5/44A3
Newick & Chailey	5E4
Newington	30G2
Newington	6B4

Station	Ref
Newland Halt	9C3
Newlay & Horsforth	21D3/42A3
Newmains	30C5
Newmarket	11C4
Newmarket Warren Hill (Racecourse)	11C4
Newmilns	29E4
Newnham	8A1/9E2
Newnham Bridge	9A2
Newpark	30C3
Newport	11E4
Newport	15E2
Newport	4F3
Newport	28E4
Newport Alexandra Dock	43A4
Newport Dock Street	43A3
Newport High Street	8B3/43A3
Newport Mill Street	8B3/43A3
Newport-on-Tay East	34E1
Newport-on-Tay West	34F2
Newport Pagnell	10C2
Newquay	1D1
Newseat	37D5
Newsham	28B5
Newsholme	24C1
Newstead	16C4/41E4
Newstead West	16C4/41E4
Newthorpe, Greasley & Shipley Gate	41F3
Newton Abbot	2C3
Newton Heath	20B1/24F1/45A2
Newton Kyme	21C4
Newton Poppleford	2B2
Newton Road	13B3/15F4
Newton St Cyres	2B3
Newton Stewart	25B4
Newton Tony	4C5
Newton	21G1
Newton	29C5/44C3
Newtonairds	26A4
Newtongrange	30C2
Newtonhill	34A1
Newton-le-Willows	20C2/24G2/45D3
Newtonmore	33A2
Newton-on-Ayr	29F3
Newtown	14C3
Newtown Halt	18E1
Newtyle	34D5
Neyland	7D2
Nidd Bridge	21C3
Niddrie	30B2
Nigg	36C4
Nigley	42A5
Nine Elms	40E5
Nine Mile Point	8B4/43B3
Ningwood	4F4
Ninian Park	43B4
Nisbet	31E2
Nitshill	29C4/44F3
No 2 Range (Military)	4C1
Nocton & Dunston	16B1/17B1
Noel Park & Wood Gren	40A5
Norbiton	5F2/39F3
Norbury	40F5
Norbury & Ellastone	15C5
Norham	31D3
Normacot	15C3
Normanby Park	22E4
Normans Bay Halt	5F5
Normanton	21E3/42C2
North Acton	46E3
North Berwick	31B1
North Blyth	28A5
North Camp & Ash Vale	4B1/5C1
North Cave	22D4
North Connel	32E4
North Crofty	1E5
North Drove	17E2
North Dulwich	40E4
North Ealing	39C3/46E3
North Eastrington	22D5
North Elmham	18E4
North Filton Platform	8C2/9G1
North Grimston	22B5
North Harrow	5A2/10G1/39A1/46F2
North Hayling	4E2
North Howden	22D5
North Kelsey	22F3
North Leith	30F2
North Queensferry	30B3
North Rode	15B320D1
North Seaton	27A5
North Sheen	39E3
North Shields	28B5
North Skelton	28E3
North Sunderland	31E5
North Tawton	2B5
North Thoresby	22F2
North Walsham	18D2
North Warbottle Colliery (Miners)	27B5
North Water Bridge	34C2
North Weald	11G3
North Wembley	39B2/46E3
North Woolwich	5B4/40C2
North Wootton	17E5
North Wylam	27B5
North Yard (Military)	1A1
Northallerton	21A3/28G5
Northallerton Low	28G5
Northam	4E4
Northampton Bridge Street	10B2
Northampton Castle	10B2
Northenden	20C1/24G1/45A4
Northfield	9A4
Northfields	39D2/46F3
Northfleet	5B5
Northiam	6F5
Northolt	39B1
Northolt Junction	5A2/39B1
Northorpe	22G4
Northorpe Higher	42C4
Northorpe North Road	42C4
Northumberland Park	40A4
North Water Bridge	34C2
Northwich	15A2/20D2/45C5
Northwick Park	46F2
Northwood	5A2/46G1
Northwood Hills	5A2/46F2
Norton Bridge	15D3/20G1
Norton Fitzwarren	8F4
Norton Junction	28E5
Norton	15A1/20C3/45D4
Norton	21E5
Norton-in-Hales	15D2/20F2
Norton Junction	9B3
Norton-on-Tees	28E5
Norwich City	18F3
Norwich Thorpe	18F3
Norwich Victoria	18F3
Norwood Junction	5B3/40G4
Nostell	42C1
Notgrove	9D4
Notting Hill Gate	39C4/46G5
Nottingham Arkwright Street	16D4/41G4
Nottingham (LMS)	16D3/41G5
Nottingham London Road	41G5
Nottingham Manvers Sidings	41F5
Nottingham Queens Road	41G4
Nottingham Race Course Sidings	41F5
Nottingham Road	16D5/41G2
Nottingham Victoria	16C4/41F4
Notton & Royston	21E3/42D2
Nunburnholme	22C5
Nuneaton	16F5
Nuneaton Abbey Street	16F5
Nunhead	40D4
Nunnington	21A5
Nunthorpe	28F4
Nursling	4D4
Nutbourne Halt	4E1
Nutfield	5D3
Oakamoor	15C4
Oakengates	15E2
Oakenshaw	21E3/42C2
Oakham	16E2
Oakhanger (Military)	4C1
Oakington	11C3
Oakle Street	8A1/9E2
Oakleigh Park	5A3/11G2
Oakley	10B1/11C1
Oakley	4B3
Oakley (Fife)	30A4
Oaksey Halt	9F4
Oakworth	21D1
Oban	32F4
Occumster	38D2
Ochiltree	29F4
Ockendon	5A5
Ockley	5D2
Offord & Buckden	11C2
Ogbourne	4A5
Ogmore Vale	7B5/43D3
Okehampton	2B5
Old Colwyn	19D4
Old Cumnock	29F5
Old Dalby	16E3
Old Ford	40B3

Note: Station closed 15 May 1944 but bus replacement service operated until 23 April 1945

Station	Ref
Old Hill	13C1/15G4
Old Hill High Street Halt	13C1
Old House Point	25B2
Old Kilpatrick	44G5
Old Leake	17C3
Old Meldrum	37E3
Old North Road	11C2
Old Oak Lane Halt	39C3
Old Roan	20B4/24F4/45F3
Old Street	46E3
Old Trafford	45B3
Old Woods Halt	14A1/15E1/20G3
Old Ynysybwl Halt	43C3
Oldbury & Bromford Lane	13B2
Oldbury	13B2/15G4
Oldham Central	21D1/45A2
Oldham Clegg Strret	21D1
Oldham Glodwick Road	21D1
Oldham Mumps	21D1
Oldham Werneth	20B1/21F1/45A2
Ollerton	16B3
Olmarch Halt	13E5
Olney	10B2
Olton	9A5/15G5
Omoa	30C5/44A2

Note: Renamed Cleland 1 October 1941

Station	Ref
Ongar	11G4
Onibury	9A1/14C1
Onllwyn	7A5/43E1
Orbliston	36D1

Ordens Halt	37C2	Palnure	25C4	Pembrey & Burry Port	7B2
Ordsall Lane	45B3	Palterton & Sutton	16B4/41C3	Pembrey	7B2
Ore	6F5	Pampisford	11D4	Pembridge	14E1
Orell	20B3/24F3/45D2	Pandy	14G1	Pembroke Dock	7D2
Oreston	1A2	Pangbourne	4A2/10G3	Pembroke Town	7D2
Ormesby	28E4	Pannal	21C3	Penally	7D3
Ormiston	30B1	Pans Lane Halt	3B5	Penarth	8D4/43B5
Ormside	27E2	Pant	8A5/43C1	Penarth Dock	8C4/43B5
Ormskirk	20B4/24F3/45E2	Pant (Salop)	14A2/20G4	Pencader	13F4
Orpington	5B4/40G1	Pant Glas	19E1	Pencaitland	30C1
Orrell Park	45F3	Panteg & Griffiths Town	8B3/43A2	Pencarreg Halt	13E5
Orton Waterville	11A1/17F1	Pantydwr	14D4	Penclawydd	7B3
Note: Used by railwaymen post closure on		Pantyffynnon	7A3/43G1	Pencoed	8C5/43D4
5 October 1942		Pantysgallog	43C1	Pendlebury	45B2
Orton	36D1	Par	1D3	Pendleton	45B3
Orwell	12D3	Parbold	20B3/24F3/45E2	Pendleton (Broad Street)	45B3
Osbaldwick	21C5	Parc	19F3	Pendre	13B5
Ossett	21E3/42C3	Parcyrhun Halt	7A3/43G1	Pengam	8B4/43B2
Osterley	5B2/39D2/46F3	Parham	12C2	Penge East	40F4
Oswestry	20G4	Park	24B5	Penge West	40F4
Otford	5C5	Park	34A2/37G3	Penhelig Halt	13B5
Otley	21D2	Park	45A3	Penicuik	30C2
Otterham	1B3	Park Bridge	21F1	Penirefelin	20G5
Otterington	21A3/28G5	Park Drain	22F5	Penistone	21F3/42E3
Otterspool	45F4	Park Parade	21A2	Penkridge	15E3
Ottery St Mary	2B2	Park House Halt (Military)	26C1	Penmaen Halt	43B2
Ottringham	22E2	Park Royal	46E3	Penmaenmawr	19D3
Oughty Bridge	21G3/42F3	Park Street & Frogmore	11G1	Penmaenpool	14A5
Oulton Broad North	12A1/18G1	Parkend	8A1/9E2	Pennington	45C3
Oulton Broad South	12A1/18G1	Parkeston Quay	12E3	Penns	15F5
Oundle	11A1/16G1/17G1	Parkeston Quay West	12E3	Penpergwm	8A3/43A1
Outwell Basin	17F4	Parkgate	20D4/45F5	Penpont Halt (Private)	14F4
Outwell Village	17F4	Parkgate & Aldwarke	21G4/42F1	Penrhiwceiber	8B5/43C2
Oval	46D3	Parkgate & Rawmarsh	21G4/42F1	Penrhiwfelin	43B3
Ovenden	21E2/42C5	Parkhead	44D4	Penrhyndeudraeth	19F2
Over & Wharton	15B2/20D2	Parkhill	37F3	Penrith	27E1
Overseal & Moira	16E5	Parkhouse Halt (Military)	26C2	Penruddock	26E1
Overstrand	18D3	Parkside Halt	38D2	Penryn	1F1
Overton	4B3	Parkstone	3F5	Pensford	3A2/8D1
Overton	29B3	Parsley Hay	15B5	Penshaw	28C5
Overton-on-Dee	20F4	Parsons Green	39D4/46E3	Penshurst	5D4
Note: Reopened 6 May 1946		Partick	29C4/44E4	Pentir Rhiw	8A5/14G3/43C1
Overtown	30D5/44A1	Partick Central	44E4	Penton	26B2
Oxenholme	24A3/27G1	Partick West	44E4	Pentreath	19D2
Oxenhope	21D1	Partington	20C1/24G1/45B3	Pentre Halt (Military)	14A1
Oxford	10E4	Parton	26B5	Pentrebach	8A5/43C2
Oxford Circus	46F5	Parton	26E4	Pentrecourt Platform	13F4
Oxford Rewley Road	10E4	Partridge Green	5E2	Pentrefelin	14A3/20G5
Oxheys	24D3	Paston & Knapton	18D2	Pentrepiod Halt	43A2
Oxshott & Fairmile	5C2	Patchway	8C1/9G1	Pentwyn Halt	43A2
Oxspring	21F3/42E3	Pateley Bridge	21B2	Penybont	14D3
Oxted & Limpsfield	5C4	Patna	29F4	Penybontfawr	14A3/19G5
Oxton	30C1	Patney & Chirton	3B5	Penychain Halt	19F1
Oyne	37E2	Patricroft	20B2/24F1/45B3	Pen-y-Ffordd	20E4
Oystermouth	43G3	Patrington	22E2	Pen-y-Graig	8B5/43D3
		Patterton	29C4/44F2	Penygroes	19E1
Padbury	10D3	Peak Forest	15A5	Penyrheol	8B4/43B3
Paddington (LU)	46D3/46G4	Peakirk	17F2	Penzance	1F4
Paddock Wood	5D5	Peartree & Normanton	16D5/41G2	Peplow	15E2/20G2
Padeswood	20E4	Peasley Cross	45D3	Percy Main	28B5
Padgate	20C2/24G2/45C4	Pebworth Halt	9C5	Perivale Halt	39C2
Padiham	24D1	Peckham Rye	40D4	Perranporth	1D1
Padstow	1C2	Peckham Rye Coal Depot	40D4	Perranporth Beach Halt	1D1
Paignton	2D3	Pedair-Ffordd	14A3/19G5	Perranwell	1E1
Paisley	29C4	Peebles	30D2	Perry Barr	13B3/15G4
Paisley Canal	44F3	Peel	23B2	Pershore	9C4
Paisley East	44F3	Peel Road	23B2	Perth Central	33F5
Paisley Gilmore Street	44G3	Pegswood	27A5	Perth General	33F5
Paisley St James	44G3	Pelaw	28A1/28C5	Perth Princes Street	33F5
Paisley West	44G3	Pellon	42C5	Peterborough East	11A2/17F2
Palace Gates (Wood Green)	5A3/40A5	Pelsall	15F4	Peterborough North	11A2/17F2
Pallion	28C5	Pelton	27C5	Peterchurch	14F1
Palmers Green & Southgate	5A3	Pemberton	20B3/24F3/45D2	Peterhead	37D5

Petersfield	4D2	Plumpton	5F3	Port Elphinstone	37F3
Peterston	8C5/43C4	Plumstead	40D1	Port Erin	23C1
Petrockstow	1A5/7G3	Plumtree	16D3	Port Gate Platform (Military)	4G5
Petts Wood	40G1	Plym Bridge Platform	2D5	Port Glasgow	29B3
Petworth	5E1	Plymouth Friary	1A2	Port Gordon	37C1
Pevensey & Westham	5F5	Plymouth Millbay	1D5	Port Isaac Road	1C3
Pevensey Bay Halt	5F5	Plymouth North Road	1D5	Port Matilda	29B3
Pewsey	4B5	Plympton	2D5	Port of Menteith	29A5
Philhorth Bridge Halt	37C4	Plymstock	1A2	Port Soderick	23C2
Philhorth Halt	37C4	Pocklington	22C5	Port St Mary	23C1
Philipstoun	30B3	Point Pleasant	28B5	Port Sunlight	45F4
Piccadilly Circus	46F5	Poison Cross Siding	6C2	Port Talbot	7B4
Pickburn & Brodsworth	21F4	Pokesdown	4F5	Port Talbot Central	43F3
Pickering	22A5	Polegate	5F5	Port Talbot Dock	7B4/43F3
Pickhill	21A3	Polesworth	16F5	Port Talbot General	43F3
Pickhill Halt	20F4	Pollokshaws East	44E3	Port Victoria	6B4
Note: Reopened 6 May 1946		Pollokshaws West	44E3	Portbury	3A2/8C2/9G1
Picton	28F5	Pollokshields East	44E3	Portchester	4E2
Piddington	10B2	Pollokshields West	44E3	Portesham	3F2
Piddington (Military)	10E3	Polmont	30B4	Portessie	37C1
Piercebridge	27E5	Polsham	3C2/8E2	Porth	8B5/43C3
Piershill	30F1	Polsloe Bridge Halt	2B3	Porthcawl	7C5/43E4
Pill	3A2/8C2/9G1	Polton	30C2	Porthywaen	14A2/20G5
Pilling	24C3	Pomathorn	30C2	Portishead	3A2/8C3/9G1
Pilmoor	21B4	Ponder's End	5A4/11G3	Portishead South	3A1/8C3
Pilning	8C2/9G1	Ponfeigh	30E4	Portknockie	37C1
Pilot	6E3	Pont Lawrence Halt	43B3	Portland	3G3
Pilsley	16B4/41D3	Pont Llanio	13E5	Portlethen	34A1/37G2
Pinchbeck	17E2	Pont Lliw	7B3/43G2	Portmadoc	19F2
Pinchinthorpe	28E4	Pontardawe	7A4/43F2	Portobello	30G1
Pinewood Halt	4A3/10G4	Pontardulais	7A3	Porton	4C5
Note: Station closed 4 August 1942 to		Pontardulais (Miners)	43G2	Porton Down	4C5
8 March 1943		Pontdolgoch	14B3	Portpatrick	25C1
Pinged Halt	7A2	Pontefract Baghill	21E4/42C1	Portskewett	8B2/9F1
Pinhoe	2B3	Pontefract Monkhill	21E4/42C1	Portslade	5F3
Pinkhill	30B3	Pontefract Tanshelf	21E4/42C1	Portsmouth	20A1/24E1
Pinmore	25A3	Ponteland	27B5	Portsmouth Arms	7G3
Pinner	5A2/39A1/46F2	Pontesbury	14B1	Portsmouth Harbour	4E2
Pinwherry	25A3	Ponthenry	7A3	Portsmouth Town	4E2
Pinxton	16C5/41E3	Ponthir	8B3/43A3	Portsoy	37C2
Pinxton & Selston	41E3	Pontillanfraith	8B4/43B3	Possil	44E4
Pipe Gate	15C2/20F2	Pontllanio	13E5	Possil Park	44E4
Pitcaple	37E3	Pontlottyn	43C2	Postland	17E2
Pitlochry	33C4	Pontnewynydd	43A2	Potter Heigham	18E2
Pitlurg	37E4	Pontrhydyfen	43E3	Potter Heigham Bridge Halt	18E2
Pitmeddon	37F4	Pontrhythallt	19D2	Potterhanworth	16B1/17B1
Pitsea	6A5	Pontrilas	14G1	Potterhill	29C4/44G3
Pitsford & Brampton	10B2	Pontsarn	8A5/43C1	Potters Bar & South Mimms	11G2
Pittenweem	34G3	Pontsticill Junction	8A5/43C1	Potto	28F4
Pittington	28D5	Pontwalby Halt	43D2	Potton	11D2
Pitts Hill	15C3/20E1	Pontycymmer	7B5/43D3	Poulton Curve Halt	24D4
Plaidy	37D3	Pontycynon Bridge Halt	43D2	Poulton	24D4
Plains	30C5/44A4	Pontyrhyll	7B5/43D3	Powerstock	3F2
Plaistow	40C2/46C3	Pontyates	7A3	Powfoot Halt (Workmen)	26B2
Plaistow & West Ham	40C2	Pontyberem	7A3	Poyle for Stanwell Moor Halt	5B1
Plas Marl	7B4/43G2	Pont-y-Pant	19E3	Poynton	15A3/20C1/45A4
Plas Powell	20E4	Pontypool	8B3/43A2	Poynton	15A4
Plashetts	27A2	Pontypool Clarence Stret	43A2	Praed Street	39C5/46F4
Plas-y-Court Halt	14A1	Pontypool Road	8B3/43A2	Praze	1E5
Platt Bridge	45D2	Pontypridd	8B5/43C3	Prees	15D1/20F3
Plawsworth	27C5	Pool	21C3	Preesall	24C4
Plealey Road	14B1	Pool Colliery	30D4	Prescot	20C3/24G3/45E3
Plean Pits	30B5	Pool Quay	14A2	Prescott Siding	9A2/15G2
Plean	30A5	Poole	3F5	Prestatyn	19C5
Pleasington	20A2/24E2	Poplar (East India Road)	40C3	Prestbury	15A3/20D1/45A5
Pleasley	16B4/41D4	*Note: Station closed 15 May 1944 but bus*		Presteign	14D1
Plenmeller Halt (Workmen)	27C2	*replacement service operated until 23 April*		Presthope	15F1
Plessey	27B5	*1945*		Preston	24D3
Plockton	35E1	Poplar	40C3	Preston Brook	15A1/20C3/45D4
Plodder Lane	20B2/24F2/45B2	Poppleton	21C4	Preston Butler Street	24E3
Pluckley	6D4	Port Clarence	28E4	Preston Christian Road	24D3
Plumley	15A2/20D2/45B5	Port Dinorwic	19D2	Preston Docks	24D3
Plumpton	27D1	Port Eglinton	44F1	Preston Junction	20A3/24E3

Preston Park	5F3	Rainford Junction	20B3/24F3/45E2	Regents Park	46F4
Preston Road	20C4/24G4/45F3	Rainford Village	20B3/24F3/45E2	Reigate	5C3
Preston Road	39A3/46F2	Rainham	5A4	Renfrew	29C4
Preston West Lancs	24E3	Rainham	6B5	Renfrew Fulbar Steeet	44F4
Prestonpans	30B1	Rainhill	20C3/24G3/45E3	Renfrew Potterfield	44F4
Prestwich	20B1/24F1/45B2	Ramsbottom	20A1/24E1/45B1	Renfrew Wharf	44F4
Prestwick	29E3	Ramsden Dock	24B5	Renton	29B3
Priestfield	13A1	Ramsey	23A3/25G4	Repton & Willington	16D5
Prince's End & Coseley	13B1/15F4	Ramsey East	11B2	Resolven	7A5/43E2
Princes Dock	44E3	Ramsey North	11A2/17G2	Reston	31C3
Princes Pier	29B3	Ramsgate	6B1	Retford	16A3
Princes Risborough	10F2	Rankinston	29F4	Rhayader	14D4
Princetown	2C5	Rannoch	32D1/33C1	Rheidol Falls	14C5
Priory Halt (Naval)	12E3	Ranskill	16A3/21G5	*Note: Summer only passenger service*	
Prittlewell	6A4	Ranskill ROF (Workmen)	16A3/21G5	*withdrawn 31 August 1939; station reopened*	
Privett	4D2	Raskelf	21B4	*23 July 1945*	
Probus & Ladock Platform	1E2	Ratby	16F4	Rhewl	19E5
Prudhoe	27C4	Ratgoed Quarry	14A5	Rhigos Halt	43D1
Pudsey Greenside	21D2/42A4	Rathen	37C4	Rhiwbina Halt	43B4
Pudsey Lowtown	21D2/42A4	Ratho	30B3	Rhiwderyn	8C4/43A3
Pulborough	5E1	Rauceby	16C1/17C1	Rhiwfron	14D5
Pulford	20E4	Raunds	10A1/11B1	*Note: Summer only passenger service*	
Pulham Market	12A3/18G3	Ravelrig	30C3	*withdrawn 31 August 1939; station reopened*	
Pulham St Mary	12A3/18G3	Ravelrig Siding	30B5	*23 July 1945*	
Puncheston	13F1	Ravenglass	26G3	Rhoose	8D5/43C5
Purfleet	5B5	Ravensbourne	40F3	Rhos	20F4
Purley	5C3	Ravenscar	28F1	Rhosgoch	19C1/23G1
Purley Oaks	5C3	Ravenscourt Park	39D4/46E3	Rhosneigr	19B2/19D1
Purton	9F4	Ravenscraig	29B3	Rhosrobin Halt	20E4
Putney	5B3/39E4	Ravensthorpe & Thornhill	42C3	Rhostyllen	20E4
Putney Bridge	39D4/46E3	Ravensthorpe Lower	42C3	Rhosymedre Halt	20F4
Puxton	3A1/8D3	Ravenstonedale	27F2	Rhu	29B2
Pwllheli	19F1	Rawcliffe	21E5	Rhuddlan	19D5
Pye Bridge	16C4/41E3	Rawtenstall	20A1/24E1	Rhydowen	13F3
Pye Hill & Somercotes	16C4/41E3	Rawyards	44A4	Rhydyfelin Halt	43C3
Pyle	7C5/43E4	Raydon Wood	12D4	Rhydryonen	13B5
Pylle	3C3/8F1	Rayleigh	6A5	Rhydymwyn	20D5
Pylle Hill	3G1	Rayne	11E5	Rhyl	19C5
Pymstock	2D5	Rayner's Lane	39B1/46F2	Rhymney	8A4/43C1
		Raynes Park	5B3/39F4	Rhymney & Pontlottyn	43C2
Quainton Road	10E3	Raynham Park	18D5	Rhymney Bridge	8A5/43C1
Quakers Drove	11A3/17G3	Reading	4A2	Ribblehead	24A1
Quakers Yard	8B5/43C2	Reading Central	4A2	Riby Street Platform (Workmen)	22F2
Quarter	29D5/44B1	Reading Southern	4A2	Riccall	21D5
Queen's Park (West Kilburn)	39B4/46E3	Reading West	4A2	Riccarton & Craigie	27A1/29E4
Queen's Road	39D5/46G5	Rearsby	16E3	Riccarton Junction	31G1
Queen's Road	40D4	Rectory Road	40B4	Richborough Castle Halt	6C2
Queenborough	6B4	Red House	14C4	Richmond	27F5
Queens Park	44E3	Red Rock	20B3/24F2/45D2	Richmond	5B2/39D3/46E4
Queensbury	21D2/42B5	Red Wharf Bay & Benllech	19C2	Rickmansworth	5A2/10F1/11G1
Queensbury	46E2	Redbourn	11F1	Riddings Junction	26B1
Queensferry	20D4	Redbridge	4E4	Ridgmont	10C1
Queensway	46G5	Redbrook-on-Wye	8A2/9E1	Riding Mill	27C4
Quintrel Downs Platform	1D1	Redcar	28E3	Rigg	26B2
Quorn & Woodhouse	16E4	Redcar East	28E3	*Note: Used by workmen's trains after*	
Quy	11C4	Redcastle	36D5	*1 November 1942*	
		Redding	30B4	Rillington	22B5
Racks	26B3	Reddish	45A3	Rimington	24C1
Radcliffe	20B1/24F1/45B2	Redditch	9B4	Ringley Road	24F1/45B2
Radcliffe (Black Lane)	20B1/24F1/45B2	Redheugh	28A2	Ringstead & Addington	10A1
Radcliffe Bridge	45B2	Redhill	5C3	Ringwood	4E5
Radcliffe-on-Trent	16D3	Redland	3F1	Ripley	16C5/41E2
Radford	16C4/41G4	Redmarshall	28E5	Ripley Valley	21C3
Radipole Halt	3G3	Redmile	16D2	Ripon	21B3
Radlett	11G1	Redmire	21A1/27G4	Rippingale	17D1
Radley	10F4	Rednal & West Felton	20G4	Ripple	9C3
Radstock	3B3/8E1	Redruth	1E5	Ripponden & Barkisland	21E1
Radway Green & Barthomley	15C3/20E1	Reedham	18F2	Risca	8B4/43B3
Radyr	8C4/43C4	Reedley Hallows Halt	24D1	Rishey Platt	9G5
RAF Cranwell	16C1	Reedness Junction	22E5	Rishton	24D2
RAF Halton	10E2	Reedsmouth	27A3	Rishworth	21E1
Raglan	8A3	Reepham (Lincs)	16A1/17B1	Risley (Workmen)	45C3
Raglan Road Crossing Halt	8A3	Reepham	18E4	Risley ROF (Workmen)	45C3

102

RNAD Broughton	26D3
Roade	10B2
Roath	8C4/43B4
Robertsbridge	6E5
Robertstown Halt	43C3
Robin Hood	21D3/42B2
Robin Hood's Bay	28F1
Robroyston	29C5/44D4
Roby	20C4/24G4/45E4
Rocester	15D5
Rochdale	20B1/45A1
Roche	1D2
Rochester	6B5
Rochford	6A4
Rock Ferry	20C4/24G4/45F4
Rockcliffe	26C1
Rockingham	16F2
Rodmarton Platform	9F4
Rodwell	3G3
ROF Bishopton	29C4
ROF Brackla	7C5/43D4
ROF Bridgwater	3B1
ROF Burghfield	4A2
ROF Cardiff	43B4
ROF Glascoed	8B3
ROF Pembury	7B2
Rogart	36A5
Rogate	4D1
Rogerstone	8B4/43A3
Rolleston on Dove	15D5
Rollestone Junction	16C2
Rollright Halt	10D5
Rolvenden	6E4
Romaldkirk	27E4
Roman Bridge	19E3
Roman Road Woodnesborough	6C2
Romford	5A4
Romiley	21G1
Romney Sands	6E3
Romsey	4D4
Rookery Bridge	15B2/20E2
Rookery	20B3/24F3/45E3
Roose	24B5
Ropley	4C2
Rose Grove	24D1
Rose Hill	21G1
Rosebush	13F2
Rosemill	34E5
Rosemount	33D5
Rosewell & Hawthornden	30C2
Roskear	1E5
Roslin	30C2
Rossett	20E4
Rossington	21F5
Rosslyn Castle	30C2
Rosslynlee	30C2
Ross-on-Wye	9D1
Roster Road Halt	38D2
Rosyth Dockyard (Naval)	30B2
Rothbury	31G4
Rotherfield & Mark Cross	5E5
Rotherham & Masborough	42F1
Rotherham Holmes	21G4/42F1
Rotherham Masborough	21G4/42F1
Rotherham Road	21G4/42F1
Rotherham West Gate	21G4/42F1
Rotherhithe	40D4/46C3
Rothes	36D1
Rothes Mill	34G5
Rothiemay	37D1
Rothienorman	37E3
Rothley	16E4
Rothwell	21D3/42B2

Round Oak	15G3
Roundwood Halt	11F1
Row	29B3
Rowden Mil	9B2
Rowfant	5D3
Rowland's Castle	4E2
Rowlands Gill	27C5
Rowley Regis & Blackheath	13C2/15G4
Rowley	27C4
Rowrah	26E3
Note: Used by workmen's trains between 11 March 1940 and 8 April 1940	
Rowsley	16B5/41C1
Rowton Halt	15E2
Roxburgh	31E2
Roy Bridge	32B2
Royal Oak	39C4/46D3
Roydon	11F3
Royds Green Lower	21E3/42B2
Royston	11D3
Royston & Notton	21F3/42D2
Royton	21F1/45A2
Royton Junction	21F1
Ruabon	20F4
Rubery	9A4
Ruddington	16D4/41G4
Ruddington Factory Halt (Workmen)	16D3
Rudgwick	5E2
Rudyard	15B4
Rudyard Lake	15B4
Rufford Colliery	41D5
Rufford	20A3/24E3/45E1
Rugby	10A4
Rugby Central	10A4
Rugeley Town	15E4
Rugeley Trent Valley	15E4
Ruislip	5A2
Ruislip (LU)	46G2
Ruislip Manor	46G2
Rumbling Bridge	30A4/33G4
Rumworth & Daubhill	45C2
Runcorn	15A1/20C3/45D4
Runcorn Docks	15A1/20C3/45E4
Rushbury	15G1
Rushcliffe Platform	16D4
Rushden	10B1
Rushton	15B4
Rushwick Halt	9B3
Ruskington	17C1
Ruspidge	8A1/9E2
Russell Square	46F4
Ruswarp	28F2
Rutherford	31E1
Rushey Platt	9G5
Rutherglen	29C5/44D3
Ruthin	19E5/20E5
Ruthven Road	33E5
Ruthwell	26B3
Ryburgh	18D4
Ryde Esplanade	4F3
Ryde Pierhead	4F3
Ryde St John's Road	4F3
Rye	6E4
Rye Harbour	6E4
Rye Hill & Burstwick	22E2
Rye House	11F3
Ryeford	9E3
Ryeland	29D5
Ryhall	16E1/17F1
Ryhill Halt	42D1
Ryhope	28C5
Ryhope East	28C5
Rylstone	21C1

Ryston	11A4/17F4
Ryton	27B5
Saddleworth	21F1
Saffrom Walden	11D4
St Agnes	1E1
St Albans	11F1
St Albans Abbey	11F1
St Andrews	34F4
St Andrews Docks	22A2
St Ann's Road	40A4
St Ann's Well	16C3/41F5
St Anne's-on-Sea	24D4
St Annes Park	3A3/8C1
St Anthony's	28C5
St Asaph	19D5
St Austell	1D2
St Bees	26F4
St Blazey	1D3
St Boswells	31E1
St Briavels	8A2/9E1
St Budeaux	1D5
St Clears	7A1/13G3
St Columb Road	1D2
St Combs	37C5
St Cyrus	34C2
St Denys	4D4
St Devereux	14F1
St Dunstan's	42B4
St Erth	1F4
St Fagans	8C4/43C4
St Fillans	33F2
St Fort	34E4
St Germains	23B2
St Germans	1D5
St Harmons	14D4
St Helen's	4F2
St Helens	20C3/24G3/45D3
St Helens Junction	20C3/24G3/45D3
St Helier	39G4
St Ives	11B2
St Ives	1E4
St James Deeping	17F2
St James' Street Walthamstow	40A3
St James's Park	40D5/46F5
St John's	23B2
St Johns	40D3
St John's Chapel	27D3
St John's Road	39C5
St John's Wood	46D3
St Kew Highway	1C2
St Keyne	1D4
St Lawrence Halt	4G3
St Leonards Warrior Square	6F5
St Leonards West Marina	6F5
St Lukes	24E4/45F1
St Margarets	11F3
St Margarets	39E2
St Marnock	29E4
St Mary Cray	5B4/40G1
St Mary's	11A2/17G2
St Mary's Crossing Halt	9F3
St Michaels	20C4/24G4/45F4
St Monance	34G3
St Neots	11C2
St Olaves	18F1
St Pancras (Goods)	40B5
St Paul's	21E2/42C5
St Paul's	46E5
St Peter's	28A1
St Quintin Park & Wormwood Scrubs	39C4
Note: Closed temporarily on 3 October 1940	

and permanently from 1 December 1940.

St Rollox West	29C5/44D4
St Thomas Cross Platform (Workmen)	26F3
Sale	20C1/24G1/45B3
Salehurst Halt	6E5
Salford	20B1/24F1/45A3
Salford Priors	9B4
Salfords	5D3
Salhouse	18E2
Salisbury	4C5
Salisbury Milford	4C5
Salt & Sandon	15D4
Saltaire	21D2/42A5
Saltash	1D5
Saltburn	28E3
Saltby	16D2
Saltcoats	29D3
Salter Lane (for Ashover)	41D2
Saltfleetby	17A3/22G1
Saltford	3A3/8D1
Saltley	13B4/15G5
Saltmarshe	22E5
Saltney	20D4
Saltney Ferry	20D4
Saltoun	30C1
Salvation Army Sidings	11F1

Note: Last in public timetable September 1942

Salwick	24D3

Note: Used by workmen's trains from 8 April 1940 until 2 November 1942 when it reopened as a public station.

Salzcraggie Platform	38F4
Sampford Courtenay	2B5
Sampford Peverell Halt	2A2/8G5
Sandal	21E3/42C2
Sandal & Walton	42C2
Sandbach	15B2/20E2
Sandbach (Ettiley Heath)	15B2/20E2
Sanderstead	5C3
Sandford & Banwell	3B1/8D3
Sandhills	45G4
Sandholme	22D5
Sandhurst Halt	4B1
Sandilands	30E4
Sandling Junction	6D3
Sandon	15D4
Sandown	4F3
Sandplace	1D4
Sandsend	28F2
Sandsfoot Castle Halt	3G3
Sandside	24A3
Sandtoft	22F5
Sandwich	6C2
Sandwich Road	6C2
Sandy Lodge	5A2/10F1/11G1
Sandy	11D2
Sandycroft	20D4
Sankey	20C3/24G3/45/45D4
Sankey Bridges	45D4
Sanquhar	30F5
Santon	23C2
Sarnau	7A2/13G3
Sarsden Halt	10D5
Sauchie	30A4
Saughall	20D4
Saughton	30B3
Saughtree	27A1/31G1

Note: Station reopened 23 August 1948

Saundersfoot	7D3
Saunderton	10F2
Savernake	4A5
Sawbridgeworth	11F3

Sawdon	22A4
Sawley	16D4
Saxby	16E2
Saxham & Risby	11C5
Saxilby	16A1
Saxmundham	12C2
Scafell (Private but advertised)	14C3
Scalby	22A4/28G1
Scalford	16E2
Scarborough Londesborough Road	22A3/28G1
Scarborough	22A3/28G1
Scarcliffe	41C4
Scawby & Hibaldstow	22F4
Scholes	21D3/42A2
Scopwick & Timberland	17C1
Scorrier	1E1/1E5
Scorton	27F5
Scotby	26C1
Scotch Dyke	26B1
Scotland Street	30F2
Scotscalder	38D3
Scotsgap	27A4
Scotstoun East	44F4
Scotstoun West	29C4/44F4
Scotstounhill	29C4/44F4
Scotswood	27B5/28A2
Scratby Halt	18E1
Scremerston	31D4
Scruton	21A3/28G5
Sculcoates	22A1
Scunthorpe	22F4
Sea Mills	3A2/8C2/9G1
Seacroft	17B4
Seaford	5G4
Seaforth	20B4/24F4/45F3
Seaham	28C5
Seaham Colliery	28C5
Seaham Harbour	28C5
Seahouses	31E5
Seamer	22A3
Seascale	26F3
Seaton	28C5
Seaton	2B1
Seaton	16F1
Seaton	26D3
Seaton Carew	28E4
Seaton Delaval	28B5
Seaton Junction	2B1
Seaton Snook	28E4
Secombe & Egremont	45F4
Sedbergh	24A2/27G2
Sedgebrook	16D2
Sedgefield	28E5
Sedgeford	17D5
Seedley	45B3
Seend	3B4
Seer Green Halt	5A1/10F1
Sefton & Maghull	20B4/24F4/45F2
Sefton Park	20C4/24G4/45F4
Seghill	28B5
Selby	21D5
Selham	5E1
Selhurst	5B3/40G5
Selkirk	30E1
Sellafield	26F3
Selling	6C3
Selly Oak	9A415G4
Selsdon Road	5C3
Semington Halt	3B4
Semley	3D4
Senghenydd	8B4/43C3
Sessay	21B4

Sesswick Halt	20F4

Note: Reopened 6 May 1946

Settle	24B1
Settrington	22B5
Seven Kings	5A4
Seven Sisters	5A3/40A4
Seven Sisters	7A5/43E1
Sevenoaks (Bat & Ball)	5C4
Sevenoaks (Tubs Hill)	5C4
Severn Bridge	8A1/9E2
Severn Tunnel Junction	8B2/9F1
Sexhow	28F4
Shackerstone	16F5
Shadwell	40C4/46C3
Shadwell & St Georges in the East	40C3
Shalford	5D1
Shakespeare Staff Halt (Military)	6D2
Shandon	29A3
Shankend	31F1
Shanklin	4G3
Shap	27F1
Shap Summit (Workmen)	27F1
Shapwick	3C1/8E3
Sharlston	21E4/42C1
Sharnal Street	6B5
Sharnbrook	10B1/11C1
Sharpness	8B1/9F2
Sharpness Docks	8B1/9F2
Shaugh Bridge Platform	2D5
Shaw & Compton	21F1
Shawclough & Healey	20A1/24E1/45A1
Shawford & Twyford	4D3
Shawforth	20A1/24E1/45A1
Shawlands	44E3
Sheepbridge	16A5/41B2
Sheepridge & Whittington Moor	16A5/41B2
Sheerness East	6B4
Sheerness-on-Sea	6B4
Sheerness-on-Sea Dock	6B4
Sheffield City	16A5/21G3/41A2/42G2
Sheffield Midland	16A5/21G3/41A2/42G2
Sheffield Nunnery	41A3/42G2
Sheffield Park	41A2/42G2
Sheffield Park	5E4
Sheffield Queens Road	16A5/21G3/41A2/42G2
Sheffield Victoria	16A5/21G3/41A2/42G2
Sheffield Wicker	42G2
Shefford	11D1
Shefford	11D3
Shenfield & Hutton	5A5/11G4
Shenstone	15F5
Shenton	16F5
Shepherd's Bush	39C4/46E3
Shepherds	1D1
Shepherdswell	6C2
Shepley & Shelley	21F2/42D4
Shepperton	5B2
Shepreth	11D3
Shepshed	16E4
Shepton Mallet	3C3/8E1
Shepton Mallet (Charlton Road)	3C3/8E1
Sherborne	3D3/8G1
Sherburn Colliery	28D5
Sherburn House	28D5
Sherburn-in-Elmet	21D4
Sheringham	18C3
Sherwood	16C3/41F5
Shettleston	29C5/44C3
Shide	4F3
Shieldhall	44F4
Shieldhill	26A3
Shieldhill Colliery	30B4

Shields Road	44F1	Sittingbourne	6C4	*1945*
Shifnal	15F2	Six Bells Halt	43B2	South Cave	22D4
Shildon	27E5	Six Mile Bottom	11C4	South Cerney	9F4
Shillingstone	3E4	Skares	29F4	South Ealing	39D2/46F3
Shilton	10A5/16G5	Skeby	16B4/41D4	South Eastrington	22D5
Shincliffe	28D5	Skegness	17B4	South Elmsall	42D1
Shiplake	10G2	Skelbo	36A4	South Gosforth	27B5
Shipley	21D2/42A5	Skellingthorpe	16A1	South Greenford Halt	39C2
Shipley & Windhill	42A5	Skelmanthorpe	21F3/42D3	South Hampstead	39B5
Shipley Gate	16C4/41F3	Skelmersdale	20B3/24F3/45E2	South Harrow	5A2/39B1/46F2
Shippea Hill	11B4	Skewen	7B4/43F2	South Hetton	28D5
Shipston-on-Stour	9C5	Skinningrove	28E3	South Howden	22E5
Shipton	10D5	Skipton	21C1	South Kensington	39D5/46G5
Shipton-on-Cherwell Halt	10E4	Skipworth & North Duffield	21D5	South Kenton	39A2/46F2
Shirley Hill	20A4/24F4/45F1	Skirlaugh	22D3	South Lambeth	40E5
Shirebrook East	16B4/41C4	Slades Green	5B4	South Leigh	10E5
Shirebrook North	16B4/41C4	Slaggyford	27C2	South Leith	30F1
Shirebrook South	41C4	Slaithwaite	21E2/42D5	South Leith Docks	30F1
Shirehampton	3A2/8C2/9G1	Slamannan	30B5	South Lynn	17E4
Shireoaks	16A4/41A4	Slateford	30B2	South Marston (Workmen)	9F5
Shirley	9A5	Sleaford	16C1/17C1	*Note: reopened for workmen's trains*
Shobhall Wharf	15D5	Sledmere & Fimber	22B4	*17 December 1956*
Shoeburyness	6A4	Sleights	28F2	South Medomsley Colliery	27C4
Sholing	4E3	Slinfold	5E2	South Merton	39G4
Shooting Range Platform (Restricted)	1C2	Sling	8A2/9E1	South Milford	21D4
Shoreditch	40C4/46C3	Slingsby	21B5	South Molton	7F4
Shoreham (Kent)	5C4	Sloane Square	39D5/46F4	South Molton Road	7G4
Shoreham Airport		Slough	5B1/10G1	South Queensferry	30B3
(Bungalow Town Halt)	5F2	Smallford	11F2	South Renfrew	44F4
Shoreham-by-Sea	5F3	Smallheath	15G5	South Shields	28B5
Shorncliffe	6D2	Smardale	27F2	South Shore, Lytham Road	24D4
Short Heath Clark's Lane	15F4	Smeaton	30B2	South Side	44E1
Shortlands	5B4/40F2	Smeeth	6D3	South Tottenham	40A4
Shoscombe & Single Hill Halt	3B3/8D1	Smeeth Road	17F4	South Willingham & Hainton	17A2
Shotley Bridge	27C4	Smethwick Junction	13B2	South Wimbledon	46D4
Shottle	16C5/41F1	Smethwick	13C2	South Witham	16E1
Shotton	20D4	Smitham	5C3	South Woodford (George Lane)	5A4/40A2
Shotton Bridge	28D5	Smithfield	40C5	South Yard (Military)	1A1
Shotts	30C4	Smithy Bridge	20A1/21E1/45A1	Southall	5B2/39C1
Shrawardine	14A1	Snaefell	23B3	Southam & Long Itchingham	10B4
Shrawardine Halt (Military)	14A1	Snailbeach	14B1	Southam Road & Harbury	10B5
Shrewsbury Abbey	15E1	Snailham Halt	6E4	Southampton Central	4G5
Shrewsbury Abbey Foregate	15E1	Snainton	22A4	Southampton Docks Empress Dock	4G5
Shrewsbury Coton Hill	15E1	Snaith	21E5	Southampton Docks	
Shrewsbury General	15E1	Snaith & Pollington	21E5	Flying Boat Terminal	4G5
Shrivenham	9F5	Snape	12C2	Southampton Docks Itchen Quay	4G5
Sible & Castle Hedingham	11E5	Snaresbrook & Wanstead	5A4/40A2	Southampton Docks Outer Quay	4G5
Sibleys	11E4	Snarestone	16E5	Southampton Docks Test Quay	4G5
Sibsey	17C3	Snatchwood Halt	43A2	Southampton Eastern Docks	4G5
Sidcup	5B4/40E1	Snelland	17A1	Southampton New Docks	4G5
Sidestrand Halt	18D3	Snettisham	17D5	Southampton Royal Pier	4G5
Sidley	6F5	Snodland	6C5	Southampton Terminus	4G5
Sidmouth	2B2	Snowdon	19E2	Southampton Western Docks	4G5
Sidmouth Junction	2B2	Soham	11B4	Southbourne Halt	4E2
Sigglesthorne	22D3	Soho	13C2/15G4	Southburn	22C4
Sight Hill	44E4	Soho & Winson Green	13C3/15G4	Southcoates	22A1
Sileby	16E3	Soho Pool	13B3	Southease & Rodmell Halt	5F4
Silecroft	24A5	Soho Road	13B3/15G4	Southend-on-Sea	6A4
Silian Halt	13E5	Sole Street	5B5	Southend-on-Sea East	6A4
Silkstone	42E3	Solihull	9A5	Southern	11A5/17G5
Silloth	26C3	Somerleyton	12A1/18F1	Southerndown Road	7C5/43D4
Silverdale	15C3/20F1	Somerset Road	9A4/15G4	Southfields	39E4/46E4
Silverdale	24B3	Somersham	11B3	*Note: SR trains ceased to use the station from*
Silverhill Colliery	41D3	Somerton	3D2/8F2	*5 May 1941.*
Silverton	2A3	Somers Town	40C5	Southfleet	5B5
Silvertown	40C2	Sorbie	25D4	Southgate	46D1
Simonstone	24D1	South Acton	39D3/46E3	Southill	11D1
Sinclairtown	30A2	South Aylesbury Halt	10E2	Southminster	12G5
Sinderby	21A3	South Bank	28E4	Southport Chapel Street	20A4/24E4/45F1
Singer	29C4/44F5	South Bermondsey	40D4	Southport Kensington Road	24E4/45F1
Singleton	4E1	South Bromley	40C3	Southport Lord Street	20A4/24E4/45F1
Sinnington	22A5	*Note: Station closed 15 May 1944 but bus*		Southrey	17B1
Sirhowy	8A4/43B1	*replacement service operated until 23 April*		Southwaite	26D1

Southwater	5E2	
Southwell	16C3	
Southwick	5F3	
Southwick	26C4	
Southwick	28C5	
Sowerby Bridge	21E1/42C5	
Spalding	17E2	
Spalding St Johns	17E2	
Sparkford	3D2/8F1	
Spean Bridge	32B2	
Speech House Road	8A1/9E2	
Speen	4A3	
Speeton	22B3	
Speke	20C4/45E4	
Spennithorne	21A2/27G5	
Spennymoor	27D5	
Spetchley	9B3	
Spetisbury Halt	3E4	
Spey Bay	36C1	
Spiersbridge	44F2	
Spilsby	17B3	
Spinkhill	16A4/41B3	
Spital	20C4/45F4	
Spitalfields (Coal)	40C4	
Spitalfields	40C4	
Spofforth	21C3	
Spon Lane	13B2/15G4	
Spondon	16D5/41G2	
Spooner Row	12A4/18F4	
Spratton	10A3	
Spring Vale	20A2/24E2	
Springburn	44D4	
Springburn Park	29C5/44D4	
Springfield	34F5	
Springfield	41D2	
Springside	29E3	
Sprotborough	21F4	
Sprouston	31E2	
Spurn Head (Workmen)	22F1	
Stacksteads	20A1/24E1	
Staddlethorpe	22E5	
Stafford	15E3/20G1	
Stafford Common	15D3/20G1	
Note: Used by RAF personnel post 4 December 1939.		
Stafford Doxey Road	15E3/20G1	
Staincliffe & Batley Carr	42C3	
Staincross	21F3/42D2	
Staines	5B1	
Stainforth & Hatfield	21F5	
Stainland & Holywell Green	21E2/42C5	
Stainmore	27F3	
Staintondale	28G1	
Stairfoot	42E2	
Staithes	28E2	
Stalbridge	3D3/8G1	
Staley & Millbrook	21F1	
Stalham	18D2	
Stallingborough	22F2	
Stalybridge	21F1	
Stamford	16F1/17F1	
Stamford Bridge	22C5	
Stamford Brook	39D4/46E3	
Stamford Hill	40A4	
Stanbridgeford	10D1	
Standish	20B3/24F2/45D1	
Standon	11E3	
Standon Bridge	15E3/20F1	
Stane Street Halt	11E4	
Stanford-le-Hope	5A5	
Stanhoe	18D5	
Stanhope	27D4	
Stanley	42B2	

Stanley Bridge Halt	3A5	
Stanley Junction	33E5	
Stanlow & Thornton	45E5	
Note: Opened 23 December 1940 for oil workers; opened to public 24 February 1941		
Stanmore	5A2	
Stanmore (LU)	46F1	
Stanner	14E2	
Stannergate	34E4	
Stanningley	21D2/42A4	
Stannington	27A5	
Stansfield Hall	21E1	
Stansted	11E4	
Stanton	9F5	
Stanton Gate	16D4/41G3	
Stanwardine Halt	14A1/20G4	
Staple Edge Halt	8A1/9E2	
Staple Hill	3A3/8C1/9G2	
Staple	6C1	
Stapleford	11F2	
Stapleford & Sandiacre	16D4/41G3	
Staplehurst	6D5	
Stapleton Road	3F1/8C1	
Starbeck	21C3	
Starcross	2C3	
Staveley	27G1	
Staveley	41B3	
Staveley & Oakes Co's Siding	16D2	
Staveley Town	16A4/41B3	
Staveley Works	16A4/41B3	
Staverton	2D4	
Staverton Halt	3B4	
Staward	27C3	
Stechford	15G5	
Steele Road	27A1	
Steelend	30A4	
Steens Bridge	9B1	
Steeplehouse	16C5/41E1	
Steer Point	2E5	
Note: Used by workmen's trains from 21 July 1941 to 3 November 1941 when passenger services restored.		
Steeton & Silsden	21C1	
Stepford	26A4	
Stepney	22A1	
Stepney East	40C3	
Stepney Green	40C2/46C3	
Stepps	29C5/44C4	
Stevenage	11E2	
Stevenston Moorpark	29D3	
Steventon	10F4	
Stewarton	29D4	
Stewarts Lane	39F4	
Steyning	5F2	
Stickney	17C3	
Stillington	28E5	
Stirchley	15F2	
Stirling	30A5	
Stirling Shore Road	30A5	
Stixwould	17B2	
Stobcross	44E4	
Stobo	30E3	
Stobs	31F1	
Stockbridge	4C4	
Stockcross & Bagnor Halt	4A4	
Stockingford	16F5	
Stockport Edgeley	20C1/21G1/24G1/45A4	
Stockport Tiviot Dale	45A3	
Stocksfield	27C4	
Stocksmoor	21F2/42D4	
Stockton	28E5	
Stockton Brook	15C3/20E1	
Stockton North	28E4	

Stockton South	28E4	
Stockwell	46D3	
Stockwith	22G5	
Stogumber	8F5	
Stoke	11D5	
Stoke	15C3/20F1	
Stoke Bruern	10C2	
Stoke Canon	2B3	
Stoke Edith	9C2	
Stoke Ferry	11A5/17F5	
Stoke Golding	16F5	
Stoke Junction Halt	6B5	
Stoke Mandeville	10E2	
Stoke Newington	40B4	
Stoke Prior Halt	9B1	
Stoke Works	9B4	
Stokesley	28F4	
Stone	15D3/20F1	
Stone Crossing Halt	5B5	
Stonea	11A4/17G3	
Stonebridge Park	39B3/46E2	
Stoneferry	22D3	
Stonehaven	34A1	
Stonehouse	9E3	
Stonehouse	30D5	
Stonehouse Pool	1A1	
Stoneywood	30B5	
Storeton	20C4/24G4/45E4	
Stottesdon Halt & Siding	9A2/15G2	
Stoulton	9C3	
Stourbridge Junction	9A3/15G3	
Stourbridge Town	9A3/15G3	
Stourpaine & Durweston Halt	3E4	
Stourport-on-Severn	9A3	
Stourton	42B2	
Stow	30D1	
Stow Bardolph	17F4	
Stow Bedon	12A5/18F5	
Stow Park	16A2	
Stow St Mary Halt	11G5	
Stowmarket	12C4	
Stow-on-the-Wold	9D5	
Stradbroke	12B3	
Stranraer	25C2	
Stranraer Harbour	25C2	
Strap Lane Halt	3C3/8F1	
Note: Station reopened 16 December 1946		
Strata Florida	10D5/14D5	
Stratford	40B2	
Stratford Lower	40B3	
Stratford Market	40B2	
Stratford-on-Avon	9B5	
Strathaven Central	29D5	
Strathaven North	29D5	
Strathblane	29B5	
Strathbungo	44E3	
Strathcarron	35E2	
Strathcathro	34C3	
Strathmiglo	34F5	
Strathord	33E5	
Strathpeffer	35D5	
Strathyre	33F2	
Stratton	9F5	
Stratton Park Halt	9F5	
Stravithie	34F3	
Strawberry Hill	5B2/39F2	
Streatham	5B3/40F5	
Streatham Common	40F5	
Streatham Hill	40F5	
Street	15F5	
Strensall	21B5	
Stretford	45B3	
Stretham	11B4	

Thorntonhall	29D5/44E2	
Thornton-in-Craven	21A1/21C1	
Thorp Arch	21C4	
Thorp Arch Walton (Workmen)	21C4	
Thorp Arch River (Workmen)	21C4	
Thorp Gates	21D5	
Thorpe Cloud	15C5	
Thorpe Bay	6A4	
Thorpe Culvert	17B4	
Thorpe Thewles	28E5	
Thorpe	10A1/11B1	
Thorpe-in-Balne	21F5	
Thorpe-le-Soken	12E3	
Thorpeness	12C2	
Thorpe-on-the-Hill	16B1	
Thorverton	2A3	
Thrapston Bridge Street	10A1/11B1	
Thrapston Midland Road	10A1/11B1	
Three Bridges	5D3	
Three Cocks Junction	14F2	
Three Counties	11E2	
Threlkeld	26E1	
Throsk Halt	30A5	
Thrumster	38D2	
Thurcroft	16A4/41A4/21G4	
Thurgarton	16C3	
Thurlby	17E1	
Thurnby & Scraptoft	16F3	
Thurnscoe	42E1	
Thursford	18D4	
Thurso	38C3	
Thurstaston	20C5	
Thurston	12C5	
Thuxton	18F4	
Tibbermuir	33E4	
Tibshelf & Newton	16B4/41D3	
Tibshelf Town	16B4/41D3	
Ticehurst Road	5E5	
Tickhill & Wadworth	21G5	
Tidal Basin	40C2	
Tiddington	10E3	
Tidenham	8B2/9F1	
Tidworth	4B5	
Tidworth Camp	4B5	
Tilbury	5B5	
Tilbury Docks	5B5	
Tile Hill	10A5	
Tilehurst	4A2/10G3	
Tillicoultry	30A4	
Tillyfourie	37F2	
Tillynaught	37C2	
Tilton	16F2	
Timperley	20C1/24G1/45B3	
Tingley	21E3/42B3	
Tinker's Green Halt	20G4	
Tinsley	21G4/42G2	
Tintern	8B2/9F1	
Tintern Quarry Siding (Workmen)	8B2/9F1	
Tintwistle (Workmen)	21F1	
Tipton St Johns	2B2	
Tipton	13B1/15F4	
Tiptree	12F5	
Tir Phil	8B4/43B2	
Tirydail	7A3/43G1	
Tisbury	3D4	
Tissington	15C5	
Tisted	4C2	
Titley	14E1	
Tiverton	2A3/7G5	
Tiverton Junction	2A2/8G5	
Tivetshall	12A3/18G3	
Tochieneal	37C1	
Tod Point	28E4	

Toddington	9D4	
Todmorden	20A1/21E1	
Toft & Kingston	11C3	
Tollcross	44D3	
Toller	3F2	
Tollerton	21B4	
Tollesbury	12F5	
Tolleshunt D'Arcy	12F5	
Tolleshunt Knights	12F5	
Tolworth	5C2	
Tomatin	36E4	
Tonbridge	5D5	
Tondu	7C5/43E4	
Tonfanau	13B5	
Tonge & Breedon	16D4	
Note: Used by troops from 10 November 1939		
until 1 January 1945		
Tongham	4B1/5C1	
Tonypandy & Trealaw	43E3	
Tonyrefail	8B5/43D3	
Tonteg Halt	43C3	
Tonypandy	43D3	
Tooting Broadway	46D$	
Tooting Junction	39F5	
Topcliffe	21A4	
Topsham	2B3	
Torksey	16A2	
Torpantau	8A5/14G3/43C1	
Torphins	34A3/37G2	
Torquay	2D3	
Torrance	29B5/44D5	
Torre	2D3	
Torrington	7G3	
Torryburn	30A4	
Torver	26G2	
Totnes	2D4	
Totnes Quay	2D4	
Tottenham Court Road	46F4	
Tottenham Hale	40A4	
Totteridge & Whetstone	5A3/11G2/46D1	
Note: Station transferred to the LPTB on		
14 April 1940 following conversion to form		
part of the extended Northern Line.		
Tottington	20A1/24E1/45B1	
Totton	4E4	
Tow Law	27D5	
Towcester	10C3	
Tower Hill	1B5	
Towiemore	37D1	
Town Green & Aughton	20B4/24F4/45E2	
Towyn	13B5	
Towyn Wharf	13B5	
Trabboch	29F4	
Trafalgar Square/Strand	46F5	
Trafford Park	20B1/24G1/45B3	
Tram Inn	9D1/14F1	
Tranent	30B1	
Trawscoed	13D5	
Trawsfynydd	19F3	
Trawsfynydd Lake Halt	19F3	
Treamble	1D1	
Treborth	19D2	
Trecwyn Sidings	13F1	
Trecynon	8A5/43D2	
Trecynon Halt	43D2	
Tredegar	8A4/43B1	
Treeton	16A4/21G4/41A3/42G1	
Trefeglwys	14C4	
Trefeinon	14F3	
Treferig	8B5/43C3	
Trefnant	19D5	
Treforest	8B5/43C3	
Treforest Halt	43C3	

Tregaron	14D5	
Tregarth	19D2	
Trehafod	8B5	
Treherbert	7B5/8B5/43D2	
Trelewis Platform	43C2	
Trench Crossing	15E2	
Trench Halt & Siding	20F4	
Note: Reopened 6 May 1946		
Trenholme Bar	28F4	
Trent	16D4	
Trentham	15C3/20F1	
Trentham Gardens	15D3/20F1	
Treorchy	43D2	
Treorchy	43D2	
Tresmeer	1B4	
Trethomas	43B3	
Trevil Halt	8A4/43B1	
Trevor	20F5	
Trewerry & Trerice Halt	1D1	
Trewythan	14C3	
Trimdon	28D5	
Trimingham	18D2	
Trimley	12E3	
Trimsaran	7A3	
Trimsaran Road	7A2	
Tring	10E1	
Trinity Road	46D4	
Troedyrhiew Garth	7B5/43E3	
Troedyrhiw	43C2	
Troedyrhiw Halt	43C2	
Troon	29E3	
Troon Harbour	29E3	
Troutbeck	26E1	
Trowbridge	3B4	
Trowell	16C4/41F3	
Trowse	18F3	
Truro	1E1	
Truro Newham	1E1	
Trusham	2C3	
Truthall Platform	1F5	
Tue Brook	20C4/24G4/45F3	
Tufnell Park	40B5	
Tufnell Park (LU)	46D2	
Tullibardine	33F4	
Tullietudlem	30D5	
Tulloch	32B1	
Tulse Hill	5B3/40E5	
Tumble (Miners)	7A3	
Tumby Woodside	17C2	
Tunbridge Wells Central	5D5	
Tunbridge Wells West	5D5	
Tunstall	15C3/20E1	
Turnberry	29G3	
Turnchapel	1D5	
Turnham Green	39D3/46E3	
Turnhouse	30B3	
Turnpike Lane	46D2	
Turriff	37D3	
Turton & Edgworth	20A2/24E2/45B1	
Turvey	10B1	
Tutbury	15D5	
Tutshill for Beachley Halt	8B2/9F1	
Tuxford Central	16B2	
Tuxford North	16B2	
Twechar	29B5	
Tweedmouth	31C3	
Twenty	17E2	
Twickenham	5B2/39E2	
Twizell	31D3	
Twyford	4A1/10G2	
Twywell	10A1	
Ty Croes	19D1	
Tycoch Halt (Miners)	7A2	
Tydd	17E3	

Watten	38D2	West Exe Halt	2A3	Weston (Ingestre)	15D4
Watton	18F5	West Fen Drove	11A3/17G3	Weston on Trent	16D5
Watton-at-Stone	11E2	West Ferry	5A3/46D2	Weston Rhyn	20F4
Waverton	15B1/20B3	West Fincheley		Weston-sub-Edge	9C5
Wavertree	45F4	*Note: Note: Station transferred to the LPTB*		Weston-super-Mare	3B1/8D3
Wavertree & Edge Hill	45F4	*on 14 April 1940 following conversion to form*		Weston-super-Mare	
Wearhead	27D3	*part of the extended Northern Line.*		Ashcombe Road	3B1/8D3
Weaste	45B3	West Gosforth	27B5	Westwood	42F2
Weatherhill	27D4	West Green	40A4	Wetheral	27C1
Weaver Down (Military)	4D1	West Grinstead	5E2	Wetherby	21C4
Weaverthorpe	22A4	West Hall Milk Platform (Restricted)	30D3	Wetherby Racecourse (Races)	21C4
Wedgwod Halt	15D3/20F1	West Hallam	16C4/41F3	Wetwang	22C4
Wednesbury	13A2/15F4	West Halton	22E4	Weybourne	18C4
Wednesfield	15F4	West Ham	40C2/46C3	Weybridge	5C2
Wednesfield Heath	15F4	West Hampstead	39B5	Weyhill	4B4
Weedon	10B3	West Harrow	39A1/46F2	Weymouth Harbour	3G3
Weedon ROD	10B3	West Hartlepool	28D4	Weymouth Town	3G3
Weeley	12E3	West Hoathly	5E3	Whaley Bridge	15A4
Weelsby Road Halt	22F2	West India Docks	40C3	Whalley	24D2
Weeton	21C3	West Jesmond	27B5/28A1	Whaplode	17E3
Welbeck Colliery	41C5	West Kensington	39D4/46E3	Wharram	22B5
Welbury	28F5	West Kilbride	29D2	Whatstandwell	16C5/41E2
Welford & Kilworth	10A3/16G3	West Kirby	20C5/24G5	Whauphill	25C4
Welford Park	4A4	West Leigh & Bedford	45C3	Wheathampstead	11F2
Wellfield	28D5	West Leigh	45C3	Wheatley	10E3
Welling	5B4/40E1	West Meon	4D2	Wheatley	21E2/42C5
Wellingborough London Road	10B1	West Moors	3E5	Wheatley Park	21G2
Wellingborough Midland	10B1	West Newport	34E4	Wheldrake	21C5
Wellington	15E2	West Norwood	40F5	Wherwell	4C4
Wellington	8G4	West Pennard Halt	3C2/8E2	Whetstone	16F4
Wellow	3B3/8D1	West Rounton Gates	28F5	Whifflet	30C5/44B3
Wells Harbour	18C5	*Note: Wednesdays only; last train*		Whimple	2B2
Wells Priory Road	3C2/8E2	*6 September 1939*		Whippingham	4F3
Wells Tucker Street	3C2/8E2	West Runton	18C3	Whissendine	16E2
Wells-on-Sea	18C5	West Stanley	27C5	Whistlefield	29A3
Welnetham	12C5	West Stanley (Goods)	27C5	Whitacre	15F5
Welsh Hook Halt	13G1	West Street	44F1	Whitburn Colliery	28C5
Welsh's Crossing & Halt	38D2	West Street	5B5	Whitburn	30B4
Welshampton	20F4	West Sutton	5C3	Whitby	28F2
Welshpool	14B2	West Timperley	45B4	Whitby West Cliff	28F2
Welton	10B3	West tinsley	21G4	Whitchurch (Hants)	4B3
Welwyn Garden City	11F2	West Vale	21E2/42C5	*Note: Station closed 4 August 1942 to*	
Welwyn North	11F2	West Wemyss	30A2/34G5	*8 March 1943*	
Wem	15D1/20G3	West Weybridge	5C2	Whitchurch	15C1/20F3
Wembley Hill	39B3	West Wickham	5B4/40G3	Whitchurch Down Platform	1C5
Wembley Park	5A2/39B3/46E2	West Wood	21F3/42F2	Whitchurch Glamorgan	43B4
Wembley Stadium	39B3	West Worthing	5F2	Whitchurch Halt	3A2/8D1
Wembley for Sudbury	5A2/39B2/46E2	West Wycombe	10F2	White Bear	20A3/24F2/45D1
Wemyss Bay	29C2	Westbourne Park	39C4/46E3	White Colne	12E5
Wemyss Castle	30A2/34G5	Westbrook	14F2	White Dale	22D3
Wendling	18E5	Westbury	14A1	White Fen	11A3/17G3
Wendover	10E2	Westbury	3B4	White Moss	
Wenford Bridge	1C3	Westcalder	30C4	Level Crossing Halt	20B3/24F3/45E2
Wennington	24B2	*Note: Became West Calder 1941*		White Notley	11F5
Wensley	21A2/27G4	Westcliff-on-Sea	6A4	Whitebrook Halt	8A2/9E1
Wentwoth & Hoyland Common	21F3/42F2	Westcombe Park	40D2	Whitechapel	46C3
Wenvoe	8C4/43C5	Westenhanger	6D3	Whitecraigs	29C5/44E2
Wern Hir Halt (Unadvertised)	8A3	Westerfield	12D3	Whitecroft	8A1/9E2
Wern Las	14A1/20G4	Westerham	5C4	Whitefield	20B1/24F1/45B2
Wern Siding	19F2	Western Jetty	22E3	Whitegate	15B2/20D2
West Acton	46E3	Westerton	44E5	Whitehall Halt	2A2/8G5
West Auckland	27E5	Westfield	30B4	Whitehaven Bransty	26E4
West Bay	3F1	Westgate-in-Weardale	27D3	Whitehaven Preston Street	26E4
West Brompton	39D5/46E3	Westgate-on-Sea	6B2	Whitehill (Military)	4C1
West Bromwich	13B2/15G4	Westham Halt	3G3	Whitehouse	37F2
West Calder	30C4	Westhead Halt	20B3/24F3/45E2	Whitehurst Halt	20F4
West Cornforth	28D5	Westhoughton	45C2	Whiteinch Victoria Road	44F4
West Craigs	30C4	Westhouses & Blackwell	16B4/41D3	Whiteinch	44F4
West Cross	43C3	Westmill	11E3	Whitemoor	11A3/17F3
West Croydon	5C3/40G5	Westminster	40C5/46F5	Whiterigg	30C5/44A4
West Drayton	5B2/10G1	Westoe Lane	28B5	Whithorn	25D4
West Ealing	39C2	Weston	17E2	Whitland	7A1/13G3
West End Lane	39B5/46D2	Weston	3A3/8D1	Whitley Bay	28B5

Whitley Bridge	21E5
Whitlingham	18F3
Whitmore	15C3/20F1
Whitney-on-Wye	14E2
Whitrope Siding	31G1
Whitstable & Tankerton	6B3
Whitstable Harbour	6B3
Whitstone & Bridgerule	1A4
Whittingham (Hospital)	24D2
Whittington High Level	20F4
Whittington Low Level	20G4
Whittington	16A5//41B2
Whittlesea	11A2/17G2
Whittlesford	11D3
Whitton	22E4
Whitton	39E1
Whitwell	16A4/41B4
Whitwell	4G3
Note: Became Whitwell Halt 1944	
Whitwell & Reepham	18E4
Whitwick	16E4
Whitworth	20A1/24E1/45A1
Whyteleafe	5C3
Wick	38D2
Wick St Lawrence	3A1/8D3
Wickenby	17A1
Wickford	6A5
Wickham	4E3
Wickham Bishops	12F5
Wickham Market	12C2
Wickwar	8B1/9F2
Widdrington	27A5/31G5
Widford	11F3
Widmerpool	16D3
Widnes	15A1/20C3/24G3/45D4
Widnes Central	45D4
Widney Manor	9A5
Wigan	20B3/24F2
Wigan Central	45D2
Wigan North Western	45D2
Wigan Wallgate	45D2
Wigston Glen Parva	16F4
Wigston Magna	16F3
Wigston South	16F3
Wigton	26C2
Wigtown	25C4
Wilbraham Road	45A3
Wilburton	11B3
Wilby	12B3
Willaston	15C2/20E2
Willenhall Bilston Street	15F4
Willenhall Stafford Street	15F4
Willerby & Kirk Ella	22D4
Willersley Halt	9C5
Willesden Green	39B4/46E2
Willesden Junction	5A3/39C4/46E3
Willington Quay	28B5
Willington	11D1
Willington	27D5
Williton	8E5
Willoughby	17B4
Wilmcote	9B5
Wilmington	22A1
Wilmslow	15A3/20C1/45A5
Wilnecote	15F5
Wilpshire	24D2
Wilsden	21D2/42A5
Wilshamstead Platform (Workmen)	10C1/11D1
Wilsthorpe Crossing Halt	17E1
Wilsontown	30C4
Wilstrop siding	21C4
Wilton	3C5

Wilton North	3C5
Wimbledon	5B3/39F4/46E3
Wimbledon Chase	39F4
Wimbledon Park	39E4/46E3
Wimblington	11A3/17G3
Wimborne	3E5
Wincanton	3D3/8F1
Winchcombe	9D4
Winchester	4D3
Winchester Chesil	4D3
Winchfield	4B1
Winchlesea	6E4
Wincobank & Meadow Hall	21G3/42G2
Winder (Workmen)	26E3
Note: Used by workmen's trains from	
11 March 1940 to 8 April 1940	
Windermere Lakeside	24A4/26G1
Note: passenger services reintroduced 3 June	
1946	
Windermere	26G1
Windmill End	13C1/15G4
Windsor & Eton	5B1/10G1
Windsor Street Wharf	13B4
Winestead	22E2
Wingate	28D5
Wingfield	16C5/41E2
Wingham Canterbury Road	6C2
Wingham Colliery Halt	6C2
Wingham Town	6C2
Winkhill Siding	15C4
Winnersh Halt	4A1
Winnington	45C5
Winscombe (Somerset)	3B1/8D3
Winsford	15B2/20D2
Winsford & Over	15B2/20D2
Winslow	10D2
Winson Green	13C3/15G4
Winston	27E5
Winterbourne	8C1/9G2
Winteringham	22E4
Wintersett & Ryhill	42D2
Winterton & Thealby	22E4
Winton	30B1
Wirksworth	16C5/41E1
Wisbech East	17F3
Wisbech North	17F3
Wisbech St Mary	17F3
Wishaw Central	44A2
Wishaw South	30D5/44A2
Wishford	3C5
Wissington	11A5/17G5
Wistanstow Halt	14C1
Wistow	21D5
Witedale	22D3
Witham	12F5
Witham	3C3/8E1
Withcall	17A2
Withernsea	22E2
Withington	9C1
Withington & West Didsbury	20C1/24G1/45A3
Withington (Glos)	9E4
Withnell	20A2/24E2
Withyham	5D4
Withymoor Basin	13C1
Witley	5D1
Witney	10E5
Wittersham Road	6E4
Witton Gilbert	27D5
Witton	13B4
Witton-le-Wear	27E5
Wiveliscombe	8F5
Wivelsfield	5E3

Wivenhoe	12E4
Wixford	9B4
Wnion Halt	14A5/19G4
Woburn Sands	10C1
Woking	5C1
Wokingham	4A1
Woldingham	5C3
Wolferton	17D5
Wolfs Castle Halt	13G1
Wolsingham	27D4
Wolvercote Siding	10E4
Wolverhampton High Level	15F3
Wolverhampton Low Level	15F3
Wolverhampton Monmore Green	15F3
Wolverhampon Walsall Street	15E3
Wolverhampton Victoria Basin	15E3
Wolverton	10C2
Wombourn	15F3
Wombridge	15E2
Wombwell	21F3/42E2
Wombwell	21F4/42E1
Womersley	21E4
Wooburn Green	5A1/10F2
Wood End	9A5
Wood Green	46D2
Wood Grange Park	40B2
Wood Green (Alexandra Park)	5A3/40A5
Wood Green (Old Bescot)	13A2
Wood Lane	46E3
Woodborough	3B5
Woodbridge	12D3
Woodburn	27A3
Woodbury Road	2B3
Woodchester	9F3
Woodcroft Halt (Military)	4E2
Woodend	26F3
Note: Used by Workmen's trains from	
11 March 1940	
Woodend Colliery	30C4
Woodford & Hinton	10B4
Woodford	5A4
Woodhall Junction	17B2
Woodhall Spa	17B2
Woodham Ferrers	6A5/11G5
Woodhay	4A3
Note: Station closed 4 August 1942 to 8	
March 1943	
Woodhead	21F2/42F5
Woodhead Dam (Workmen)	21F1
Woodhill Road Halt	45B1
Woodhouse	16A4/21G4/41A3/42G1
Woodhouse Mill	16A4/21G4/41A3/42G1
Woodkirk	21E3/42B3
Woodland	24A4/26G2
Woodlands Road Halt	45B2
Woodlesford	21D3/42B2
Woodley	21G1
Woodnesborough	6C2
Woodside	15A1/20C3/45E4
Woodside & South Norwood	5B3/40G4
Woodside Park	5A3/46D1
Woodvale	20B4/24F4/45F1
Woodville	16E5
Wooferton	9A1
Wookey	3B2/8E2
Wool	3F4
Woolaston	8B2/9F1
Wooler	31E4
Wooley	41D2
Wooley Colliery	27D5
Woolfold	20B1/24F1/45B1
Woollerton Halt	15D2/20G2
Woolmer (Military)	4C1

Woolston	4E4	Wragby	17A1	Yaxham	18E4
Woolwich Arsenal	40D1	Wrangaton	2D5	Yaxley & Farcet	11A2/17G2
Woolwich Dockyard	5B4/40D2	Wraysbury	5B1	Yeadon	21D2
Wooperton	31E4	Wrea Green	24D4	Yealmpton	2E5

In 1899, a line was built to the Foreign Coal Market, Deptford, that resulted in the railway passing through Grove Street. The depot passed to the War Office in 1915; the War Office also took over maintenance of the line in 1927. Seen here in March 1940, Class D1 0-4-2T No 2215 runs through the south London streets. The depot and branch would finally close in late 1963. *Ian Allan Library*